THE DIAR'
A YEOMANR_ ...

EGYPT, GALLIPOLI, PALESTINE
AND ITALY

BY

CAPTAIN O. TEICHMAN, D.S.O., M.C.

CROIX DE GUERRE, CROCE DI GUERRA

Royal Army Medical Corps (T.F.)

WITH ILLUSTRATIONS AND MAPS

T. FISHER UNWIN LTD
LONDON: ADELPHI TERRACE

First published in 1921

TO

THE MEMORY OF

CAPTAIN M. C. ALBRIGHT ("TOBY")

1/1 WORCESTERSHIRE YEOMANRY,

WHO FELL AT THE HEAD OF HIS SQUADRON

WHEN CHARGING THE GUNS

AT HUJ (PALESTINE)

NOVEMBER 8, 1917

NOTE

Throughout the late war, the author of this book kept a diary, often under considerable difficulties and on odd scraps of paper, owing to the order which forbade the taking of diaries into the front line: occasionally these had to be written in cipher or destroyed when there seemed a possibility of the writer being captured. Apology is made for the apparently trivial incidents of the daily routine during the quiet periods, which are retained in the text in order to make the narrative continuous. Owing to the first year's diary having been lost, this period, which contained little of interest, has been covered by a brief synopsis. The narrative does not pretend to be in any way a full or accurate account of current events, being merely the experiences of the writer and his deductions, the latter often proving erroneous when subsequent facts became known at a later date. If it should prove of some slight interest to those members of Mounted Units and Medical Officers who took part in the campaign, the time spent daily in compiling it will not have been in vain. A chapter has been added on the last phase of the war in Italy, where the writer had the good fortune to accompany the Twenty-second Infantry Brigade which captured the Island of Papadopoli (Piave). Acknowledgment is made to the official Dispatches, official intelligence, and to extracts and maps from The Times (*Weekly Edition*).

O. T.

November 1, 1920.

CONTENTS

ILLUSTRATIONS

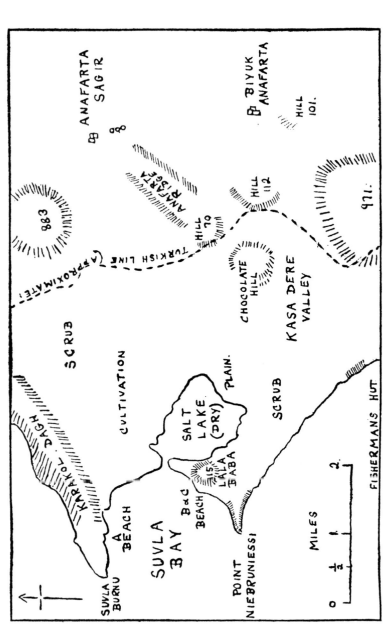

SKETCH MAP OF SUVLA BAY DISTRICT.

(Based on *The Times* map.)

THE DIARY
OF A YEOMANRY M.O.

CHAPTER I

ENGLAND—EGYPT—GALLIPOLI

On the evening of August 4, 1914, the momentous telegram arrived containing the one word "Mobilize," and on the following day the writer of this diary joined his regiment, the Worcester Yeomanry, at Worcester. According to the mobilization orders, the last copy of which we had received a year ago, exactly one week was allowed to complete the former, but on the fifth day our C.O. was able to telegraph to Headquarters that mobilization was complete. Two days later we moved to Warwick, where we joined the Gloucester and Warwick Yeomanry, whom we had been brigaded with in 1913 at Bulford, in order to form the old First South Midland Mounted Brigade. A few days later the whole Brigade moved to the vicinity of Bury St. Edmund's, our regiment being billeted at Rushbrook Park and in the neighbouring villages. During the next few days there were a certain number of "invasion" alarms, generally at midnight, which resulted in the Brigade making hasty and fruitless dashes towards the coast. Towards the end of August we joined the rest of the Second Mounted Division, in the area of the Berkshire downs, our own Brigade being under canvas on the Newbury Race-course. We were told that we should shortly be proceeding to France, and were inspected by His Majesty the King and also by General Sir Ian Hamilton. One day in October the Brigade received sudden orders to entrain for an unknown destination, but after travelling through the night we were disappointed to find in the grey dawn that we had arrived at Sheringham. There was evidently another big invasion scare, and a number of guns of a large size arrived during the morning. Nothing, however, happened, and after being stationed a few miles behind Cromer during November and December, turning out about once a week on account of the usual invasion scare, we eventually found ourselves more or less permanently billeted at King's Lynn. Just before the end of the year we took part in one of the first Zeppelin raids, and our bearers had their first experience of dealing with real wounded.

1915.

For the first three months of 1915 strenuous training was indulged in, and we took our part in patrolling the roads along the coast. On April 8th our period of waiting actually came to an end, and the 1st Worcestershire Yeomanry entrained for Avonmouth. Two days later the whole of the Second Mounted Yeomanry Division embarked in order to join the British Mediterranean Force. Our own Brigade actually sailed between April 10th and 13th. Eleven officers of our regiment, with 100 N.C.O.'s and men and 530 horses, sailed on a horse-boat, by name the s.s. *Eloby* ; the rest of the regiment sailing on a large troopship, together with other units. We were accompanied by a destroyer, which left us on the following morning, but at about 4 p.m. we passed the Warwickshire horse-boat, the s.s. *Wayfarer*, which had been torpedoed. A collier was standing by her, but apparently our orders were to make for the open sea as quickly as possible. On April 21st Malta was reached, but our arrival appeared to be unexpected and we received orders to proceed to Alexandria. Unfortunately, we lost about thirty horses from what was said to be pneumonia, possibly owing to the bad ventilation in the hold of our ship and the sudden change of climate from the cold of the east coast to the heat of the Eastern Mediterranean. Amongst these horses was an old friend whom I had had for many years.

On April 24th the regiment disembarked at Alexandria
and with the rest of the First Brigade moved into camp
on the beach at Chatby, about a mile outside the town.
For the next two months we were used for garrison purposes, and began to wonder whether mounted troops would
ever be needed in Gallipoli. During July the Brigade
moved out to Aboukir Bay for training, which could not
well be undertaken near Alexandria. On August 11th,
when we had almost begun to forget that there was a
real war, our Division received orders to proceed to the
Dardanelles dismounted. Each regiment was instructed to
leave one hundred men and four officers behind in order
to look after the horses in Egypt; as this would make
the regiments very weak it was arranged that only one
regimental medical officer per Brigade was to proceed
to Gallipoli, the other two being left in Alexandria, where
there was a great lack of R.A.M.C. officers. Infantry
web equipment was served out to all ranks, and it took
us some time to get accustomed to its intricacies, as not
a single officer or N.C.O. had seen anything except
cavalry equipment before. On August 13th the Brigade
was finally inspected in marching order on the outskirts
of Alexandria.

August 14th.

The First Mounted Brigade, the whole of the Divisional
Staff and some details of the Second and Fourth Mounted
Brigade Field Ambulances embarked on H.M.T. *Ascania*
at 9 a.m. At midday we began to inoculate the men
against cholera and were kept hard at it until 7 p.m.
The heat was terrific, in the small space available amidships below the deck.

August 15th.

We heard that the *Royal Edward* had been sunk with
great loss of life on the previous day about twelve hours
ahead of us in the Ægean Sea. By sunset we had completed the cholera inoculation, which amounted to 900
for the day.

August 16th.

The ship steamed through the Greek islands of the
Ægean Sea. The boat was a comfortable one and meals
were excellent. It seemed strange that although we
were shortly going into action and would have to live
on the simplest rations, the normal routine went on
on board as if we were crossing the Atlantic. We had
our bedroom stewards, bathroom stewards, table stewards,
etc. During the day we all had our heads shaved by
the ship's barber, as prevention was better than cure.
It being our last night on board, a successful concert was
held. Little did we think that four days hence at this
hour some of those present would be lying dead on the
plains of Suvla Bay. Before turning in, two brilliantly
lighted hospital ships passed us, a double row of green
and white lights over the portholes and an illuminated
red cross amidships and at either end. We, of course,
were steaming with all lights out.

August 17th.

We arrived off Lemnos early in the morning, but as
it was not possible to enter Mudros Bay until a fixed
hour, our ship kept moving about until we were signalled
to come in. We entered the Bay and finally the inner
" harbour." Considerable rolling hills flanked the Bay,
and it was full of an enormous amount of shipping—British
and French battleships, cruisers, torpedo-boat destroyers,
mine-layers, mine-sweepers, transports, colliers, provision
boats, captured Turkish steamers and Greek sailing
boats. Naval picket boats and pinnaces were dashing
about in all directions. As we entered the Bay we were
followed closely by a French troopship, which cheered us
and was cheered in return. Then followed the other
transport which had conveyed our Division (now fourteen
yeomanry regiments strong). In the distance lay the
town of Mudros, and numerous white-tented camps were
to be seen extending down to the water's edge. The
harbour itself was a buzz of activity. It was here that

the early landings on the Peninsula were rehearsed before they actually took place. Before reaching our anchorage we passed two French troopships packed with Senegalese soldiers and tirailleurs Algériens. At 1 p.m. orders were received that the Headquarters of the First Brigade, the Worcestershire Yeomanry Machine Gun Detachment, and also that of the Gloucester and Warwick Yeomanry, were to be ready to leave the ship at 2 p.m. The remaining regiments and staff were to leave at a later hour. At 3 p.m. a paddle-wheel steamer, painted grey (which was formerly an Isle of Man passenger boat), came alongside, and the units before mentioned began to embark. We found that there were already on board the Hertfordshire Yeomanry and drafts of numerous infantry regiments. Much to the disappointment of those concerned, four officers per regiment were left behind as first reinforcements. This turned out, as will be seen, to be a very wise procedure. At 5 p.m. we were all aboard, and amidst cheers from the *Ascania* we cast off. The little steamer carried about 2,500 men, and every inch of deck space was occupied. Orders were issued that no man was on any account to move from the deck space he occupied, for fear of capsizing the boat. Maps were now issued, and we received one of the Gallipoli Peninsula and one of Suvla Bay (Anafarta region). As we steamed out of the harbour the crew of a battleship gave us a cheer and wished us good luck, and a yeomanry officer responded with a " Gone away " blast on his hunting-horn, and we realized that after many months of waiting the Second Mounted Division was at last going into action. After leaving the harbour and Bay of Mudros we turned northwards and passed several mine-sweepers and destroyers. As darkness came on we could just see the heights of Imbros on the west and Cape Hellas to the east. From the latter place we could hear the thunder of guns and occasionally see the flash. We were steaming as fast as possible, with all lights out in order to avoid submarines, and one could not help thinking that hardly a single man would be saved should an accident occur to our little paddle-wheel steamer. The officer on the bridge told me that he had been performing this journey every night for some months. One night was quite enough for us. Before leaving the *Ascania* all ranks had been supplied with two days' emergency ration, so that even if no supplies were forthcoming for two days after landing we should have enough food to go on with. At 10 p.m. our boat stopped, and after exchanging signals with some one, proceeded in pitch darkness through the submarine nets into what we were told was Suvla Bay. Every man now put on his equipment, and we patiently waited for the next stage in our journey. A steam launch came alongside and was quietly hailed from the bridge. We discerned six large tows following behind a launch, and began to disembark into the former. Each boat carried about fifty men. When all the boats were full the little launch moved quietly off into the darkness. After steaming for about ten minutes we narrowly avoided collision with six boats which were returning empty from the shore, their launch having broken down, and the sailors on board were waiting for another one to take them on. How they were ever found again that night in the pitch darkness without any lights was difficult to understand. In another ten minutes we ran up alongside of a little jetty made of pontoons and made fast. As soon as we had landed our men on the jetty, one of them disappeared through a hole in the planks, caused by a shell that afternoon. However, he was not quite out of his depth, and two of his fellows soon got him out. It was lucky it was not deeper, as a man in full equipment sinks like a stone. I reported myself to the Landing Officer, whose instructions were somewhat vague : " Go up the hill a little way, turn to the left, and try to find your unit directly the sun rises." It was very lucky for us that we landed in the dark, as the Turks shelled all landing parties by day—a fact which we soon realized when we saw the destruction at the land end of the jetty. They seldom fired at night, as they were afraid of giving away their positions. It was very hard work for my men, as they had to " man-handle " all the equipment, as they stumbled up the hill over rocks and through the scrub. We passed an A.S.C. food and ammunition dump which had evidently recently suffered from shell fire. About every twenty-five yards we were challenged by sentries. I learned from one of these that a Field Ambulance belonging to our Division had landed an hour previously and was only a short distance ahead. Eventually I heard a friend calling me, so decided that we had better lie down where we were until morning. As we lay in the scrub more and more troops kept arriving in the Bay from the transports at Lemnos, some being conveyed in destroyers, others in mine-sweepers and small packet-boats similar to the one we had come in. The strings of tows kept returning and fetching more men. Everything proceeded in perfect order, and hardly a sound was heard. All through the night drafts passed us asking for the whereabouts of the Manchesters, the Inniskillings, the Munsters, etc.

August 18*th.*

I was told that we should have to be on the move early, as we were lying in a very exposed position, as shown by certain ominous holes in the ground. We had landed at " A " Beach (west) Ghazi Baba, at the northern side of Suvla Bay. Directly it got light I came across the Gloucestershire Yeomanry, and we all received orders to move off in a north-westerly direction in order to take up a position behind a slight ridge on the rising ground. As we moved off the enemy began to shell our landing-place, where the rest of the Division, who could not be all disembarked during the night, were being landed. It was their baptism of fire, but they did not take the slightest notice of it, in spite of casualties. Eventually the whole division took up its position on the south-western slopes of Karakol Dagh, behind a low ridge which partially concealed them from enemy guns. Every man now set to work to dig himself a dugout.

At about 6 a.m. the Turkish guns got to work and heavily shelled " A " Beach, " A " Beach west, and Kangaroo Beach. This firing appeared to come chiefly from the positions on Baki Baba and Anafarta Sagir. The landing stages at the beaches mentioned and the A.S.C. depots seemed to be their special objective, but every now and then a shell would drop in our camp.

I established my dressing station in a little ravine between the first regiment of our Brigade and Brigade Headquarters. From this spot the wounded were evacuated to the Second Mounted Brigade Field Ambulance, and from this unit they were conveyed by mule ambulance transport to the beach at the extremity of Suvla Burnu. Here was situate the East Anglian Casualty Clearing Station. A steam launch towing three barges took the wounded from this point to the hospital ships in the Bay. It was a wonderful panorama that lay spread out before us as we sat in our dugouts on this heath-covered slope. A few hundred yards below was Suvla Bay with its battleships, transports, destroyers, monitors and hospital ships. The gunboats kept up an intermittent fire on the enemy's positions to the east, while the latter bombarded them in return. Fountains of spray kept appearing all round the ships where the enemy's shells had missed their mark. One of the former was apparently hit and left the line for a time, probably to repair some slight damage. Looking across the Bay to the southern side, one could see the hill called Lala Baba and " B " and " C " Beaches. The latter were protected by a spur which ran from Lala Baba to Point Niebruniessi, and behind this spur could be seen numbers of our troops and guns encamped. To the south-east of our position could be seen the white-coloured Salt Lake and Chocolate Hill (Yilgin Burnu) in the distance. North of this point could be seen the Anafarta Hills, and nestling in a depression in the latter the little white village of Kutchuk (small) Anafarta, with its slender minaret and row of little windmills set amongst the cypress-trees.

About midday the bombardment ceased and a few of us went down to bathe. We found a secluded cove to the west of Kangaroo Beach and enjoyed the refreshing swim. While in the water a shell hit a transport (? the *Minneapolis*), standing about half a mile out, and carried away part of her superstructure. A gunboat immediately placed herself between the transport and the enemy's line of fire and tried to locate the battery, which it apparently silenced—anyhow, for a time. Our water supply was derived from two springs near the beach and also from condensed water supplied from the ships. In the afternoon sixty men per regiment were ordered to make a road from " A " Beach in an easterly direction towards the Salt Lake. Some of them never returned to the camp, and others, severely wounded, passed through my hands, as the Turks saw them at work and shelled them heavily. At 5 p.m., while at tea, an aeroplane suddenly appeared from over the Anafarta Hills, and every man was ordered to lie down where he was. This was our first sight of " Fritz," who, we were told, came over daily at 5 p.m. to have a general look round. As he appeared almost over us with the evident intention of seeing what new troops had landed, suddenly little white clouds of smoke appeared above, below and in front of him. At the same time we heard the sound of firing, and then realized that the white puffs of smoke were the shells exploding from the anti aircraft guns of the ships in the Bay. It was all very new to us. He did not venture any further than our ridge, and was then compelled to return to his base, but apparently none the worse. It is doubtful whether he was able to estimate our strength or that of the Infantry Division situated behind us. During the night we heard very heavy rifle fire from the trenches in the plain to the east, and heard afterwards that a trench had been lost and retaken.

August 19th.

In the morning, while our men were drawing rations and water on the beach, some more casualties occurred.

The East Anglian Casualty Clearing Station lost several of its personnel and had to change its position. Our Second Mounted Brigade Field Ambulance also had to move further up the hill, as shells, meant apparently for " A " Beach, kept falling in its dugouts. From a slight eminence we watched another wonderful sight—the ships in the Bay bombarding the enemy's positions vigorously. We identified the positions of the various troops, which could be seen like a map spread out below us. On climbing the path that led right up the summit of Karakol Dagh, we found some of the Eleventh Division holding trenches on the summit. To the north these hills fell precipitously to the sea, and in a little bay below us a small gunboat was firing shells right over our men into the Turkish lines. Sitting in the old Turkish trenches on the south-eastern slope, we had a good view of the plain 400 feet beneath us, which extended eastwards to the hills where the enemy's big guns were located. Below us we could see our own guns, hidden almost entirely ·from view by the scrub, in most cases only the openings into the gunners' dugouts which faced towards us being visible. About 2 miles in front of the guns we could see parties in the open moving forward to the trenches and the wounded being carried back to the Welsh Field Ambulances near the beach. While we watched, the enemy did not locate our batteries, but we saw some men wounded who were apparently carrying up stores or ammunition. As the enemy's gunners had now suddenly selected the site of our Third Brigade Camp as their favourite target, this Brigade was compelled to change its position. Luckily the R.E. and Wireless Camp, situated next to us, was not interfered with. On our way down to the beach for our afternoon bathe, while the Turkish gunners were apparently having their siesta, we passed the Turkish prisoners who had been recently taken, in a barbed wire enclosure guarded by our men. They were chiefly fair complexioned, looked well fed and well equipped, in dark-brown khaki uniforms with khaki fez. From our bathing place we had a good

view of the islands of Samothrace and Imbros, the latter
being G.H.Q., M.E.F. At 5 p.m. "Fritz" appeared
again, received his usual greeting from the anti-aircraft
guns, and retired. We found it best to dine before dark,
as no lights were allowed. One had to be rather careful
with the water, but food was plentiful.

August 20th.

In the morning an aeroplane suddenly appeared over
our camp, and caused some alarm, until by the use of
glasses we recognized that it was one of our own. It
then circled round and round several times, and came
very low down, then, rising suddenly, flew off towards
the south. It transpired afterwards that it had brought
a message, which had been dropped in our camp for the
G.O.C. At midday the five Brigadiers met the General
and there was a rumour that we should soon be on the
move. At 5 p.m. we were told to be ready to move off
at six, and to carry extra ammunition, two days' emergency rations, and picks and shovels as well as the ordinary
entrenching tools. At 7 p.m. the Division commenced
to leave camp and at 8 p.m. I followed our Brigade with
my men. As we had no transport, it was very heavy
work for the medical and machine gun detachments, as
all equipment had to be man-handled. The large medical
and surgical panniers had to be carried on open stretchers,
and we organized a system of reliefs every quarter of
an hour, in order that the men should not be tired out.
All the officers' valises and the men's packs were left
behind in camp with a few sentries. After leaving camp
we followed the coast for about a mile, and then struck
out due east through the dense scrub, where our field
battery lay concealed. We saw the ghost-like figures
of the gunners as they stood just outside their shelters,
and the Indian Mule Corps bringing up their ammunition
in the dark. These little mules were wonderful, the way
they got over the rough ground. We had seen them
previously moving through our camp, on their way up
to the Eleventh Division on the summit of Karakol Dagh.

After going another half-mile we turned due south and, after passing a little cultivated land, got on to sound turf where the going was good. In front of us appeared what looked like rows of bathing machines in the dark, but they turned out to be the covered ambulance waggons of a Field Ambulance. Here we halted and rested for twenty minutes : we could hear very rapid and loud rifle fire from the trenches 2 miles to the east, and a message came through for the loan of two machine guns at once. The Derbys sent their detachment for a few hours and rejoined the column on the following morning. We now followed the coast line again, marching over .heavy sand, passing the Welsh Field Ambulances and the First Welsh Casualty Clearing Station, whose dugouts were in the sand-dunes near the water's edge. Here was situated the pontoon jetty, from which the wounded were dispatched by barge to the hospital ships in the Bay. Our way now lay through some soft ground, a sort of swamp, which, in winter, was the communication between the Salt Lake and Suvla Bay. Here was another wireless station, erected by the R.E. As we plodded on, the ground on our left gradually rose, until we were on the beach beneath the sandy cliff. On this beach we were astonished to find horse lines, the first we had seen on the Peninsula ; they were those of the heavy draught-horses belonging to the 60-pounders, which had been recently landed. We were now on what is called " B " Beach, which we had previously looked at from across the Bay. An Irish regiment passed us who were going to a " Rest Camp," after doing their turn in the trenches. As a matter of fact, such a thing as a Rest Camp did not exist in the Suvla Bay district, as every part of the beach was under gun-fire. After passing two Field Ambulances stationed near " C " Beach, we skirted the western slopes of Lala Baba and halted behind the commencement of the spur which leads from that hill to Point Niebruniessi. Here, after each man had dug himself in, the Division spent the night.

August 21st.

As soon as it was light we were awakened by terrific reports. A 60-pounder gun fifty yards to our left had opened fire on the enemy's position, and shells from our battleships were roaring over our heads. As the enemy were obviously searching for the 60-pounders, the Brigade nearest to them took up a position further to the south and nearer the beach. It was very interesting, watching the precision with which these guns were fired. There appeared to be regular danger zones between our Division and Lala Baba and between ourselves and the ground occupied by the next Infantry Division. No troops were encamped in these zones, and when one had to cross them, one did so at the double. Along the top of the crest behind which we were dug in was situated an old Turkish trench captured at the original landing about ten days before. Our Divisional Headquarters were established on the western slopes of Lala Baba. At 8 a.m., as the enemy's shells had become unpleasantly frequent, most of us left our temporary shelters, and ate our breakfast in the tiny ravines that ran down through the cliffs to the sea. Afterwards we had an enjoyable bathe. We were told that our Division was to take part in a general attack on the Turkish positions that afternoon. Some of us crawled over the ridge and lay down in the low scrub to examine the position through our glasses. Looking almost due east across the Salt Lake, we could see the low brown-coloured hill known as Chocolate Hill or Yilgin Burnu (53 m.), and in the foreground some low scrub. Under cover of the hill could be seen a Brigade of our infantry in their temporary dugouts ; these we supposed were part of the Tenth Division. To the north of Chocolate Hill we could see Hill 70 (Burnt Hill or Scimitar Hill), which is the commencement of the Anafarta Ridge. Immediately behind Chocolate Hill could be seen Hill 112 (or,ᵢ" W " Hill), on whose summit were the guns which caused most trouble to " B " and " C " Beaches and to the southern part of Suvla Bay.

We fully realized that when our time came to march across the plain these guns would be very troublesome. South-east we could see what looked like a series of cliffs at the foot of 971, running up towards Hill 101. These cliffs were partly occupied by the Australians, and a fertile valley lay between them and Chocolate Hill. Having had a good look, we returned to a safer place for lunch near the beach. At 1.30 p.m. I climbed the western side of Lala Baba in order to see our A.D.M.S. at Divisional H.Q. and to receive my orders ; I was told to carry all equipment on stretchers and make my own arrangements with regard to the wounded, and that the latter would have to be carried from the Field Ambulances to the beach by hand, as the country to the south was too rough for mule transport. At 2 p.m. all the battleships and monitors in Suvla Bay steamed in as near to the shore as possible, and two cruisers which had appeared south of Lala Baba promontory did the same. A few minutes later an observation balloon rose from one of the cruisers south of Lala Baba, and then commenced what appeared to us the most terrific bombardment of the enemy's position, chiefly Hills 70 and 112, by our battleships, cruisers, field guns and heavy howitzers. The enemy's positions appeared to be swallowed up in clouds of dust and smoke ; the Turks replied, but without any very obvious result as far as we could see. At about 3 p.m. our firing ceased, and four hospital ships, two in Suvla Bay and two south of Lala Baba, steamed in to within half a mile of the shore, taking care to give the battleships a wide berth. One of our aeroplanes, returning from over the Turkish trenches, brought news of the latest dispositions. From what we could gather, the dispositions of our own forces were as follows :

A Brigade of the Tenth Division and part of the Twenty-ninth Division were to attack Hill 70, aided by our own Second and Fourth Mounted Brigades. A Brigade of the Eleventh Division was to attack Hill 112, aided by our First, Third and Fifth Mounted Brigades, with another Brigade in reserve ; while the Divisions holding the trenches in the plain to the south were to rush the Turkish trenches in their front, then turn northwards and converge on Hill 112 from the south. Meanwhile the Fifty-third, Fifty-fourth and Eleventh Divisions in the trenches to the north of Hill 70 were also to advance, and in the extreme south the Australians and Ghurkas from Anzac were to advance on Hill 60 and link up their line with our own trenches. The remaining Brigades of the various Divisions were in reserve. At 3.10 p.m. our Division and part of the Tenth formed up behind Lala Baba, and then, crossing the ridge, commenced to descend to the Salt Lake plain. We were in the following order : Second Brigade (Berks, Bucks and Dorset Yeomanry), Fourth Brigade (three London Yeomanry Regiments), First Brigade (Worcester, Warwick and Gloucester Yeomanry), Third Brigade (Derbyshire and two Notts Yeomanry Regiments), Fifth Brigade (Hertfordshire and Westminster Yeomanry). Each Medical Officer and bearer party followed his own Brigade. Not a shot was fired until we had gone a quarter of a mile and were well into the plain, when suddenly we seemed to walk into an inferno of shrapnel and H.E. Our first casualty was a Worcester yeoman with a spent bullet in his thigh. After that, men seemed to be dropping like flies. Finding an old Turkish trench, we made it our first Aid Post ; this was soon full of wounded, dressed and labelled and fairly safe, as it was deep. I then looked for a Field Ambulance, but ours was at that moment only just starting down the hill behind the last Brigade, and the only Red Cross flag to be seen was 2 miles away across the Salt Lake. So, noting the position of our trench, we moved on. Selecting another Aid Post in a slight depression behind a stunted oak-tree, we were soon busy again bringing in the wounded. It was heartrending work, as so many were past hope of recovery ; the proportion of killed was very great and many were quite unrecognizable. Three slightly wounded men were killed in our Aid Post as a shell burst over us. The H.E. caused ghastly effects, as men were literally blown to pieces. My bearers worked splendidly, and brought the wounded in in a perfect inferno of bursting shells. We found that we were now picking up chiefly Notts, Derbys, Inniskillings, Irish Fusiliers, Sherwood Foresters and Hertfordshire Yeomanry, as our Brigade had turned slightly northwards and we, being busy, had not noticed this, and had kept straight on. Our Aid Post now contained about fifty wounded and dying, and I was very relieved to suddenly see a Red Cross flag appear about 200 yards behind our position. This turned out to be our Second Mounted Brigade Field Ambulance, so, after detaching an orderly to inform them of the position of our first Aid Post and the one we were just vacating, we pushed on to form our third. We now entered a piece of land covered with tall rushes, which made the search for wounded difficult. Here I was working with several M.O.'s, but we each had our own zone to draw. On one occasion practically nothing was left of what had been two stretcher-bearers carrying a man. I came upon a group of five yeomen, quite dead in realistic attitudes, without a scratch on them, probably the concussion effect of H.E. Several men unwounded had completely lost their reason and some were blind. Huge holes seemed to be torn in the squadrons as they advanced, but, to quote Ashmead-Bartlett's report, "they moved as if on parade, and losing many, they never wavered but pressed steadily on." The Indian Mule Corps advancing with us to bring up ammunition showed the greatest contempt for the enemy's fire. Our men bore their wounds with the greatest courage, and our stretcher-bearers worked in the calm routine fashion, as if they were working at a Field Day on the Berkshire Downs or on the marshes of the East Coast. One recognized now how important discipline and routine are on these occasions, when one saw each squad of three or four men performing their duties methodically. As we advanced the men of the Signal Companies, R.E., kept on laying their field telephone, and if one man, rolling his wheel over the ground, fell, there was always another behind to take it on. Here and there one came on large holes made by the H.E. shells; they were useful to put men into, as they were safe from rifle fire. We had to work as fast as possible in order to keep ahead of our Third and Fifth Brigades, which were following us, as we knew that if they passed us they would draw more fire on our wounded. My next Aid Post was just in front of a little wood of scrub ; there were now more bullet wounds, as we were nearer to the trenches. The fleet in the Bay now opened fire again, and we could hear the big shells roaring overhead. To quote Ashmead-Bartlett : " The rifle fire was deafening, and I do not think that I have ever heard such a din as that produced by the ships' guns, field pieces, bursting shells and thousands of rifles, on any battle-field before." Snipers in the low scrub in front of the hill now became very troublesome, remaining behind and firing on our men when they had passed. My Aid Post was now full, so, sending back another messenger, we pushed on again. We came to a point where a little path forked in the wood, and there we found quite a pile of men, evidently all shot by the same sniper as they passed that spot. As we were removing one of them another man was shot by the sniper. About this time the scrub on our right caught fire and burnt furiously. This made the immediate search for wounded very urgent. We could hear those who could not move crying for help as the flames crept up. Some men of another Division advanced along little footpaths amongst the flames, and when they were wounded badly, it was very difficult to remove them. I now moved on to form my next Aid Post at the base of the hill, but to get there we had to leave the scrub and double across two fields, which were continually being searched by snipers ; some of these were left exposed by the fire and were shot by our men on sight.

The Second Brigade Field Ambulance, which till now had been taking our cases, had been passing them on to the Casualty Clearing Station on the beach south of Lala Baba promontory, whence the wounded, after receiving their anti-tetanic inoculation, were removed by barge to the hospital ships.

On forming my Aid Post under the hill, I saw a Field Ambulance in a small wood just beyond the reach of the flames. This turned out to be our Fourth (London) Brigade Field Ambulance, and we then commenced to evacuate our wounded to it. From this spot the stretchers were carried to the dugouts of the advanced dressing station of the 32nd Field Ambulance on the Salt Lake. At this point mule transport took them across the bed of the lake to the Welsh Casualty Clearing Station on the beach. On arriving at the hill we were told that the Second and Fourth Brigade had gone on to the left, that the First Brigade had gone to the right, and that the Third and Fifth were resting under it. The latter then moved off to the right and our machine guns moved up the hill itself, with some of the Tenth Division. We received orders to leave all heavy equipment at the foot of the hill, and when this had been done we started to follow our Fifth Brigade, which had gone to the right, according to orders. The Brigade had moved off round the hill about twenty minutes before, and after going a short distance we came under very heavy fire and met a Major in an Irish regiment, who said it was quite impossible to get round that way now, as the enemy had just got a fresh machine gun in position and were enfilading that path ; so, realizing that I should be quite useless if I lost my bearers, I decided to retrace my steps, climb the hill, and descend on the other side. While we were attending to some wounded on the hill, I walked towards the northern end and must have become temporarily concussed, as two hours later I found myself walking between the advanced post of the 32nd Field Ambulance and Hill 70, without knowing how I got there, having lost most of my equipment, including my pack. However, I found my men, three of whom were now missing, on the top of the hill with our Brigade machine guns, and learnt that both our Field Ambulances were now established under the hill. It was now 11.30 p.m., and we began to descend the eastern exposed slopes of Chocolate Hill in very open order. There was little moon, and we could see, as we approached Hill 112, the fires which had broken out all over that hill, and also on Hill 60 to the south and Hill 70 to the north. As these fires increased, the surroundings were brilliantly illuminated. We did not know at the time that there was a large communication trench leading from the top of the hill to our advance trenches. We were told that if we went on about half a mile we should come to a lane which passed behind the trenches held by our First Brigade. We missed the lane, but stumbled into a trench held by the Sherwoods. We were glad to get into it, as the rifle fire was getting hot and bullets meant for this trench were breaking the ground at our feet. Here we attended to some wounded, and then proceeded along the trench in a north-easterly direction to where we heard cries for help. Doubling across the open, we found ourselves in a hot position, so dropped into the nearest trench, which turned out to be a Turkish one recently evacuated. I proceeded carefully, thinking that we might meet the Turk any moment; however, we did not meet any live ones. The fires on Hill 112 were now burning low, but one could see the neutral ground between our lines, with heaps of Turkish dead. Our Brigades had advanced up this hill, but had had to retire. I got out of our trench and found one of our machine guns at work, and waited for a time in a well-built Turkish shelter. Thus ended August 21st.

The following is an extract from Sir Ian Hamilton's dispatch (*The Times*, January 7, 1916):

The advance of these English yeomen was a sight calculated to send a thrill of pride through anyone with a drop of English blood running in their veins. Such superb martial spectacles are rare in modern war. Ordinarily it should always be possible to bring up reserves under some sort of cover from shrapnel fire. Here, for a mile and a half, there was nothing to conceal a mouse, much less some of the most stalwart soldiers England has ever sent from her shores. Despite the critical events in other parts of the field,

I could hardly take my glasses from the yeomen ; they moved like men marching on parade. Here and there a shell would take toll of a cluster ; there they lay : there was no straggling ; the others moved steadily on ; not a man was there who hung back or hurried.

August 22nd.

The fires on the hills had now burnt out : it was 2 a.m., and not knowing the general scheme of the trenches, I thought it best to wait until daylight before making a move. At 3 a.m. two infantry subalterns, evidently having lost their units, tumbled in on the top of us and immediately fell asleep. At 4 a.m. we got the order to retire, and fell in with the Worcester Yeomanry, who skirted the hill and formed up with the remains of the Division on the west of Chocolate Hill. The greater part of the Division then retired over the same ground which we had crossed on the previous day and returned to the ridge behind Lala Baba. Fortunately, in the dim dawn the enemy did not see our move, or we should have been shelled again. By 7 a.m. regiments were formed up again and were going through the sad ordeal of the roll call. We then learnt that the Second and Fourth Mounted Brigades had made an heroic attack on Hill 70, had reached the top, and had then been thrown back by sheer force of numbers. Their losses were very great, including two Brigadiers. It transpired that during the advance from Lala Baba to Chocolate Hill alone there had been five hundred casualties in our Division before it came within rifle range, and that our total casualties had been 30 per cent. A message now came up that sixty wounded were still lying on the edge of the Salt Lake, at the original first position of the Second Mounted Brigade Field Ambulance. They had been left there, under cover of a slight ridge, the afternoon before, but owing to the extreme pressure of work it had not been found possible to evacuate them to the southern beach. The Field Ambulance bearers were quite worn out with twelve hours' continuous carrying ; volunteers were therefore called for to carry them to the beach, as it was now light and shells were beginning to fall in the plain again. My own bearers were not fit to go, but we managed to get ten men per regiment in the Brigade, and I accompanied them, as, not having done any manual work, I was fairly fresh in spite of the last sixteen hours. We ran down and got to work at once, and acting as a bearer, I realized what hard work it was as I helped to carry a fat Major over very rough ground to the Casualty Clearing Station on the beach. Here we were rewarded with enormous bowls of tea and bread, which was very much appreciated, as we had eaten nothing since the previous afternoon. At this Casualty Clearing Station every wounded man was redressed if necessary, received hot food, his anti-tetanic injection, and was shipped off to the hospital ships in the Bay. On returning to our position behind Lala Baba we found most of our men asleep, in spite of the 60-pounders which were firing only a hundred yards away. Meanwhile, the sections of our Field Ambulances which had remained under Chocolate Hill, I could see with my glasses, were having a rough time. After a bathe we lunched again in the little ravines by the sea ; it was quite peaceful when the guns ceased to fire for a while, but we were not the merry party we had been twenty-four hours before—some were missing, some killed and some wounded. At 7 p.m. we again left Lala Baba and crossed the Salt Lake to Chocolate Hill. Not a shell was dropped on us, only an occasional rifle shot. What a scene of desolation—dead men, mules, rifles, ammunition, helmets and emergency rations lay everywhere. As we marched slowly along, we came across some of our dead and hastily buried them while it was possible. Most of these had not fired off any ammunition, as they had been killed by shell fire long before they were within rifle range of the enemy. It was sad work, burying these men, mostly yeomen farmers in the prime of life and of splendid physique—this senseless slaughter of war seemed appalling, when viewed calmly after the excitement of battle was over. Even-

3

tually we caught up our Brigade, who were lying at the foot of the hill. While sitting on the ground, one man gave a little cough and rolled over against his neighbour quite dead. We could not find the cause of death at first, but it turned out that a dropping spent bullet had entered the left lung just behind the clavicle, leaving hardly any wound. The Division now ascended the hill ; each Brigade had a small area allotted to it, and we all began to dig in for the night. It was very hard work in the stiff clay, but a certain amount of corrugated iron and balks of timber were obtainable. Extra sandbags were issued to the men, as they had used up those which they carried on the previous day.

August 23rd.

At daylight we found that we were not in the correct position, so we took over other dugouts further to the north, while part of the Brigade moved into the front-line trenches. At 8 a.m. the enemy, knowing that the western slope of the hill was covered with troops, shelled it furiously, and searched for the battery just below us. During the morning we improved our dugouts, which were built into the side of the hill. We were within fifty yards of the top of the hill, where our main communication trench started : the top of the former was an impossible place, as anyone who showed himself on the skyline was immediately sniped. Bullets were continually whistling over this ridge. Our water supply, which was limited to one gallon per man for twenty-four hours (to include drinking, washing and cooking), was drawn from the two wells at the bottom of the hill and from the mule water-convoys which crossed the Salt Lake at night from " A " Beach. Water was fetched at 6 a.m. and 6 p.m., and indents had to be in the night before ; it seemed a novel idea to us to have to indent for water ! The supply was organized by the D.A.D.M.S. and was in charge of an A.S.C. officer. Each regiment sent two R.A.M.C. water-duty men to assist at the distribution—unfortunately, the enemy got to know of the queue of men waiting under the hill morning and evening, and we had many casualties on this account. Eventually it was arranged that the men should wait on the hill and run over in pairs to fetch their water. All the condensed water brought from the ships by the mule transport was carried in old petrol-tins, which proved invaluable. A high wall of sandbags was built round our two Field Ambulances at the bottom of the hill, but in spite of this their casualties were frequent. Ammunition and ration dumps were formed nearby and were replenished nightly by the Mule Corps. Parties were sent out over the battle-field to bury the dead and collect equipment and ammunition. Whenever the mule convoys had to cross the Salt Lake by day they were shelled, and a line of dead mules marked the way from Chocolate Hill to Suvla " A " Beach. Whenever any number of men crossed this plain they were shelled, but single individuals were left alone. The advance post of the 32nd Field Ambulance on the Salt Lake lost so many of its personnel from shell fire that it had to be abandoned. I established my Brigade Dressing Station in our camp, and soon afterwards lost one of my men from a " spare." These spares were probably meant for the top of the hill, but being spent, they dropped on to us.

Intelligence reports informed us that the Turks were massing for a counter-attack, which might be expected in the early dawn. At midday our ships' guns got to work again, and as we sat on our hill the shells passed directly over us. After lunch a letter was read from our Divisional General congratulating the Division on its magnificent behaviour under fire, and especially the Second Mounted Brigade (Berks, Bucks and Dorset Yeomanry) on the splendid way they had attacked Hill 70. Numerous telephone wires ran from the crest of our hill to Lala Baba and the beach, so that observation officers could inform our ships and Field Artillery of the effect of their fire.

August 24th.

During the morning one of our wells ran dry and we were limited to one water-bottle a day each and a little extra water per ten men for making tea. One was afraid of eating one's fill of bully beef, as it caused such a thirst. After lunch I obtained permission from the General for myself and orderly to walk over to Suvla " A " Beach, in order to fetch some warm clothes, as the nights were now cold. It was a distance of about 4½ miles each way, by the route across the Salt Lake. There was a certain amount of risk, but that was certainly not as great as that of our usual position on the hill. Although parties were always shelled when crossing the open, I knew, from watching on previous days, that the Turks considered it a waste to shell single men. The only danger was from spares coming over from the trenches 1½ miles to the east, but these we also had on our hill. We passed the position formerly held by the 32nd Field Ambulance, whose dugouts had been completely flattened out, and then followed the track over the lake, which was punctuated by dead mules. It had been found impossible to bury these animals, as the clay forming the bed of the lake was very hard and any party of men digging would have been immediately shelled. A tremendous thunderstorm suddenly came on, which made our progress across the lake very slow, as the dry clay became wet and slippery. On reaching our former camp we found the Quartermaster and three other officers whom we had left at Lemnos as a first reserve ; they had just arrived on a destroyer, so I promised to conduct them to Chocolate Hill. After my servant had collected a few things and we had had a good bathe, we commenced the return journey. Walking one behind the other, at an interval of two hundred yards, Chocolate Hill was reached without any incident. In the evening an order was read out that we were to stand to arms every morning at 4.30 a.m., as that was apparently the usual time for a Turkish counter-attack.

August 25th.

We stood to at daylight, but bar the usual rifle fire nothing was doing. After breakfast I attended to some Irish wounded, brought into the reserve trenches at the top of the hill. During the morning we were heavily shelled, and had several men killed and wounded in their primitive dugouts. Fifty men per regiment were sent into the advance trenches to strengthen the Eleventh Division and learn their duties in stationary trench warfare. Burial parties were again sent out into the plain to search for missing and collect equipment. After supper our Divisional General joined us ; he told us that one of his R.E. officers had discovered a new Turkish well, and that probably our supply of water would be increased.

August 26th.

In the afternoon two of us walked across to the Welsh Casualty Clearing Station on the beach ; taking a different route across the lake, we came across several unexploded shells embedded in the clay, and examined the large craters formed by the enemy's H.E. Here were situated some of the hastily made Turkish trenches of the original landing. They contained Turkish equipment, broken rifles and dead Turks. On arrival at our hill we found that an Intelligence report had just come in (aeroplane) announcing the appearance of six large red cylinders behind the village of Kutchuk Anafarta ; these were supposed to contain gas. Respirators (of the most primitive type !) were served out to all, and Brigade M.O.'s instructed the men how to use them.

In the evening a large packet of maps was delivered at Brigade H.Q. ; we were all very pleased, as the maps which had been served out were scarce and lacking largely in detail. When the packet was opened it was found to contain maps of the Cromer, Sheringham and King's Lynn districts where we had been stationed in 1914 !

August 27*th.*

While having tea with the officers of the Second Mounted Brigade Field Ambulance in the tunnel in which they were living (they could no longer exist aboveground in their exposed position at the bottom of the hill), we heard a tremendous bombardment going on about two miles to the right of our position. Seizing our glasses, two of us ran up the hill and lay down in the scrub on its right-hand shoulder. Here we had a wonderful view of an Australian and a Ghurka Brigade advancing south of the Kasa Dere valley on Hill 60. We saw these troops, aided by the Connaughts and the South Wales Borderers, drive the enemy out of three rows of trenches amidst clouds of H.E. smoke and ultimately take the hill. It was a brilliant piece of work.

August 28*th.*

There was an alarm at 1.30 a.m.—very heavy rifle fire on the other side of our hill and thousands of bullets whistling over us. The enemy had sapped and taken one of our front trenches. We began to think that we might have to evacuate the hill. However, the trench was retaken with bombing, and things quietened down. At 8 a.m. the Turks got a new gun in position and began to enfilade our hill with shrapnel. This was a new experience, as hitherto they had always fired over the hill. Our dugouts which looked east and west were now not so useful, as shells came from the north. Just before breakfast three Gloucesters were killed and four wounded ten yards above us, and ten minutes later, while the men were having breakfast, three shells exploded in the midst of C Squadron, Worcester Yeomanry, killing three and wounding nineteen. Meanwhile the Yeomanry Brigades lower down the hill were faring little better, and both our Field Ambulances suffered ; however, one of our big guns behind Lala Baba saw our trouble and silenced the enfilading gun for a while. At 10 a.m., while attending to a man in my dressing station below the ridge, this

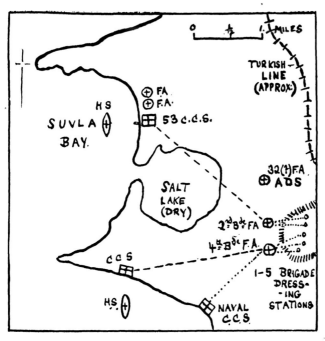

- - - - Light Ambulance Waggon.
.... Stretcher.

EVACUATION OF WOUNDED (SECOND MOUNTED DIVISION),

AUGUST 22-28, 1915.

(Based on *The Times* map.)

troublesome gun got to work again, and this time I was one of the victims. On coming to, I found myself being carried face downwards on a stretcher by my own men. Suddenly another shell burst, covering us with lumps of clay ; one bearer stumbled, recovered himself, and we went on. Ultimately they deposited me at Brigade Headquarters, where I was dressed. I now started on the usual journey of the wounded to the coast. They carried me to the bottom of the hill to the Second Mounted Brigade Field Ambulance, where a mule ambulance cart was standing to convey wounded to the beach. While four of us were waiting to be lifted into the cart, a shell burst and killed the two leading mules. They were cut away from the survivors, but it was an hour before new ones could be procured. Meanwhile, more wounded were accumulating in the Field Ambulance. It was the most uncomfortable hour I had ever spent, lying on one's face on a stretcher unable to move and getting stiffer and stiffer, and never knowing where the next shell would fall, as the mules were killed about ten yards from where we lay. However, we were off at last, four lying and four sitting cases, jolting over the bed of the Salt Lake. The blinds were drawn and we could see nothing, but twice a shell fell near the waggon ; the good little mules plodded on and eventually brought us to the Welsh Casualty Clearing Station. Here we each received our injection of anti-tetanic serum, and after waiting about two hours were carried on to the barges. On the way out to the hospital ship a shell meant for a monitor gave some of us rather a shock. On coming alongside, those who could walk went up the steps, and the rest of us were slung on board by means of winches, the stretchers being placed in a sort of crate before being hoisted out of the barge. We found ourselves on board that excellent ship, H.S.F.A. *Rewa*. My wound was just below the right shoulder, and the shrapnel bullet had tracked up to the cervical spine ; it was stiff and painful. Most of us managed to enjoy our dinners, which, although " light diet," were delicious, after the food we had been accustomed to lately. Best of all, we were allowed as much water to drink as we liked, as the ship had her own condensing plant on board.

August 31*st.*

At dawn the *Rewa* entered Mudros Bay ; here the walking cases were transferred to the stationary hospital and other stretcher cases were embarked. . . . After an uneventful voyage Devonport was reached on September 9th, and we were all transferred by hospital train to London.

CHAPTER II

MUDROS—MENA CAMP

November 5th.

At 2 p.m. H.M.T. *Andania* left Devonport carrying drafts of various regiments to the Dardanelles ; many of us had been there before, and had recovered from our wounds.

November 12th.

Our troopship entered Malta Harbour about midday ; the latter contained numerous British and French gunboats, destroyers and transports—amongst these we saw the troopship *Mercia*, carrying the Lincolnshire Yeomanry, which had preceded the *Andania* and had suffered considerably from an attack by a submarine. Two of us spent an interesting day in the town visiting the splendid collection of armour in the palace of the Knights of Malta. Before returning to our ship we were shown all over the submarine which we were told Commander Boyle, V.C., had navigated through the Dardanelles.

November 13th.

The *Orange Prince* was reported to have been submarined outside Malta. We sailed in the early morning.

November 15th.

Our escort of T.B.D.'s met our ship amongst the Greek islands and convoyed us to Mudros Bay, which we reached on the following day.

November 16*th.*

Although no official landing orders were received, six of us, anxious to know the whereabouts and the strength of our units, were given permission to go ashore in one of the ship's boats on the condition that we were back by 5 p.m. By mistake we rowed to East Mudros, which appeared to be entirely occupied by French, European and native troops. After ascertaining that there were no British troops in the vicinity, we put off in our boat, chiefly manned by officers and men of an Australian Bridging Train, for the opposite side of the Bay, and landed at West Mudros. After spending a couple of fruitless hours looking for our units, we returned to our rowing boat and embarked. By the time we had reached the transports in the Bay it was dark, and an hour was spent in searching for the *Andania*. It was after 5 p.m., and a voice from our ship informed us that the " steps " were up, and that we were to come on board by a rope-ladder hung over the bows. Climbing on to a barge, three of us commenced to ascend ; the first man had just got on board when suddenly I found a large bale descending on my shoulder. I started to descend, but could not do so fast enough ; my right arm became useless, and thoughts of letting go passed through my mind as the pressure became greater, but I remembered that I should fall not into the sea but on to the iron deck of the barge far below. However, the first man up heard my shouts and attracted the attention of the donkey-man, who in the nick of time reversed his engine and thus took the load off my shoulder. It was an unpleasant experience, and I eventually arrived on deck in a somewhat shaky condition.

November 17*th.*

As a gale was blowing it was not considered safe to land, so we remained at anchor in the Bay. In the afternoon a large supply barge, in calm weather propelled by a small motor, drifted by us, making for the open sea stern first and completely out of control. Hearing the agonized cries from the two A.S.C. men on board, wire hawsers were thrown from the *Andania* and the men were rescued.

November 18th.

During the morning we were landed in tugs at West Mudros; after reporting at H.Q. Lines of Communication, a walk of four miles brought us to the Ninth Corps Rest Camp, where the remains of the Second Mounted (Yeomanry) Division were under canvas. Only ninety of our original regiment were left, and only one of the attached R.A.M.C. The camp was situate in a bleak valley and the weather was bitterly cold.

November 20th.

On climbing to the summit of a hill surmounted by a Greek chapel we obtained a fine view of the Bay full of shipping, the latter being dwarfed by the enormous *Olympic* and *Aquitania*.

November 21st.

Many tents were blown down by the gale; one unfortunate officer woke in the night feeling remarkably cold, but in time to see his tent departing in the direction of Imbros.

November 22nd.

As we were merely awaiting embarkation orders no work was undertaken, and expeditions in the island were the order of the day. The village of Condia was first explored, but it was found to be an uninviting place. The road between this village and our camp was patrolled by a Greek gendarme; he did not quite know what his duties were, as the road was already patrolled by our M.F.P.'s; however, he solved the difficulty by opening a little stall, where he did a thriving trade in chocolate and cigarettes.

November 23rd.

On the way to Castro, the capital of the island, one of our party shot a vulture, and we saw it fall about a quarter of a mile away. A Greek peasant ran to secure it; however, one of us got there first and seized the bird, only to be rewarded with a nasty wound on the arm, caused by the former in its death struggle. Castro proved to be a picturesque town, reminding one of the Balkans, and boasted an inn which produced an excellent omelette and good white wine. On the return journey we took a different route, and not having the requisite passes to present to the pickets on the road, we left the latter and struck across country instead.

The natural hot baths at Thermopylæ proved a great boon to the men, as the bitterly cold weather did not make cold baths popular.

November 24th.

Orders were received to embark at West Mudros. One Brigade, having disposed of all its mess stores and handed over its tents to other units, marched down to the beach to find that orders were cancelled, and was compelled to return to its bare bleak camp for another three days.

November 26th.

The remains of the Worcester, Berks, Dorset, Bucks, Herts and Westminster Yeomanry, accompanied by the London Mounted Brigade Field Ambulance, left the Ninth Corps Rest Camp and embarked on a large flat ferry steamer, and were transferred to H.M.S. *Hannibal* in the Bay. During the proceedings several valises fell overboard, and after bobbing up and down for a few minutes quietly sank. Except for the owners it was an amusing spectacle.

November 30th.

H.M.S. *Hannibal* arrived at Alexandria and we entrained for Cairo.

December 1st to 20th.

During the next three weeks the fourteen Yeomanry regiments of the Second Mounted Division, which had now returned to their horses, were camped in the desert near Mena, close to the Pyramids. The weather was beautiful, and it was a delightful change after the bitter cold experienced at the Dardanelles. The camp was situate well above the Nile flood water, amidst intensely interesting and historic surroundings. The sunsets were wonderful, especially when the Mokattam Hills became tinged a delicate pink.

December 25th.

About this date the Division left Mena, the First Brigade proceeding to Salhia Kantara and El Ferdan (the latter two on the Canal), the Second Brigade taking part in the Senussi campaign on the western frontier, the Third Brigade embarking for Salonika, and the Fourth Brigade marching to Abassia. The author of this diary, having been admitted to Mena House Military Hospital with enteric fever, was for a period unable to keep himself informed of current events.

1916.

February 12th.

At sunset the hospital ship *Oxfordshire* left Alexandria with her complement of sick and wounded.

February 15th.

Our ship arrived at Malta at 9 a.m. ; here some of the convalescents were disembarked for Palermo and some Salonika wounded were taken on board.

February 22nd.

We arrived at Southampton in a snowstorm ; what a contrast to the warm weather in Malta a week ago ! The usual hospital train was waiting and carried us swiftly to London.

CHAPTER III

THE SINAI DESERT

May 10*th.*

Off to the East again for the third time in thirteen months ; this time it was on the empty hospital ship *Carisbrooke Castle,* outward bound from Southampton to Alexandria.

May 21*st.*

Alexandria was reached at 10 a.m., the sight of which now appeared quite familiar. Being in charge of R.A.M.C. drafts for the Fifty-second Division, my first duty was to march the men to the Base Details Camp at Mustapha.

May 24*th.*

At 8 p.m. a troop train, containing drafts for all the regiments on the Canal, left Sidi Gaba station. The draft for the Worcester Yeomanry contained many of our Gallipoli wounded, two of my personal friends being in charge.

May 25*th.*

At 4.30 a.m. our train arrived at Ballah, a post on the western side of the Canal, between Kantara and El Ferdan. Horses had been sent to meet us, as our camp was some distance across the desert. Here we found the remains of our regiment, which had suffered so severely at Katia and Oghratina on Easter Sunday. In addition to our regiment there were in this camp two squadrons

of Warwickshire Yeomanry, "B" Battery H.A.C., our
Field Ambulance and A.S.C., A.V.C. and R.E. details.
Nearer the Canal was a part of the 33rd Field
Ambulance and the 26th Casualty Clearing Station ; on
the opposite bank were some Brigades of the Eleventh
Division. Two squadrons of Gloucester Yeomanry were
at El Ferdan and one squadron of the Warwickshire
Yeomanry were at Ballybunnion. Our drinking water
supply came by pipe from Ismailia and was carried from
a depot near the station by water-cart. Washing water
was obtained from a branch of the Sweet-water Canal ;
this water contained *Bilharzia hæmatobia*, and in order
to render it safe for ablution purposes it had to be
pumped into tanks and allowed to stand for forty-eight
hours before use—the organism, whose habitat is the
snail, dies twenty-four hours after it leaves its host. A
sentry was always on duty at the tanks and an R.A.M.C.
water-duty man was in charge.

May 26th.

It was most curious to watch the large steamers passing
through the Canal : at a little distance they appeared
to be sailing through the desert. Numerous flamingos
were to be seen, of a delicate pink colour, but of no
use as food.

May 27th.

Bathing in the Canal was most refreshing in the evening,
but we were not allowed to swim across to the other side.
A picket patrolled the opposite side of the Canal day
and night to prevent native spies from placing mines
in the fairway. Every night a detachment of the Bikanir
Camel Corps dragged a sort of wooden sledge along the
bank, so that footprints on the smooth track could be
detected at once in the morning ; by this means, at a
later date, Turkish prisoners were caught after they had
crossed the Canal. After bathing, we usually remained
a while and watched the evening steamers passing by.
All neutral vessels had a guard of soldiers on board for

the Canal passage ; they were sent on board at Suez or Port Said in order to prevent the benevolent neutrals from sowing mines.

May 29th.

In the morning two of us took the train to Port Said in order to do some mess shopping ; it was a disappointing town, and the only thing that appeared to be of interest was the statue of De Lesseps at the end of the pier. We were rowed across to the Asiatic bank, where we visited some of our wounded in the Thirty-first General Hospital.

May 30th.

A case of smallpox having occurred in this area, orders were received to vaccinate everyone. This disease appeared to be common amongst the natives. No one was allowed to leave the camp during the morning, as the Ballah guns were practising. After lunch we found our first chameleon, which proved most useful in eating all the flies in the mess ; later on we kept quite a large number of these little animals, which became quite tame and used to live on the tent-poles ; one of these, known by the name of Cuthbert, held the record for eating fifty flies before breakfast.

June 1st.

To-day we heard that there was a rumour of a move ; this usually happened when we had put in a lot of work and got thoroughly settled. The men had been working for weeks building reed mess-huts and sun-shelters over the horse lines.

June 2nd.

Orders were received to march to Kantara on the 5th.

June 3rd.

" Intelligence " stated that a German Turkish offensive was maturing at El Arish.

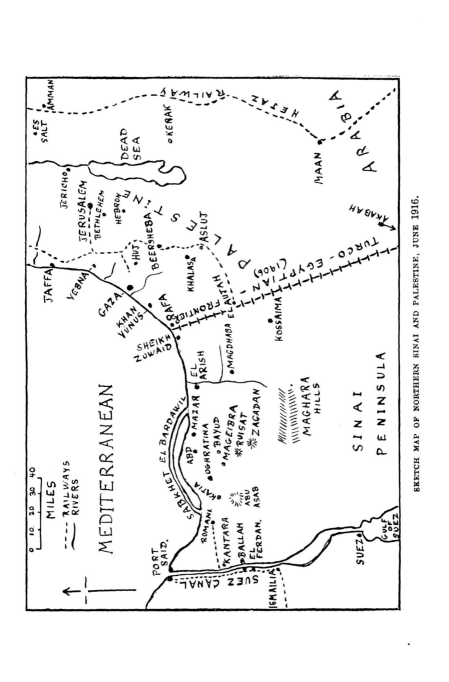

SKETCH MAP OF NORTHERN SINAI AND PALESTINE, JUNE 1916.

June 5th.

At 4 a.m. two of us, with eighty men, marched down
to the Canal, where we found a large barge, on which
our heavy materiel had been loaded the day before.
After embarking the men we woke up a Sapper and had
some breakfast with him on his river steamer; he was
building a road between Ballah and Kantara. At 5 a.m.
a tug came along with the Gloucester barge from El
Ferdan; we tied on, and proceeded up the Canal to
Kantara. The rest of the Brigade came across country with
the camels. We arrived about 8 a.m. and disembarked
above the pontoon bridge. Kantara, at this time a very
small place and on the eastern side of the Canal, consisted
only of the quarantine house and the tents belonging
to two or three regiments. Our camp was about a mile
along the old caravan route, which leads through the Sinai
Peninsula to Palestine, and was situate between part of
the Fifty-second Lowland Division and the Scottish
Horse Brigade; on the opposite side of the track was an
aerodrome, and between our camp and the Canal was an
artillery park. In the evening several of us walked
through the gunners' lines to the Canal, where we found
a good bathing place off an old barge. As swimming
across this part of the Canal was not forbidden, we
amused ourselves by swimming from Asia to Africa and
back again.

June 6th.

Machine guns had now been mounted round our camp,
in order to be ready for "aviatiks," should they appear.
We were inlying regiments for the day, ready to move out
in case of an alarm. In the evening we walked round
some of the trenches and posts protecting our camp;
the trenches were well revetted in the loose sand. Special
orders were issued as to procedure in the event of an
aeroplane attack. As our Fifth Mounted Brigade Field
Ambulance had remained at Ballah, I received orders to
evacuate any sick and wounded to the 2nd Lowland

Field Ambulance. The evening Intelligence report stated
that enemy concentration was rapidly proceeding at
El Arish. An " agent " reported one German aeroplane
made of gold ! The Germans had apparently given this
out in order to impress the natives. The " agent " also
reported numerous foreign officers with fair hair and
yellow (sic) eyes, followed by long dogs with short
legs which came to heel when whistled to ! Inference
of " agent "—probably Germans ! These agents were
generally Bedouin, employed by both sides as spies.
They had, however, to prove their identity before
entering our camp.

June 9th.

In the evening our Brigade moved into the trenches
which would be occupied by us in the event of an attack
on Kantara ; these consisted of a series of barbed wire
entanglements and an intricate system of trenches with
occasional strong posts. The artificial inundations from
the Canal completed the defences north and south. The
idea in those days was that we should hold out until all
other troops and materiel had been removed across the
Canal.

June 10th.

In the morning some of us rode out to a post known
as Hill 40, where the Australi. n Light Horse and some
Scottish regiments were stationed. The flamingos on
the edge of the inundation were most picturesque.

June 11th.

It was a very hot day, with absolutely no breeze. At
2.45 p.m., while we were resting in our tent, we were
awoken by several explosions, and ran out to find an
" aviatik " immediately overhead. An explosion followed
close to the 2nd Lowland Field Ambulance. In all nine
bombs were dropped : two fell in the Canal, one near
the station, two behind the R.F.C. sheds and some in
the A.V.C. lines. Very little damage was done, two or

three men being wounded and twelve mules killed. The regiment, except for one man to every six horses, paraded outside the camp, according to orders. Our machine guns responded without any success. One of our battle-planes ascended, but the enemy had done his work and had got a good start for the east. He was chased as far as Bir El Abd, and was then lost in a cloud. This was my first experience of being bombed in the Sinai Peninsula.

June 12th.

To-day it was rumoured that Baghdad had fallen—rumours travel fast in the East. Two fresh battalions of infantry reinforced us during the day.

June 18th.

Early this morning ten aeroplanes collected on the aerodrome, three having joined up from Ismailia. By 7.30 they had all left, flying due east ; this was our revenge for last Sunday. Later in the morning seven returned ; two were said to have been shot down at El Arish, where the others had caused considerable damage to the Turkish camp outside the town.

June 20th.

It was decided that two of us, accompanied by two sergeants and twelve men, should march to Katia, in order to re-bury and identify some of our dead. A few days after the battle these had been buried by the Australian Light Horse, but news had reached us that the wind had uncovered the graves in the exposed position. At 10.30 p.m. a message came through from Ismailia stating that a cyclone was approaching the Canal area at 90 miles an hour, and that our tents and huts would be blown away unless strengthened. A few minutes later every tent-peg in Kantara was being driven deeper into the sand, and the tapping of the mallets resounded throughout the camp. Everyone stood by for the expected cyclone ;

this, however, never arrived. It is supposed that it must have taken a different course, as, with the exception of a stiff breeze, nothing occurred.

June 21st.

At 1 a.m. our little party left the camp, accompanied by the Padre. Our way lay through Hill 40, and passing through this post in the dark was quite jumpy work, as the sentries were very much on the alert and suddenly leapt out of obscurity into the middle of the track with bayonet fixed and gruff challenge. By 2.30 a.m. it was getting light as we arrived at the last fortified camp, known as Hill 70. Here we watered our horses as the sun rose behind the great sand mountain Katib Abu Asab, a landmark for miles around. Up till now we had been following a desert track by the side of our narrow-gauge railway, laid down by the R.E., but now we struck across the open and met the broad-gauge railway which then ran from Kantara to Romani, and which was destined to connect Egypt with Syria. Some miles to the right of our path lay the camp of Dueidar, where six weeks ago a company of the Royal Scots Fusiliers made such a brilliant stand. To our left lay the plain of Tina, with the Bay in the distance, and the site of the ancient Roman city of Pelusium ; the latter the Romans called the key to Egypt, as in those days the Nile is supposed to have flowed out into Tina Bay. The going now became very heavy, over undulating sandy country heavily dotted with clumps of " camel-grass." A wonderful mirage appeared in the Bay of Tina, rows of white houses being seen apparently standing in the water ; this was evidently caused by a reflection of Port Said, some 25 miles to the west. We now followed a field-telephone wire which would eventually lead us to Romani. A few large birds flew overhead, kites and bustards, the only other signs of animal life being jerboas (kangaroo rats), lizards and chameleons. After stopping for breakfast we crossed a ridge of sandy hills, the spurs of which extended down to the plain, and obtained a wonderful view of the surrounding country. The landscape had altered and we had begun to enter the great Katia water-belt, or the land of Hods. A Hod is usually a depression in the desert, studded with palm-trees and containing water, of a varying degree of brackishness, just below the surface of, the ground. This water can sometimes be drunk by human beings, and horses will generally drink it unless the degree of salinity is very high. When drunk by the former, intestinal catarrhs are apt to follow. The water is usually obtained by sinking a shaft four to six feet deep, revetting the sides with sandbags, and then letting in a cylinder of corrugated iron. It was considered essential that the Katia waterbelt should be held by our troops, as it was the last district the Turks could obtain water from, and thus constituted a jumping-off place for an attack on the Canal. From our position we could see several of these Hods scattered about over the landscape. It was ten o'clock and getting very hot as we rode through a large Hod, the water of which was so brackish that the salt lay deposited on the sand, and saw part of the Romani camp at the end of a long sandy valley. We had now been riding for ten hours and had covered some 30 miles, this being the average horse pace (including halts) through the heavy sand. The first camp was that occupied by the Bikanir and Egyptian Camel Corps. Here we saw thousands of camels, which carried out all the transport of supplies and water to the isolated posts. Romani was, at this time, both railhead and pipe-head. We rode on a mile or two through the various camps, which were very much spread out on account of recent enemy bombing, until we reached Brigade H.Q. of the Second Australian Light Horse Brigade, situated in a little Hod by itself. The Brigade was out on recon-naissance, but we found the Staff Captain and Supply Officer, from whom we drew three days' rations for our men and horses. We also procured the regulation amount of water in " fanatis " [1] and a certain number of camels.

---

[1] *Fantassi* (plural *fanatis*) = zinc water-container of about ten gallons capacity, two of which are usually carried by a camel.

After lunch we tried to get some sleep, but the extreme heat down in the hollow and the enormous number of flies made this difficult. It was agreed that we should start at three o'clock next morning, with an Australian guide to show us the best way to Katia and Oghratina. We were informed that we should have to return immediately after the patrols between the former place and Bir El Abd came in.

June 22nd.

We left Romani, after watering just outside camp, at 3 a.m., with our Light Horse guide. After going a short distance one camel sank in some boggy ground and had to be unloaded before he could be extricated ; luckily, we saved the two fanatis of drinking water which he carried. The desert was very picturesque, so different from the endless sandy wastes of Libya. To our left lay the sea and the camp of Mahamdiya. The camels were rather troublesome, so I took one party on while my companion went back to try a little persuasion. We rode over some very deep sand drifts, sand ridges, and " saddles," whose conformation was continually changing according to the prevailing wind. In one Hod which we passed there was actually standing water, and in most of them there was evidence of former Bedouin encampments. These Bedouin had now been cleared from this district, as they were often found to be enemy agents. The palm-trees were loaded with dates, but these were still green. As we were passing through a little sandy valley we came across footmarks, which greatly excited our guide, who assured us that they were recent, since the dew, and not those of our patrol. We hastily got our camels down off the sky-line, and all took cover behind a small ridge. One of the enemy's patrols could be seen about a mile away ; thinking it best to be cautious, we waited until the Turk had disappeared before continuing our journey. By 9.30 we were on firm ground and were entering the northern Oghratina Oasis, known as Hod En Negiliat. At this point we came across the old Sinai telegraph line

which formerly connected Kantara with Jerusalem. In
the Hod were congregated a large number of camels,
with supplies and drinking water for the Australian
Light Horse Brigade, which was doing the two days'
patrol between this spot and Bir El Abd. Three wells
had been sunk in this Hod in April, at the time of the
recent fighting, in order to water camels and horses.
All drinking water had to be carried out in fanatis from
pipehead at Romani. At 11 a.m. two of us climbed
the northern face of Oghratina Hill ; this was very steep
and of loose sand. The hill itself was horseshoe shaped
and we were at one extremity ; it was here that
one and a half squadrons of our regiment, with some
R.E.'s and R.A.M.C., had been surrounded and attacked
early on Easter Sunday morning, in a white mist, by a
force of 2,000 Turks with artillery. Our visit was in
order to estimate the number of bodies to be re-buried.
Everywhere there was evidence of a stubborn resistance,
and a very large number of Turkish corpses lay on the
western slope. All the bodies and graves were round the
circumference of the hill ; each man lay where he fell.
Most of the bodies had been stripped by the Bedouin of
their clothing, identification discs and boots. We now
descended to our palm grove again and rested till three
o'clock, when a camel was loaded with 500 sandbags and
spades and the whole party climbed the hill. The sad work
now proceeded of reinterring, and covering the graves with
sandbags, where necessary. Most of these had been
lightly covered with sand, which had, in many cases, been
blown away by the wind on the exposed western slopes.
By 7 p.m. we had completed our work, and descended
to the palm grove again. As the Brigade which was
operating in the vicinity was to be withdrawn next
day, we were told that we must be ready to move
at 1 a.m.

June 23rd.

We left Oghratina at 3 p.m. and marched on a compass
bearing of 260°, leaving Katia on our left. Here some

squadrons of the Worcester and Gloucester Yeomanry had been attacked by 3,000 Turks and Germans with artillery. The bodies had been properly interred a day or two after the engagement, but it was now almost impossible to approach, on account of the very large number of dead horses and camels. As we approached the sandhills which protect Romani to the eastward, we noticed how strongly the latter place was defended with trenches, wire, guns and strong posts. Passing through a narrow defile in the sandhills, we arrived at the water-troughs at 6 a.m ; after resting in the heat of the day we rode straight back on a compass bearing of 240° through Hills 70 and 40 to Kantara, where we arrived at 9.30 p.m., having done about 40 miles since three o'clock in the morning.

June 25th.

Dummy hangars and dummy guns were erected on the aerodrome, as retaliation was expected for our recent successful raid on El Arish.

June 27th.

Enemy aeroplanes approached during the morning, but were driven off by our scouts. A large boxing contest took place at night between the Fifty-second Division, Fifth Mounted Brigade and the Scottish Horse Brigade. In the evening the G.O.C. Third Section distributed the prizes.

June 28th.

An " aviatik " appeared over camp during the morning, but did no damage. Later in the day one large Haviland machine was brought down by the enemy ; one of our aeroplanes was also brought down near El Arish, but the pilot and observer managed to escape by walking along the coast to Mahamdiya. A mounted patrol tried to save the machine near El Abd, but was beaten off by the Turks.

June 29th.

The Warwickshire Yeomanry proceeded to Hill 70, their camp being taken over by a regiment of the New Zealand Mounted Rifles.

July 3rd.

While at dinner our patrols brought in 150 camels captured from the Bedouin. From our mess tent we watched searchlights of the steamers in the Canal flashing across the desert. The old pilgrim route along which the caravans have journeyed for thousands of years passed just outside our camp ; this was the route which connected the Holy Land with Egypt, and must have been traversed during the Flight into Egypt soon after Our Lord was born. This little caravan must have used the same Hods for water which the British troops were using now. Probably at that time the Nile ran out into Tina Bay, near Romani, where the ancient city of Pelusium, the " key of Egypt," was situated. One could not help wondering what could have been the determining factor in altering the course of such a mighty river.

July 19th.

The Brigadier and General Commanding the Third Section dined with us at night. In the middle of dinner they both received urgent messages and were compelled to leave ; intelligence had come through that a force of Turks had collected at El Abd and was advancing towards us. There were 8,000 at El Abd, and our patrols had also been engaged at Oghratina. Several infantry regiments reinforced us from the other side of the Canal during the night.

July 20th.

More regiments from the Fifty-third and Forty-second Divisions marched in. At twelve o'clock orders were received for one squadron of the Worcesters, one squadron of the Gloucesters and two squadrons of the New Zealand Mounted Rifles to be ready to move off if required.   I was ordered to go in medical charge of this composite regiment.

At 10 p.m. we moved off, consisting of Gloucesters, Worcesters and New Zealand squadrons ; the desert seemed to be alive with infantry battalions and guns, which kept bumping into us in the dark, and a brilliantly lit hospital ship passing down the Canal gave a sort of omen of what was to come. We halted at Hill 40, where the Adjutant of a New Zealand regiment told us that patrols had been in action near Oghratina, in the vicinity of which 10,000 of the enemy were said to be entrenched. Hill 70 was reached before midnight, here the air was still more pregnant with rumours, and after watering our horses we bivouacked for the night.

July 21*st*.

When it got light we found the Warwickshire Yeomanry, who had been here three weeks, camped close by. The following order was issued :

It is forbidden to drink water from desert wells, which are nearly always polluted. At the same time it is recognized that there may be cases where it is unavoidable—for instance, a wounded man left out, etc. ; to meet such cases, and in order to treat water from the wells, each man will be supplied with one bottle of sulphate tablets ; should a man find himself in such a position that he must drink well water, he will add two tablets to the contents of the water-bottle each time he fills it. He will then shake the whole thoroughly, and not drink the water until a full half-hour has elapsed.

These tablets were issued to units, and when the occasion arose were extremely useful. Whenever it was possible, all water was properly sterilized by medical officers with chloride of lime. At this time the water allowance was good—one gallon per man per day. Of this, five pints were used in the cook-house (for cooking, tea, etc.), two pints were used for filling the man's water-bottle, and

one pint was allowed for washing purposes. During
the morning we could hear the Ayrshire R.H.A. shelling
the Turkish position at Oghratina. The Leicester and
Somerset R.H.A. were lying next to us. At midday we
sent an officer to the Hill 70 fort to look out for hostile
aircraft : his duty was to telephone down to the camp,
whence the warning was passed to Hill 40 and Kantara.
An officer from each regiment in the camp took this duty
for two hours at a stretch.

Intelligence.—A large body of the enemy located yesterday
cannot be accounted for to-day ; they are probably moving south.
The Turks have dug in along a line N. to S., Oghratina to Mageibra
(7 miles), with 6,000 men. Another 1,500 are at Bir El Abd.

It appeared that the Turks now held a strong position,
and a line behind which they could easily bring up reinforcements. We were about 15 miles from that line.
During the day the Australian Light Horse fell back
on Romani. One could not help thinking how pleased
the enemy must have been to have found our well-
prepared wells at Oghratina.

Intelligence.—Large reinforcements are now on their way from
El Arish.

July 22nd.

At 7.30 an " aviatik " came over, evidently observing
and counting us ; he was signalled to Kantara, and one of
our battle-planes came out, but by this time the former
was on his way home. In this camp the alarm consisted
of three blows on a whistle, following which all the horses
were taken off the lines. Then another three whistles
and all horses were taken outside camp. During the day
we procured a few tents, as we had come without any
transport and our only shelter from the sun consisted of
one horse-blanket each. The Turks were evidently in
a good position, and it was wonderful how quickly they
had crossed the 47 dry miles from El Arish to
Bir El Abd. We were now part of a mobile column,

consisting of the Gloucester Yeomanry, the New Zealand Mounted Rifles, two R.H.A. batteries and ourselves, and were ready to " strike " at a moment's notice. The idea apparently was to lure the Turks on to our defences at Romani and Dueidar. Later in the day two of our officers rode over from Kantara and we heard about the prisoners who had already been sent down ; the latter stated that Romani was to be attacked and the railway and pipe-line cut. We were ordered to send out mounted patrols day and night to guard both of these. After a conference of C.O.'s we were informed that the mobile column would strike when the Turks crossed the line Romani–Dueidar.

July 23rd.

After standing to from 3 to 4 a.m. the regiment practised an attack at Turk's Top Post.

July 24th.

The Turks were said to be still entrenching, and Intelligence reported that large numbers of machine guns were being brought up. We received orders that while on the move no one was to touch his water-bottle between dawn and sunset, and that even then he was not to empty his bottle until he knew for certain that more water was to be issued.

July 25th.

An " aviatik " came over at 7.30, but was soon driven off.

Intelligence.—The Turks are firmly established at Bir El Abd, where they have a good landing-ground for aeroplanes.

July 26th.

Intelligence.—The enemy have now advanced to Hod Er Reshafat, which they now hold. Two thousand camels have been seen at Mageibra.

During the afternoon an " aviatik " dropped a message asking us to mark our hospital tents more clearly.

July 27th.

The following mobile column order was issued :

Attention of O.C.'s is called to the following : 1. As the number of sand-carts and cacolets is limited, great care should be exercised that they are only indented for when absolutely necessary. An indent should bear the signature of a responsible or medical officer. 2. As it is probable that the troops will be fighting without their tunics, O.C.'s will take steps to ensure that when this occurs all field dressings are extracted from the pocket of the tunic and pinned to the breeches. 3. All ranks are reminded that when dressing the wounds of a comrade the field dressing belonging to the wounded man should be used, and not that of the man who is dressing the wound.

With regard to order 2, I was very against this, and strongly advised that our men should continue to wear their tunics in order to avoid sunstroke, and also in order to make it possible to wear the cavalry equipment, which it was difficult and painful to carry without shoulder-straps ; eventually this was agreed upon, and our men fought in their tunics and preferred it.

We were all now getting very impatient, as the Turks were steadily advancing and no orders were received to attack.

Intelligence.—The Turks are now at Hod Es Sagia, a point midway and well in front of the Oghratina–Mageibra lines.

A few weeks ago we had been told that the Katia water-belt district must be held at any price, as it was considered a jumping-off place for the Turks before attacking the Canal ; and now, directly the Turks advanced all these places (with wells made by our engineers) were evacuated.

July 28th.

Intelligence.—The enemy have had a skirmish with the Light Horse and have advanced the line Oghratina–Mageibra at the following points : (1) Hod Umm Ugba ; (2) Hod El Amoia, and at (3) Hill 245. These places are connected by a series of rifle-pits and machine-gun emplacements.

Later.—There has been a general advance from 1, 2 and 3; patrols have been in action: one killed, several Turks killed.

We received orders to be ready to move at any moment, each man to carry three days' rations for himself and horse and all water-bottles to be filled overnight.

July 29th.

We were ready to move off all night, with horses and camels saddled, but no orders arrived. In the afternoon one of our aeroplanes flew over rather lop-sided and very low. On arrival at Kantara the pilot, who had been shot through the chest, died of wounds.

Intelligence.—Near Hod Umm Ugba, the Wellington Mounted Rifles attacked the Turks and drove them back 100 yards, with casualties on both sides. Later the Turks advanced their previous line in a semicircle (concavity forward), and the Ayrshire Battery shelled them while pitching camp at Ugba.

During the day a squadron of the Duke of Lancaster's Own came into our camp.

Intelligence (later).—Tracks are reported at Hod Krush (this would extend their northern line to the sea), and, commencing at Hod El Khirba, a new line of trenches exists west of Hod Ed Dhakar and Hod El Mahari ; gun-tracks seen near Mageibra. Many camps have been seen at Mazar and Bir El Abd. Prisoners taken by our patrols near Ugba are from the 31st Infantry Regiment. Patrols found enemy entrenching west of Hod El Mezahmi, on Ridge 100 ; there was firing all along the line east of Katia (which we still hold). Posts are also reported between Hills 200 and 245. One Austrian officer was caught at the latter post; he died of wounds.

July 30th.

While standing to at 3 a.m., the Somerset R.H.A. moved out to Bir En Nuss ; the Royal Lancashire Fusiliers came in next to us.

Intelligence.—We have evacuated Katia.

August 1st.

During the morning a monitor in Tina Bay shelled the Turks at Oghratina. Romani was heavily bombed by enemy aeroplane.

August 2nd.

Intelligence.—There is almost complete absence of Turks to-day —they have evacuated Mageibra, as the wells are dry.

It seemed that the monitor had " annoyed " them ; the enemy were wonderful at disappearing and appearing again. We were now uncertain whether we were part of the Fifth Mounted Brigade or of the New Zealand Mounted Brigade.

August 3rd.

Our G.H.Q. at Ismailia was bombed during the morning. An advance guard of our composite regiment left at dawn to prepare a camp at Gilbaan.

Intelligence.—The Turks have reappeared, and are advancing. They now hold Katia, Bir El Hamisar and Bir Nagid (the most westerly point, about 6 miles from Dueidar). Our patrols have met the Turks between Romani and Katia.

During the afternoon we received orders to march to Gilbaan at dawn on the next day. We heard that we were now in the Fifth Mounted Brigade again, under our own Brigadier. I realized that if we went into action on the morrow we should have no Field Ambulance with us, as ours would not be able to arrive in time, and that we had no claim on the New Zealand Field Ambulance, as we were no longer in that Brigade.

THE BATTLE OF ROMANI.

August 4th.

We heard heavy firing at dawn, which sounded near at hand. Orders were received to proceed to Gilbaan at once, but these were countermanded at 5 a.m. and the order was given to ride as fast as possible to Dueidar, that all camel transport was to be left behind, and that only pack-ponies were to be taken. I had my camels quickly unloaded and only absolute necessaries were transferred to pack-horses. Soon after 5 a.m., after watering, we were on the caravan route to Dueidar. Here the going was not quite so heavy, and one could distinguish the track most of the way. Our column was preceded by a small advance guard, and patrols were thrown out on either side. After going for about half an hour we became aware of rifle fire and machine-gun fire ahead of us. A little later a cloud of dust appeared, and some riderless horses came galloping up. They were evidently part of a gun team which had been stampeded by one of the enemy's shells ; after securing these, we soon arrived at the fortified camp of Dueidar. Here our C.O. found orders from the Brigadier—" the composite regiment was to proceed to Point 8 (Shohat) and at once engage the enemy by attacking his left flank, after having first detached one troop at Point 6 (Hod Abu Gharab) and another at Point 7 (Hod El Bikriya) " ; these two posts fell to two of our troop-leaders, the idea being apparently to protect the infantry which would detrain at K 25 on the railway. These were the two most vulnerable places, through which a southern detachment of the enemy might force itself. Signallers were left with each post, in order that Regimental H.Q. could at once be informed if any considerable body attacked them. While maps were being studied and arrangements made, I called on the M.O. of the Scottish Horse Regiment in the fort. After telling him my difficulty about having no Field Ambulance to depend on, he said that he would telephone to his Field Ambulance for sand-carts, and promised to send me some if they turned up ; meanwhile, he had aid posts in the trenches of the fort, and as far as our posts 6 and 7 were concerned, if I could manage to get the casualties to his trenches, he would guarantee to get them down into the camp and evacuate them. I also got into communication with the Forty-second Division and informed them of our difficulty with reference to the wounded. After halting for twenty minutes at Dueidar, we rode out on a bearing of 60°. As we advanced we could see the enemy's shells exploding in

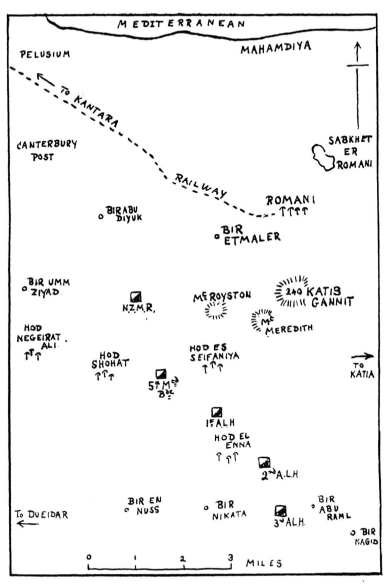

SKETCH MAP OF ROMANI AND DISTRICT, WITH APPROXIMATE POSITIONS
OF MOUNTED BRIGADES AT 11 A.M., AUGUST 4, 1916.

Second and Third Australian Light Horse Brigades) was to attack the enemy's left flank and prevent him from advancing south of Mount Meredith, and to make him detach such a large force that his main body would be materially weakened. This Division early in the day (August 4th) occupied approximately the line Bir Abu Diyuk, Hod Shohat, Hod El Enna, Bir Abu Raml. The Mounted Brigades occupied this line in the order detailed above. The right wing of this Division was eventually intended to sweep round left-handed and take the Turks in the rear. In addition to these dispositions, reserves of the above-mentioned Infantry Divisions were at Pelusium, Hills 70 and 40, and Kantara.

Medical arrangements—for August 4th. New Zealand Mounted Field Ambulance near Bir Abu Diyuk. First and Second Australian Light Horse Field Ambulances at Romani. Lowland Field Ambulance at Romani Railhead, and another at Bir Et Marler. East Lancs Field Ambulance, one at Pelusium (special arrangements for wounded Turks) and one at Mahamdiya.

It may be of interest here to give some " Intelligence " notes received at a later date :

Composition of the Enemy Force which attempted to reach the Suez Canal, July–August 1916.

The Turkish Force which was destined for an attack on the Canal by the North Road was collected at Bir Saba, Shellal and Sheria during June. It seems from captured documents that the attack would have been made in October, when about 40,000 men would have been available, but the views of General Kress Von Kressenstein prevailed, and the expedition was launched in June.

Infantry.
3rd Infantry Division—Rifaat Bey :
31st Regiment—Ismael Hakki Bey.
32nd Regiment—Hassan Basri Bey.
39th Regiment—Kiamil Bey.
(Approximate number, 12,000.)
Each regiment contained four battalions of 1,000 men each
27th Infantry Division ;
81st Regiment—Haddi Bey.
(About 4,000 strong.)

Mounted Troops.
2 Companies Syrian Dromedary Corps—400, and some horsemen.

Artillery.

1 Battery 4 20-cm. Howitzers (Austrian), oxen.
1 Battery 4 15-cm. Howitzers (German), oxen.
1 Battery 4 10-cm. Guns (German), horses, 450.
1 Battery 8 10-cm. Howitzers (Austrian), oxen, 200.
3 Batteries 4 " 75 " Mountain Guns (Turkish).
5 Anti-aircraft Guns (German), oxen, 150.

Engineers.

3 Pioneer Companies, 600.
1 Composite Battalion, 750.

Medical.

Attached Battalion Units, 1 Officer, 36 O.R., 500.
Attached Division (1 Medical Company), 250.
Attached to Force (1 Base Hospital), 250.

Machine Gun Companies.

8 German Companies, Nos. 601–608, 800.

Aircraft.

Aviatik, Albatros, Fokker, 12.

Arab Irregulars commanded by Sami Bey.

Number uncertain.

Progress of Force.

German Machine Gun Companies arrived at El Arish
    July 15th.
3rd Division arrived at Bir Saba July 15th.

Infantry Marches.

Djemain–Sheikh Zowaid, 24 hours.
    –El Arish, 24 hours.
    –El Mazar, 48 hours.
    –Bir El Abd, 48 hours.
    –Katia, 48 hours.

Grouping of Force before Attack.

Group 1 at Hod El Rabah ; Commanders, Rifaat Bey and
    Graf Zu Rentzau.
Group 2 at Bir El Mamluk ; Commander, Major Von Istonk.
Group 3 at Abu Thila ; Commander, Kaiamel Bey.
Group 4 at Hod El Masia ; Commanders, Colonel Von Shonsky.
    and Major Bolmann Bey.

The following particulars were obtained from prisoners on August 3rd :

Medical Services.
> Each Battalion has 1 M.O. (Captain), 4 corporals, 32 men and 8 stretchers. Each Machine Gun Company has 1 M.O. (Lieutenant).

Divisional Services.
> 1 Medical Company; O.C. is a combatant officer (Captain). There are 3 doctors, 1 Major and 2 Captains, one of whom is a surgeon.
> There is 1 chemist (Lieutenant), 54 orderlies, 198 stretcher-bearers, 70 camels, 140 cacolets, and 30 supply camels.

Expeditionary Force Hospital.
> 1 Major, 2 Captains, 1 chemist, 4 large Baumann marquees and 200 beds.

System of Evacuation.
> A Medical Company sends forward camels with cacolets to collect serious cases from Battalion Dressing Station ; all light cases walk.
> The Expeditionary Hospital and Divisions had apparently one Field Kitchen each, with a personnel of 22 men, of whom 2 were cooks.

August 4th.

I arranged with the M.O. of the Warwick Yeomanry that we should get all our casualties to the Headquarters of the Composite Regiment on Shohat Hill. Considering the nature of the fighting, casualties were not heavy. By 3 p.m. our Mounted Brigades had forced the enemy over the first ridge on which we had found the Turks on arrival. We now occupied this ridge and were firing on the Turks in the valley beyond. About this time we suffered rather severely from the enemy's shrapnel. Our Second-in-Command had a very narrow escape near Hod Es Seifaniya : an unexploded shell dropped a few feet in front of him, took the sand from under his feet, and sent him flying head over heels in the soft sand. On returning to my dressing station I met the Brigadier, who told me to send a reliable man to look for our Brigade camel convoy ; the latter was on its way from Pelusium to Hod Negeiret Ali, and I was told to get it diverted to Shohat. My messenger never found the convoy, as owing to an aeroplane swooping down and peppering it with a machine gun it had to alter its course. Later in the evening, however, we spotted it with our glasses and had it brought in to a valley behind us. Our Brigade was now over the first ridge and in the valley beyond, and was gradually forcing the enemy over the second ridge (the part opposite the Worcesters being called Mount Royston) down into Hod Abu Adi. Suddenly white flags and white sand-bags were held up, and a stream of prisoners began to come in with their hands up. Meanwhile the Light Horse Brigade on the right of the Warwicks wheeled round left-handed and swept the enemy in. While these prisoners were coming in, German machine gun detachments to the east, which had not surrendered, fired on them unmercifully. Our regiment had previously captured a battery of mountain guns by first shooting the camels and thus preventing their escape. While the prisoners were being taken over, I returned to my dressing station to make some arrangements about evacuating the wounded, when suddenly an aeroplane dropped a smoke-ball immediately above us, and a few seconds afterwards we found ourselves being heavily shelled. I shouted to the men who were holding the led horses to gallop away, and a second later a shell fell where they had been. The Brigade now came in. It was seven o'clock and dusk was coming on. We were fortunately able to bring all our dead back with us for future burial. On moving down into a little Hod, our camel transport supplied us with water from fanatis. The order was then given that the water out of water-bottles might be drunk ; this was much appreciated, as we had been fighting throughout that grilling August day and had had no water since 5 a.m. In spite of these circumstances there had been very few cases of collapse. The wounded Turks were most grateful for the water and food, as they only had with them a few dates and a little dirty water. They looked so grateful when they found that we were not going to leave them out in the desert, and made no sound while we dressed their wounds. One great bearded fellow, badly shot through the thigh, had the grateful look of an injured dog in his expressive eyes as we lifted him on to a horse. Some of these men must have suffered greatly as they rode in with us that night ; we only had a few empty ammunition limbers, and our worst cases were conveyed in them. It transpired that the Brigade had taken some 500 prisoners, including several German officers and N.C.O.'s, and four guns. It seemed very horrible to think of the number of wounded and dying Turks who must have been left out. We did what we could, but had no organization to deal with the large numbers ; a Turkish Field Ambulance which had been captured was left to work on the field and an Australian unit from Romani did excellent work amongst the enemy. It was extraordinary how one's feelings changed after a battle—during the fight, while our men were getting hit, one felt delighted every time one saw a Turk drop ; but when it was all over and we had got all our wounded safely back, one thought of the number of wounded Turks who would probably never be found in this undulating country, condemned to die of thirst. A Turkish N.C.O., through an interpreter, told us that their German officers had promised them that they would reach the Suez Canal during the first days of Bairam (the month of Ramadan was just over), and that the English only had one Division in our section of the Canal. As a matter of fact, this would have been partly true a month ago, when the Fifty-second was the only complete Division, apart from numerous separate units. According to the Turkish time-table found in their " Orders of the Day," Romani railhead was to be seized at 8 a.m. on August 1st. Many of the prisoners wore a ribbon which they said was that of the Gallipoli medal. At 8.30 p.m. we moved off in the dark, making for Pelusium via Canterbury Post. So ended the Turkish attack on Romani and the Suez Canal, for from henceforth the Turks were fighting rear-guard actions. Desultory shelling still went on on our right, but it gradually ceased towards midnight. On leaving, our Brigade handed over the positions which we had occupied to some regiments of the Forty-second Division which had detrained at midday at K 25. On passing through Canterbury Post our column threaded its way through numbers of resting infantry and eventually arrived at Pelusium. Here we found what seemed in the dark to be indescribable confusion—mounted troops coming in to water, infantry detraining and marching out, busy A.S.C. depots, camel convoys loading up, ammunition columns on the move, wounded arriving in sand-carts, and large columns of prisoners being marched in. After long delay our horses were watered (the first for eighteen hours) and our horse lines were put down. It was extraordinary how the horses could smell the water long before they reached it ; my horse got very excited before I had any idea that we were near water, and then made a rush for it. Our horses were now so used to camels that although the lines were only a few feet away from the camel camp they took no notice. Fires were lit, and we gathered round to drink our tea and eat some food ; we had seldom enjoyed a meal more, as we had been unable to eat a midday meal on account of the lack of water. It was a picturesque sight when the fires lit up the camp and the motley collection of Turkish prisoners, many of whom were supplied with tea from our dixies. There seemed to be representatives of many races amongst them, from the desert Arab and negro soldier to the fair-haired and blue-eyed European Turk. Infantry wearing the enverene hats, brown fezzes or skull-caps, dressed in dark-brown khaki and corduroy breeches (most unsuitable for this climate), gunners in astrakhan caps and blue uniforms, Arab irregulars in flowing garments, transport drivers with red facings to their uniforms and yellow sashes, and German machine gunners in khaki drill and wearing yachting caps. I had charge of a Turkish medical officer ; after he had had some food and tea I told him (in French) that he would be taken over to one of the Field Ambulances, where he would spend the night. He had been captured on one of the little white Arab ponies which most of the Turkish officers had been riding; he was immaculately dressed in lemon-coloured drill, with the snake of Æsculapius on his tunic and the red crescent on his arm, and wore a yellow silk turban and kid gloves! He told me that his name was Jahat. On arrival at the Field Ambulance we found a very large number of Turkish wounded, some waiting and others being dressed in a large tent. Three R.A.M.C. officers were hard at work, assisted by Red Crescent orderlies. I brought Jahat in and announced that he was going to help them; after explaining this to him he was very disgusted, but we compelled him to take off his coat and get to work amongst his own wounded. It was evident that he had previously concluded that his work was over after surrendering. Another Turkish medical officer told us that he had been in charge of the Field Hospital in Anafarta Village, which reminded us of our days at Suvla Bay. By midnight we had bivouacked for the night, with orders to move off at 4.30 a.m. on the next day.

THE SECOND BATTLE OF KATIA.

August 5th.

By 3.30 a.m. we were up, and quickly watered, fed and breakfasted. Just before starting I was given two captured camels loaded with Turkish medical equipment; unfortunately, there was not time to go through it and it had to be left behind. Our column marched to Bir Umm Ziyad (8), where we halted for half an hour. It was known that the enemy had retired eastwards through Katia, where a very strong force had been left to cover the retreat of the main army. It was now the duty of all the Mounted Brigades to " make good " the country west, north-west and south-west of Katia before an attack was launched on that place. For this purpose the western district was assigned to the Fifth Mounted Brigade.

The latter now spread out, and, advancing cautiously, proceeded to scour the country in a south-easterly direction between Hod Shoat and Mount Royston, signal connection being maintained continuously with Katib Gannit, across yesterday's battle-field, through Hod El Enna and Bir Nikata to Bir Abu Raml. At the latter place we sighted the Imperial Camel Corps, which was carrying out a reconnaissance to the south ; a little later we met a lonely horse in very poor condition ; on examination he was found to have the Worcester brand and a Gloucester saddle. Evidently he had been captured three and a half months ago and had now come into his own again. It is probable that this horse had been carrying a Turkish officer who had been killed the day before. We now turned due north and eventually reached the 100-foot contour of Katib Gannit. Wellington Ridge, on which the Turks had actually gained a footing the day before, was now held by a Lowland regiment, while the higher part to the north, 100 to 240, was lined by a Manchester regiment. A few men went down with sunstroke about midday, and being near Romani they were removed to the First Australian Light Horse Field Ambulance. After half an hour's halt we proceeded due east towards Katia. Everywhere we came across Turkish equipment which had been thrown away during the retreat and large numbers of killed and wounded Turks. Many of the latter were lying under the little sun-shelters, which their comrades had presumably erected for them before retiring. It was a pleasing sight to see an Australian and a Turkish Field Ambulance working side by side amongst the wounded. As we advanced slowly, more cases of sunstroke developed, and these were sent into Bir Abu Hamra, where we had already collected some Turkish prisoners. Our line now consisted of the following units, taken in order from north to south : Warwickshire Yeomanry, Gloucester and Worcester Yeomanry, the New Zealand Mounted Brigade (who had advanced from Bir En Nuss) and two Australian Light Horse Brigades (who had moved up from Bir El Hamisah).

The Somerset R.H.A. accompanied the New Zealanders; the Ayrshire and Leicestershire R.H.A. batteries were probably somewhere to the south. At about two o'clock the enemy opened fire on us with shrapnel and H.E., and as we galloped forward we soon came under rifle fire. " Action dismount " was given, and the Brigade proceeded to line a low ridge and to open fire on the enemy, who could now and then be seen in their trenches outside Katia. The ground, being uneven, afforded us a good deal of cover, as it abounded in small hummocks and ridges. After advancing to another position, Regimental H.Q. was established behind a little sandhill. Here I established my dressing station, and had just attended to some casualties when a shell exploded in the middle of our little group. I was thrown to the ground after being struck by a fragment of the shell, and realized at once that my leg was broken. I was carried back a short distance, and my orderlies dressed the wound and fixed up the leg with improvised splints. It was extraordinarily lucky that the fragment did not strike my leg " full on," otherwise the whole foot would certainly have disappeared. Meanwhile the enemy's big guns in Katia were very troublesome, and some Turkish infantry with machine guns and a field gun, who had moved out of Katia towards Abu Hamra, proceeded to enfilade us in a most uncomfortable manner. Our " left " (Warwick Yeomanry) was in the air, except for a squadron of Glasgow Yeomanry who moved up late in the afternoon. A few prisoners were taken, but on the whole the enemy was very stubborn. We could not understand why the infantry had not been brought up for this frontal attack, as there was at least one Division behind us. We thought that if they had been in our position, and the Cavalry Division had deployed on either side of and in rear of Katia, the enemy's retreat would have been cut off and a large number of guns and prisoners would have been taken. I was not quite aware what happened during the next two hours, as the morphia which I had taken to allay the pain had begun to make me drowsy. At 5 p.m. the C.O. told me that we should have to retire about a mile, as our position was becoming untenable on account of the concentrated enfilading fire from the north. As soon as some infantry supports came out we were to advance again. Meanwhile, I could not be left where I was, or I should have been captured by the enemy—an unpleasant predicament, especially in the state I was in. A couple of men put me on my horse, and with my sergeant supporting me on one side, we galloped back through the open, under a desultory fire from the north. My horse pecked once, and I was nearly off, but he recovered himself; he had been touched in the hind-quarters by a bullet. After a painful ride of about half an hour we reached Brigade H.Q., and I arranged with the M.O. of the Warwick Yeomanry to look after the wounded from the composite regiment. Together with my sergeant and six wounded men who could ride, we started back, passing on the way our Acting Staff Captain, who, together with his horse, had just been wounded. The Brigadier told us not to take the route through Abu Hamra, as the Turks were working round on that side. Accordingly, we set out for Katib Gannit, intending to ride round under its defences until we could reach Romani through a narrow defile which I knew of, close to Bir Er Romani, where we intended to water the horses. Although we were now out of rifle fire the Katia guns worried us with shrapnel and H.E., bursting all over the ground ; this was chiefly intended for the New Zealand H.Q., which had apparently been spotted. The desert here was still scattered with wounded and dead Turks, a grim reminder of yesterday's battle. It was very sad to see the wistful way they regarded us—I remember one man who was nursing his shattered leg, as he sat in a rifle-pit waiting to be picked up ; but we could do nothing : we were but a party of wounded men, some hardly able to keep in the saddle, riding tired horses through heavy sand. I knew they would be picked up eventually, but when ? Some had already been lying out twenty-four hours.

About a mile from the foot of Gannit we met a party

of Turks with rifles. We thought we were going to have an awkward moment; however, they seemed to be in a dazed condition and took no notice of us. At the foot of Katib Gannit we came across the barbed-wire entanglements, trenches and redoubts, which extended from the foot of that mountain to Bir Er Romani. Here again were many corpses of Turks who had been killed on the previous day while attempting to cut our wire. After riding along outside the wire for about half an hour, we came to a redoubt where a Scottish officer let us through. The ground behind this fort was strewn with pieces of shell and unexploded shells. When we had watered we met several battalions of infantry (Forty-second Division) who were marching out to relieve the mounted troops; also a procession of sand-carts, which I had got our Signalling Officer to helio for earlier in the afternoon. My sergeant went back with this convoy to show them where our wounded were. On riding up the steep defile we reached the Romani plateau, and avoiding the large holes made by the enemy's big guns, arrived at the First Australian Light Horse Field Ambulance.

Some of us were hardly conscious what happened during the last part of the journey, and were eventually lifted off our horses by willing hands. I found myself in the same tent with two wounded friends from our Brigade.

August 6th.

On waking in the morning I found that one of my companions, though shot through the arm, had returned to the field. We were well looked after, our wounds were dressed, and we were supplied with excellent rations. On asking when we should be removed to railhead, we were told that the line was so congested with Turkish prisoners that it would be impossible to evacuate us at once. During the morning a Major from the Canterbury Regiment was brought into our tent, and he told us that the mounted troops and infantry had cleared Katia, and that the Turks were putting up another rear-guard action at Oghratina; he had met some of our infantry in a fearful state through lack of water, with blackened lips and swollen tongues. After all, we mounted troops did not know what it was to march through heavy sand. In the afternoon there appeared to be still no chance of moving the wounded, and the various Field Ambulances became very full. The larger part of the personnel of the Australian Light Horse Field Ambulances went out again to collect more wounded, both ours and Turkish.

August 7th.

There was still no sign of our being moved to railhead, and as some of us were suffering considerable pain, our wounds were re-dressed. At midday we were visited by several friends from our regiment who were on their way up to the front line. We heard that cholera had broken out amongst the Turks and that some cases had occurred amongst our troops. It appeared that after a stiff resistance the Turks had evacuated Oghratina and were making for Bir El Abd. At the former place they had left a note saying that Lieut. ——, of the Australian Light Horse, was safe and a prisoner; that he had dined with the officers of one of their batteries the night before, and that he was a gentleman. Another note said: "How did you like the six ladies from Katia?" This referred to their heavy guns, which they had succeeded in removing. During the pursuit a large amount of timber and felled palm-trees were found on the track; the former had been brought on camels and was used in the transit of the guns over the sand. At 4 p.m. we were relieved to hear that we were to be moved at last. Two of us were placed in a sand-cart drawn by four mules and taken down to the Lowland Field Ambulance at railhead. This was the end of the desert railway, which was being rapidly pushed out across the Sinai Peninsula. The Field Ambulance was very congested, and there were many rows of us lying on stretchers, together with numerous wounded Turks. At 5.30 we were taken out of the tents and placed in the train. This "hospital train" consisted of one engine

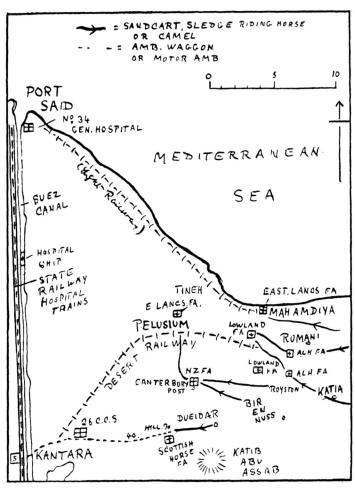

EVACUATION OF DESERT WOUNDED, AUGUST 4-8, 1916.

(Based on *The Times* map.)

and a number of open trucks, the latter containing nothing
—not even straw. As a matter of fact, we were lucky to be
even in trucks, as, had the railway not been built so far
at this period, we should have travelled most of the way
to Kantara probably on camels. The stretcher cases
were placed on the floor of these trucks, while the walking
cases sat on the sides. When we started off there was
the usual " bump, bump, bump " which one hears from a
goods train, and pitiful groans escaped from the badly
wounded and fracture cases. A trooper in a New Zealand
regiment who lay next to me, and had been shot through
the spine, kept up a pitiful wail until he was finally
exhausted; he was just alive when eventually taken out,
but could not have survived long. After we had been
going for a time the noise of the train overcame the
groans of the sufferers. On reaching Pelusium our engine
broke down and the train waited for a considerable time ;
then the shrieks and groans of the wounded broke the
stillness of the quiet night. But worse was to come :
we had to be shunted in order to let a supply train pass
through. It seemed a cruel thing to shunt a train full
of wounded in open trucks, but it had to be done.
Every bump in our springless truck was extremely
painful. At midnight we arrived at Kantara, and after
being unloaded were transferred by motor-ambulances
along the newly made road to the 26th Casualty
Clearing Station. Here we were laid out in rows and
waited our turn to be examined. The M.O.'s and
orderlies at this Casualty Clearing Station had been
working for forty-eight hours continuously and were
absolutely worn out, but in spite of this the tired men
handled us most carefully. Each of us was then
examined and dressed again. I was labelled Cairo
instead of Port Said, as that hospital had been already
filled on the first day. Eight of us were then removed to
a tent, and our stretchers were placed on trestles instead
of on the ground ; this appeared to be the great difference
between a Field Ambulance and a Casualty Clearing
Station. Opposite me was a Captain of the New Zealand

Medical Corps, who had been brought in the day before, but was in such a critical state that he could not be moved: machine-gun fire had removed a large part of his femur and the greater part of his thigh. It was a bad night, and one could not forget the horrors of that train journey.

August 8th.

During the morning we were visited by several friends from Kantara, and heard that there had been more cases of cholera, and that the Turks had left a note in one of the Hods through which our force had passed, saying " Beware of cholera." Some dead Turks were found in the same place who had died of the disease. The Turk was indeed a gentleman; not many enemies would have given this warning. At 2 ~ we were taken in motor-ambulances to Kantara West station, where we were transferred to a Red Crescent train. The latter was perfect luxury after what we had gone through. Before midnight our train arrived at Cairo and we were distributed amongst the various hospitals.

October 31st.

Together with a friend who had also been discharged from hospital, I arrived at our Brigade Base Details Camp at Kantara. We found that the latter place had grown enormously during our three months in hospital, and that a railway ferry and large railway station had been erected.

November 2nd.

We left Kantara in the early morning and proceeded by train along the new railway to Bir El Abd, which was at that time railhead. A 12-mile ride across the desert on a compass bearing, there being practically no landmarks, brought us to Hod Bayud. The country was here more hilly and was on the edge of the waterless district. Half-way to our destination we halted at Hod El Gamel, where we found a squadron of the Warwick-

shire Yeomanry. On reaching our camp we found a
number of new officers who had come up as reinforcements.
The men were living in bivouac, chiefly in huts made of
palm-trees, as no tents were allowed on account of the
enemy aeroplanes. The 7th Battalion of the Imperial
Camel Corps were camped 1 mile to the east. Our
camp was situate on a hill above the little oasis called
the Hod Bayud. The hill was so steep in places that
one could actually slide down some 200 feet on the loose
sand to the watering-place below. Owing to the shifting
configuration of the sandhills, some of the tallest palm-
trees, which had originally been on the edge of the Hod,
were now embedded in sand and only the topmost branches
were showing. The water was brackish, but not sufficiently so to prevent horses drinking it. Close by lay
the remains of a rear-guard force belonging to the
Turkish left flank, which had been harried by our aeroplanes and mounted troops in the recent August fighting.
The landscape was grand and austere ; the enormous
vista of endless desert, here and there interrupted by
gigantic sand mountains—fashioned into fantastic shapes
according to the caprices of the wind—and by occasional
palm-studded Hods nestling in tiny valleys, was most
impressive. In this clear atmosphere the visibility was
wonderful. Perfect silence reigned, and there appeared
to be no sign of life except an occasional vulture hovering
over the old Turkish battle-field or a jackal slinking
homewards to his lair. At sunset the sky assumed most
marvellous colours, which it is useless to try to describe.
Then followed the deathly stillness of the desert night,
broken occasionally by the hideous shrieking of the
jackals as they quarrelled over their prey.

November 3rd.

The dawn found us " standing to " with all eyes
turned to the east as the sun rose behind the forbidding
Maghara hills, which were held by the Turks. Our duty
at this post was to watch this flank, lest the followers of
the Prophet should swoop down and cut our main com-

munications—we depended entirely on camel transport for rations and drinking water, which were conveyed to us daily over 12 miles of desert from railhead at Bir El Abd.

November 4th.

During the day we arranged a new camp for our " A " Squadron, which was coming in to join us from Mageibra. Fritz came over in the afternoon, and a few minutes later we watched him through our glasses bombing railhead. Our patrols rode out to Mount Ruisat and thence to Zagadan, about 15 miles away, daily ; this procedure was adopted in order to watch the Turks who held the Maghara hills. It was hard work for the horses, as the distance covered in heavy sand was altogether about 30 miles.

November 6th.

During the day an Australian Wireless Section arrived, and erected their station just above our camp.

November 7th.

At dawn two of us rode out and visited the Yeomanry and Australian squadrons who were encamped at Hod Gamel, Hod El Wilegha, Hod El Salmana, Hod Ce Eilia, and returned to Bayud at sunset. At this period the Warwickshire Yeomanry were at Hassanya and Mageibra. The Gloucestershire Yeomanry were at Narbit and Gamel, and the 7th Imperial Camel Corps were camped at Worcester Hill, just outside Bayud.

November 8th.

In the evening our patrols returned from the Maghara foothills via Ruisat (where water had previously been buried), and brought with them one Bedouin prisoner and two goats. The former, although an old man, kept up with the horses on foot the whole of the 15 miles, and when he arrived in camp drank one whole canvas bucket of water ; he appeared to be disgusted with the Woodbine cigarettes which were offered him, and proceeded to make his own out of some priceless Turkish tobacco.

At night we received a message that a hostile camel patrol was passing between us and Hod El Wilegha, and soon afterwards one of the patrol was shot, the rest of the enemy escaping in the dark.

November 9th.

During the morning several " aviatiks " bombed railhead, a proceeding which we watched through our glasses.

November 11th.

About ten o'clock in the morning two Staff officers rode over to investigate our wells. One of them asked our C.O. whether we had suffered from hostile aircraft; the latter replied that as we were such a long way from railhead and so inconspicuous we had probably not attracted Fritz's attention. At that moment, however, Fritz appeared and proceeded to drop five bombs in our lines. Luckily, no damage was done, but our monkey had a very narrow escape, as a bomb fell within two yards of the perch on which she lived. The bombs were evidently of German manufacture, as the instructions, which were found on the fragments, were printed in that language. Our C.O., on looking round to continue his conversation with the Staff officers, found that they had entirely disappeared. They had evidently jumped on to their horses directly Fritz appeared, and had adopted the wise procedure of galloping into the " blue."

November 12th.

A warning was received during the day that a spy, in the uniform of an Australian officer, riding a grey horse, had been seen in our neighbourhood. It was evidently very easy for a spy to patrol the country between our scattered posts; and it would be easy for him to visit a yeomanry squadron, dressed as an Australian, without attracting much attention.

November 16th.

In company with the Second-in-Command I rode over to Hod El Muhammam, where we saw evidence of the fighting between the Imperial Camel Corps and the retiring Turkish left flank which had taken place August 7th–10th last. Most of the trees in the Hod had had their tops knocked off by the Turkish shells, and enemy ammunition-boxes, equipment and shell-cases were scattered far and wide. In this Hod we noticed an interesting old Bedouin graveyard, with aloes plants at the head and foot of each grave. Here there had evidently been a permanent Bedouin encampment. The date palms were heavy with their golden fruit, and fig-trees and pomegranate-trees also flourished round the native wells. Outside the Hod, towards the north, we found the graves of some Pembroke and Shropshire yeomen who had been attached to the Imperial Camel Corps. We rode through Hod El Balein, Hod El Dhaheihal, Hod Abu Dhahao to Hod El Hassaniya, where we found our Brigade Headquarters established. A letter had been picked up in the desert, written in French, from Djemal Pasha to Kress Von Kressenstein in a sarcastic vein, and complaining of the failure of the August expedition, and asking how many guns, etc., Von Kress had lost. This was interesting, in view of the fact that Djemal Pasha had proposed that the expedition should take place in October, when 40,000 men would have been available (see Turkish " Intelligence " received in August), and that the views of Von Kress had prevailed, i.e. to launch the attack with a much smaller force in August.

November 20th.

We ascertained that a pariah dog visited the camp nightly from the Maghara direction, and the C.O. considered that this might possibly be a means of communication between our native camel-drivers and the enemy. Accordingly, it was decided that we should try to poison it with some meat, in order to procure any letter it might be carrying.

November 21*st.*

During the morning two of us tracked a pariah dog for some 6 miles towards the Maghara hills and then gave up the quest. It was probable that these dogs merely came to feed on the old Turkish battle-field and returned to Maghara in the early morning. Eventually we found our poisoned dog, but he was carrying no information. We discovered later that both pariah dogs and jackals will travel an enormous distance over the desert, as, when the wind is in the right direction, they can scent their prey very many miles away.

November 22*nd.*

During the next few days our patrols made daily excursions to Mount Ruisat and Zagadan, usually returning with a few hostile Bedouin, whom the Turks used as scouts.

November 24*th.*

Orders were received for the Brigade to march to Hill 70 in order to go into reserve.

November 25*th.*

At midday our regiment was relieved by the 6th Australian Light Horse ; each of our outposts on the outlying hills was separately relieved by detachments from the Australian regiment before we were able to move off. The camel transport had previously been dispatched to Khirba, and the regiment marched out at 1 p.m. At Hassanya we found that the Australian Brigade Headquarters had moved in and taken the place lately occupied by our own Brigade Headquarters. We watered at the Hod, and rode out to Khirba through Hod Abu Hattat and Hod Saht, passing on the way numerous infantry outposts belonging to the Forty-second Division. Khirba was reached at sunset, and the water was found to be so salt that the horses would scarcely drink at all.

November 26th.

We marched at an early hour to Bir En Romani, passing through Oghratina, Reshafat and Er Rabah. At Oghratina we saw the large wooden cross which had recently been erected on the hill in memory of those who had fallen in the April fighting. At Romani we bivouacked near the old salt lake, together with Sikh Pioneers and a West Indian regiment.

November 27th.

The Worcesters and Warwicks marched to Hill 70, and the Gloucester Yeomanry received orders to proceed to Dueidar. We passed north of Abu Diyuk and watered midday at Pelusium, where a strong camel battalion passed us on their way up to the front. On entering the camp of Hill 70 we met the One Hundred and Sixty-sixth Infantry Brigade, who had bivouacked just outside.

November 28th.

The regiment was inspected by the G.O.C. East Force, this Force having been recently constituted.

November 30th.

It was evident that the men, and particularly the horses, would benefit by their rest while in reserve, as the Brigade had been constantly in the front line since August 1, 1916. During the morning some of us rode over to Dueidar, where we found the Gloucester Yeomanry and the 5th Battalion of the West India Regiment encamped. The last time we had been in this spot was under very different conditions, a few minutes before going into action on the first day of the battle of Romani.

.   .   .   .   .

December 5th.

After spending a few days' leave in the Canal Zone, two of us returned to Hill 70; here we came across the first hospital train that we had ever seen in the Sinai Peninsula. Intelligence reports stated that El Arish had been strongly reinforced.

Our Brigade received orders to march in a few days' time in order to take part in the advance on El Arish. So, after all, our men and horses had very little rest.

December 9th.

The Brigade moved out at 8 a.m., watered at Pelusium, and bivouacked at Romani.

December 10th.

On the move again at dawn; this time our march took us to Hod El Khirba. We heard that the Turks were strongly entrenched before Fort Massaid, 3 miles to the west of El Arish, and that our patrols had been in touch at Bir Lahfan (8 miles south of El Arish), cutting off the Turkish communications with Maghara.

December 11th.

The Brigade marched to Bir El Abd, crossing the August battle-field on the way. We now belonged to a force which was known as Desert Column.

December 12th.

We received an account from our liaison officer, who was with the Australian Light Horse, of the movements of the Turks between Mazaar, Massaid, and Lahfan; it appeared to be doubtful whether the Turks would make a stand at these places or retire on El Arish.

December 13th.

R.M.O.'s received new instructions with regard to sterilizing and mapping new wells in the country occupied by units during the intended advance. Each squadron was for this purpose to have its water-duty man specially trained in the procedure.

R.M.O.'s were made responsible for the wells in the wake of their units, and were instructed to furnish their

C.O. at the end of each day with a list of the wells treated, stating their exact location on the map. These lists were to keep Divisional Headquarters informed of the efficiency with which this duty was being carried out, and also to show which areas had escaped treatment. The Divisional C.R.E. would then make arrangements for the disinfection of any well which had been missed.

The regimental personnel consisted of one trained man per squadron. Each man would be allotted a strip of area covered by his advancing unit and would maintain touch with the men on either side of him. He would note the positions of all wells treated, and the time at which each one was treated, and at the end of the day's march he would hand the day's list to the R.M.O. of his unit.

During the next few days, while in bivouac at Abd, the water-duty men were thoroughly instructed in the disinfection of wells and were given the necessary equipment.

December 14*th.*

During the morning two of us rode out to the Sabkhet El Bardawil, a large partially dry salt lake, north of Abd and separated from the sea by a narrow strip of land ; the " going " was somewhat treacherous, and the larger part of the lake was encrusted with firm white salt, in places a foot thick, and occasionally intersected by stretches of blue water ; here and there the effect of an H.E. shell had tinged the " salt ice " a brilliant yellow. We returned through the Hod Hisha, where we found the remains of many dead horses and also some large shells, probably the result of gun fire from our monitors.

December 15*th.*

The regiment practised an attack from Hod Zaganiya on Hod Amara ; here we found more evidence of the late Battle of Abd. In the evening we heard a rumour that Germany was suing for peace !

December 16*th*.

The Brigade marched from Bir El Abd to Hod Salmana, and we noticed much activity on the newly made line.

December 17*th*.

We marched from Hod Salmana via Bir Moseifig to Abu Tillul. The track lay partly along the edge of a salt lake and was marked by the carcasses of many oxen, horses and camels, which had been left by the Turks in their retreat.

December 18*th*.

The regiment marched to Bir El Mazar (the Turkish advance base in August) due east via Sabkhet El Mustabig. At the latter place we passed one of our large aerodromes, recently erected on the bed of the dried-up lake, the surface of which was as flat as a billiard-table and firm enough to permit the transit of motor-lorries ; the latter were the first we had seen used in the Sinai Peninsula. As we entered the camp at Mazar an " aviatik " dropped some bombs and was fired at by the anti-aircraft batteries ; our Brigade, however, sustained no casualties. We watered at the Bir, passing on the way the tomb of Abu Gilban. Our whole Brigade bivouacked on a hill surrounded by Turkish trenches, just outside the main camp. We were now only 26 miles from El Arish. To the south we had a good view of the north-eastern end of the Maghara hills (which we used to see from Bayud), with Geb El Lagama and Mount Barga, both occupied by the Turks, in the foreground. Close by us was encamped a battery of our heavy (6-inch) guns, each of the latter being drawn by twenty-four fine Shire cart-horses, ridden four abreast by twelve drivers.

December 19*th*.

At 7 a.m. two "aviatiks" came over and bombed the camp severely. Several men were killed and wounded at the Ordnance Depot, ammunition dump and railway sidings. Our regiment was lucky, the nearest casualties being four camel-drivers, who were killed about 400 yards away. The "aviatiks" took little notice of our anti-aircraft guns and calmly circled round the camp until they had dropped all their bombs. While they were flying immediately over the anti-aircraft guns the latter were unable to fire, and it was said that two of the gunners were killed. Fritz apparently always came up from the east with the sun behind him in the early morning, so that he could only be spotted with considerable difficulty.

December 20*th.*

At 11.30 a.m. we marched to Maadan, riding most of the way across another firm Sabkhet. This firm going was a great relief for our horses after the heavy sand of the Sinai Peninsula, which they had been traversing for almost a year. At Maadan we bivouacked with part of the Fifty-second and Forty-second Divisions in a sandy valley, which was studded with Jerusalem artichokes ; the latter Division had just received orders to return to railhead and entrain for France.

December 21*st.*

It was uncertain whether the oasis of Bittia was still occupied by the Turks, and at 2 a.m. the Brigade commenced an advance on that place. We passed the infantry outposts and proceeded carefully along the old caravan route ; it was bitterly cold, but the track was a good one. On reaching Bittia our scouts reported that it was unoccupied. The Turks had left twenty-five wells, but as dead animals had been thrown into most of them they were not fit for drinking purposes, although some of them were good enough for watering our horses. From our bivouac we had a good view of El Arish and also of the Mediterranean 1½ miles to the north. Helio communication was obtained with 1st Australian Light Horse, who had just entered El Arish, and we learnt that the Turks had evacuated that town and also Fort Maidan.

THE SINAI DESERT   91

During the day our patrols brought in a few prisoners, and we were joined by the Leicestershire and the Inverness-shire R.H.A. batteries. At 2 p.m. Fritz paid his usual visit, but without doing much damage. One of our aeroplanes dropped a message saying that Bir Lahfan and 8 miles beyond El Arish were also clear. We were now only 4 miles from that town, and orders were received to develop and treat all water supplies in the Bittia district for the rest of Desert Column, who were following on ; this duty devolved on us, as we were the first regiment to enter Bittia after the Turks had left. Assisted by our R.E. troop, we cleaned out some of the old wells, but on testing, the water was found to be so highly polluted that all the wells had to be condemned, and our engineers supplied us with water from a couple of spear points.

December 22nd.

After a very cold night we had a delightful bathe in the blue Mediterranean ; the climate at this time of year was delightful during the daytime. We met the armoured cars proceeding along the beach to El Arish and saw a gunboat, which we later heard firing further up the coast. During the afternoon railhead was bombed, and the Fifty-second Division joined us, their advance Brigade having already reached El Arish. We were very short of food, as our camel convoys from railhead failed to arrive for two days in succession, and were therefore reduced to a few biscuits and what little provisions we carried with us.

December 23rd.

At 9 a.m. a few of us obtained permission to visit El Arish. We passed through the recently evacuated Turkish defences at Ujret El Sol, passing south of Fort Massaid, and entered the town 1 mile to the north of the landing-place. We were warned not to touch any ropes lying about near the shore, as land mines were in some cases attached—two men were killed in this way. The town was full of people, but all the troops, including irregulars, had left. We watered our horses at a picturesque old stone well, sixty feet deep, the natives letting down little boys who filled the buckets at the bottom. A landing stage had been constructed, and lighters from Port Said were already landing stores. The inhabitants seemed quite friendly, but very curious and anxious to be photographed. Amongst the various types which we observed the tall red-haired and blue-eyed natives seemed to predominate ; these were said to be the descendants of the ancient Philistines. We rode through the chief streets of the town, which had suffered considerably from our aeroplane and naval bombardments during July-October 1916, and saw the two large mosques. The shops were open, but the Turks had seen to it that little was left behind. The One Hundred and Fifty-sixth Brigade of the Fifty-second Division were encamped just outside. We heard firing to the east, and ascertained that the Anzac Mounted Division were engaged about 8 miles away. The inhabitants of the town were very scared whenever our aeroplanes flew over, as they had suffered so severely during the last few months. To the north of the town we saw the fine green cultivation on the banks of the Wadi El Arish ; the latter, which in summer is merely a dry watercourse, was now in flood and appeared to be a river of some importance. While in the town I picked up a German newspaper, dated August 5th, which described the Turkish advance on the Suez Canal and prophesied that the latter would be an unqualified success. This was interesting, in view of the fact that the very day on which the paper was printed in Berlin the Turks were receiving the final beating which caused them to commence their retreat through Sinai and Palestine. At this period the Warwickshire Yeomanry were at K 181 (railhead), performing convoy duties to El Arish, the Gloucesters were at Malha, while we remained guarding the right flank just outside El Arish. Although we were now 10 miles ahead of railhead, the latter would reach us in a week. It was extraordinary the pace that this railhead

moved, provided it was not held up by actual hostilities.
First came a troop of yeomanry doing advance guard,
then the surveyors of the line, often themselves under
fire, then some thousands of Egyptian natives belonging
to the Labour Corps, who either built up an embankment
or else dug a cutting, and finally the construction train
itself. The natives performed their work almost entirely
by using little spades and fig-baskets, the sand being
scooped into the latter and removed as quickly as
possible.

December 24th.

We heard in the morning that the Anzac Mounted
Division had, after some strenuous fighting at Magdaba,
taken 1,200 prisoners; some "aviatiks" by way of retaliation bombing the landing-stage at El Arish and the troops
in its vicinity.

December 25th.

A perfect Christmas Day, though not in a European
sense—brilliant sunshine and beautifully warm. A football match was played in the afternoon, and a concert
was held around the big camp fire at night.

December 27th.

Two of us took some camels out in the morning to
collect loot from the old Turkish camp. We were very
hard up for firewood, and the Turkish water-barrels were
very useful. We rode through the Turkish fortifications,
which extended from Fort Massaid on the sea down to Bir
Masmi.

The Maghara hills were now reported clear, and the
Turks were said to be in retreat from Kossaima across
the Turko-Egyptian frontier. At three o'clock a regiment
from the Anzac Division marched their Turkish prisoners
along the seashore towards railhead; they were a motley-
looking crew, mostly Syrians and Arabs; many were
dressed in quaint canary-coloured uniforms, which combined with light blue trousers looked somewhat theatrical.

It seemed strange that they should be marched through El Arish again as prisoners, when they had garrisoned that town for the last two years. One of our aeroplanes was washed up on the beach, but there was no sign of the pilot. The pariah dogs were rather troublesome at night, as unless food was carefully hidden they often used to steal it ; this was due to the fact that we were just outside a town, where the dogs were not afraid of human beings.

December 28*th*.

On waking up in the morning we were astonished to see that railhead had reached us, and 300 yards away a large embankment had appeared, which was covered with Egyptian Labour Corps, swarming like ants all over it. During the next few days we had heavy rain, the only rain which falls in this district during the whole year.

December 29*th*.

The wet weather was very depressing, and was accentuated by the fact that owing to submarines no Christmas parcels had arrived.

1917.

January 1*st*.

In the morning I rode out with the C.O. by the coast route via El Daheisha and Bir Massaid to the new landing-stage which had been constructed on the beach north of El Arish. Here was a big supply depot, and two steamers from Port Said were landing stores. After passing the tomb of Nebi Yesir we crossed the Wadi [1] El Arish, which at this time of the year was a considerable river. It was fringed on either side by mighty palm-trees and native cultivation. This green cultivation was a great relief to one's eyes after the sandy desert, occasionally dotted with scrub, of the Sinai Peninsula. A few minutes later we heard machine-gun fire and saw an " aviatik "

[1] *Wadi*=a watercourse, generally dry in summer.

Palestine campaign appeared to us to have very little effect on the Turkish and German aeroplanes. The Hong-Kong and Singapore Mountain Battery, which was attached to Desert Corps, was always very active on these occasions, and being a certain distance from our camp, generally dropped some shrapnel shell-cases into our lines. We heard, through an agent who obtained the information from the Turkish Intelligence, that the French had landed a force at Akaba. New orders were received for Desert Column to start at 4 p.m. on " Z " day for Sheikh Zowaid ; the plan of attack was now to be generally more south. The Fifth Mounted Brigade were to lead the attack on the east, headed by the Worcester Yeomanry, and " D " Squadron of that regiment was to make a cordon round the village of Sheikh Zowaid to prevent the population from giving information before the general attack on Rafa commenced. At 9.30 p.m. (full moon), just as we were turning in, we were startled by a big explosion just outside the tent, and rushed out to find the two " aviatiks " back again and flying very low over our camp, bombing and spraying our lines with their machine guns. It was a bad night and, as usual, the " aviatiks " escaped unscathed.

January 8th.

During the morning the following orders were received from the medical authorities :

At 3.30 p.m. Desert Mounted Column will proceed to Sheikh Zowaid, where the main Division Dressing Station will be established, to which lightly wounded will ride direct. Any casualties during the afternoon on the line of march will be left with one man and picked up by the following Field Ambulances. On the morning of the 9th the Fifth Mounted Brigade Field Ambulance will arrive at the Magruntein–Darba fork roads at 5.30 a.m., and will proceed along the Rafa telegraph track. The tent subdivision will halt at the T in Sultanieh, and the bearer subdivision (with sand-carts and sledges) will report to the Worcester squadron at a given point on the Magruntein road at dawn. If successful, pursuit of the enemy will not be carried out beyond Khan Yunus. If there is a standing fight at the enemy's trenches, each R.M.O.

7

will keep his Field Ambulance informed of his position, and maintain constant communication with it when an advance occurs. From Field Ambulances camel cacolets will evacuate to the Divisional Dressing Station at Sheikh Zowaid, and thence wounded will be conveyed by sand-carts to El Arish. When the action is over, R.M.O.'s will let officers commanding Field Ambulances know at once when all wounded have been collected. R.M.O.'s are especially warned that the wounded must be collected as quickly as possible when night comes on, as there is a native hostile tribe in the neighbourhood which are known to have the reputation of mutilating their enemies.

The following orders were received from the G.O.C. Fifth Mounted Brigade :

1. The enemy are in an entrenched position between El Magruntein and Rafa.

2. The Desert Mounted Column will attack Rafa at dawn on January 9th from Sheikh Zowaid.

3. The Fifth Mounted Brigade, less one rear-guard squadron, leaves Sheikh Zowaid at 1 a.m., and proceeds to Point 210 by the southern road.

4. Order of march : Fifth Mounted Brigade, Desert Column H.Q., First Australian Light Horse Brigade, Third Australian Light Horse Brigade, New Zealand Mounted Brigade, Camel Corps, H.A.C. Battery, Somersetshire R.H.A., Leicestershire R.H.A., Inverness-shire R.H.A., and Hong-Kong and Singapore Mountain Battery ; the whole will move off from El Arish at 4 p.m., January 8th. Signal troops will march with Brigades, and R.E. troops will remain at Sheikh Zowaid. A rear-guard squadron of Worcester Yeomanry will leave Sheikh Zowaid at dawn, and move as a feint along the bifurcation of the Rafa road (some way north of 210) ; they will observe these roads and report any enemy in the sandhills. The rest of the force proceeds at 1 a.m. to 210 as above.

It was pointed out by our Second-in-Command, on seeing the Medical and Brigade Orders, that the bearer sub-division of our Field Ambulance, with its sand-carts and sledges, would arrive at its destination before the Worcester squadron, and that the former would probably be the first to get in touch with the enemy, a proceeding which actually occurred, as will be seen later. The Wadi El Arish was at this time a roaring torrent, owing to recent 'rains, and it was difficult to obtain communication with the town in our rear. At midday Fritz appeared, evidently to reconnoitre, and found Desert Column still bivouacked. At 4 p.m. our force started east, accompanied by R.F.C. scouts to prevent Fritz being aware of our movements; he appeared, however, but was rapidly driven away. At 10 p.m., after riding some 20 miles, we arrived in the vicinity of the village of Sheikh Zowaid, and " D " Squadron and two troops of " A " Squadron Worcester Yeomanry immediately pushed on and made a cordon round the village, to prevent the natives from giving warning of our advance. One troop was also thrown out as an advance guard on the southern road to 210. While we were resting and eating a little food, we became aware of our immediate surroundings, which were most picturesque in the brilliant moonlight—in the foreground was the silver lake, here and there dotted with little islands of white salt, resembling snow, and surrounded by patches of green cultivation and giant dark palm-trees, which stood out boldly against the sky. At one end of the glistening water nestled the sleepy little village around which our cordon had been drawn; not a sound was heard; the silence was uncanny; a few miles to the east lay an unknown Turkish force. Many thoughts flitted through our heads : Were the enemy's outposts aware of our advance ? Should we, on the morrow, be able to defeat and capture his outlying force, and return again to El Arish before he was able to call up his large reserves from Khan Yunus and Shellal ? It was evident that our cavalry force was relying entirely on its mobility, and it was a big undertaking to advance 30 miles, fight all day, and then retire again the way we had come on the evening after the battle. We were all supplied with two days' rations for man and horse, and were warned that no water would be obtainable until we returned to Sheikh Zowaid after the engagement.

January 9th.

At 1.30 a.m. our Brigade moved out of Sheikh Zowaid to 210 south-west of Rafa, and then proceeded a mile and a half north-east along the El Magruntein road ; at this point Corps and our Brigade Headquarters were established, and the former at once set up its wireless plant and its white cross signs on the ground for the use of our aeroplanes. At 6 a.m., soon after dawn, the enemy fired his first shots at our Field Ambulance Column, which was proceeding solemnly towards the enemy in advance of the Worcester squadron, just as had been predicted by our Second-in-Command. However, within a few minutes the Worcester squadron dashed up in front of the sand-carts. The former were met by the troop of " A " Squadron which had been sent out from Brigade Headquarters to reconnoitre. The New Zealand Mounted Brigade, with the Inverness-shire R.H.A., proceeded round to the south-east (behind Rafa) over the boundary into Turkish territory—on their way to this position they fell in with a force of 4,000 Arab irregulars bivouacked outside the village of Sheikh El Sufi ; these were surprised, and after some Sheikhs had been taken as hostages the remainder were rendered harmless. This was the tribe which was known to be hostile to us, who we were particularly afraid would mutilate our wounded. The First and Second Australian Light Horse Brigades, covered by the Somerset R.H.A. and the Leicestershire R.H.A., now approached Rafa from the south, having the Imperial Camel Corps on their left ; the latter were covered by the Hong-Kong and Singapore Mountain Battery. Meanwhile, the Fifth Mounted Brigade (Yeomanry) were still 1½ miles north-east of 210, facing Rafa from the south-west. At 8 a.m. the Gloucester Yeomanry moved across the open grass plain near E. Rasum, and proceeded up under the sandhills, where they came into action. Our battery (the H.A.C.) took up a position about 2 miles north-east of 210, with " C " Squadron Worcestershire Yeomanry as their escort, and immediately opened fire over open sights on the enemy's " B " and " C " trenches. The Warwickshire Yeomanry came into action on the left of the battery. A few minutes later our C.O. took out the rest of the Worcesters with his Machine Gun Detachment (the latter immediately proceeded due north to a position in the sandhills) and galloped into action opposite the C 1 trenches—this position turned out, however, to be an impossible one for the time being, owing to heavy shrapnel and close range machine-gun fire, so we left-wheeled and for action dismounted about 1,000 yards due west of the A 2 trenches. By this time the action was becoming general, and Divisional Headquarters on our right was being heavily shelled. We advanced by rushes, with absolutely no cover, firing on the Turks, who we could plainly see getting in and out of their trenches (they apparently had no communication trenches) in the most nonchalant manner ; we then returned to our led horses, with our wounded, to a position behind a small sandhill. From this position we had a good view of the trenches in front of us, of which the redoubt known as 255 was the most noticeable feature, with the houses of Rafa to the left ; the latter were occupied by a Turkish garrison, especially the large square police barracks, which were being shelled by our batteries. We now mounted and galloped into the sandhills north of the Jerusalem tele-graph line, and I sent an orderly back to the C.O. of our Field Ambulance to notify him of our new position. About 2 miles north-east of 164 we found " D " Squadron Worcester Yeomanry, who had worked up to that point after doing advance guard in the early morning with only a few casualties. Our " A " and " D " Squadrons opened fire on Rafa and the redoubt from the sandhills, with the Gloucester Yeomanry below them. While this was going on the New Zealand Brigade had got into Rafa, supported by the Inverness-shire R.H.A., from the east, and were attacking the redoubt from behind. The First Australian Light Horse Brigade were closing on the C 5 and C 4 trenches, supported by the Hong-Kong Battery. The Third Australian Light Horse Brigade were concentrated on the C 2 and C 3 trenches, assisted by the Somersetshire and Leicester batteries. The Camel Corps also attacked the latter trenches after they had rushed the B 1, B 2 and

B 3 trench system. In fact, with the exception of the northern (sea) sector the enemy's system of redoubts and trenches was surrounded. The former, however, were very strong, as they were situate on a steep hill sloping south and south-west, with a perfect field of fire for the defenders. During this time I had had a strenuous task getting sand-carts up into almost inaccessible places in the sandhills overlooking the A 1 and A 2 positions. There was every chance of single mounted men being wounded amongst these sandhills and never being found. Especially in the direction of 183, snipers were very active, and one was found buried up to the armpits in the sand behind a small aloes plant; these men continued to fire at close quarters until all their ammunition was expended and then surrendered, knowing full well that there could be but one ending. At 3.30 p.m. the position was unchanged, and the Turks, evidently expecting reinforcements, were holding out stubbornly; the Worcester Yeomanry then received orders to charge the C 1 trenches, supported by the Warwicks on the right and the Gloucesters, who also attacked the A 2 trenches, on the left. We debouched from the sandhills and galloped across the open grass plain to a depression in the ground, where the regiment dismounted and left their horses. Luckily we had only had a few casualties crossing the open. " C " Squadron Worcester Yeomanry, which had been escorting our battery, now joined up, somewhat depleted by casualties, and the regiment commenced a dismounted attack on the C 1 trenches. Meanwhile, the Worcester, Warwick and Gloucester machine guns, brigaded, opened fire from the sand-dune 2½ miles south of 183. I selected a dressing station behind a ridge as the attack started. The Turks fought stubbornly, although almost surrounded, but by this time their guns had been silenced. Their rifle and machine-gun fire, however, were intense, and we had many horses hit behind the dressing station. Casualties dribbled in, but they were not very numerous. The regiment attacked by short rushes and behaved splendidly, and just before dusk rushed their trenches at the

SKETCH MAP ILLUSTRATING EVACUATION OF FIFTH MOUNTED BRIGADE WOUNDED,

same moment that the Turks were seen to be surrendering on the top of the redoubt to the New Zealanders, who had charged with the bayonet. I had a certain number of sand-carts concealed behind my dressing station, and as well as our own men evacuated a number of Warwicks and Gloucesters from the other side of the plain. The wounded were taken from the regimental dressing station to the Field Ambulance at 210, and thence were conveyed by camel cacolet 7 miles to the Corps Collecting Station at Sheikh Zowaid. Each Brigade had no doubt a similar arrangement. (From the Corps Collecting Station the wounded were moved by a large convoy of carts 20 miles to El Arish, where they were accommodated in the 2nd Lowland and 3rd Australian Light Horse Field Ambulances, both acting as Casualty Clearing Stations; thence they were moved by hospital train from railhead to the Casualty Clearing Stations and stationary hospitals at Kantara, to be ultimately transferred across the Canal for distribution amongst the hospitals of Egypt.) The slightly wounded men who had had their horses shot we mounted on the horses of the killed and severely wounded, and arranged for them to follow the regiment. It was now dark, and our regimental sergeant-major was our last casualty—chest wound, serious. As there was some delay about getting another sand-cart in the dark, and his condition after the first field dressing had been applied appeared to be very serious, I managed to stop one of our motor machine gun cars and sent him direct into Sheikh Zowaid. About an hour previously the regiment had formed up and started back to the same place in order to water. Rainclouds obscured the moon and it was pitch dark. Luckily we had accounted for all our missing, but the Warwicks and Gloucesters still had a considerable number of wounded to be picked up, especially in the sand-dunes. On such a night a compass became a vital necessity in order to find one's way about the battle-field. R.M.O.'s were each given an escort of six men when the regiments moved off, as the ground was still partly occupied by prowling Arabs of the Sufi tribe, ready to mutilate or plunder the wounded. Some of these surrendered to small parties during the night. In addition to my six men I had a friend with me who had remained when our R.S.M. had been hit, and the former accompanied me to the Field Ambulance, where we had been told to report when all casualties had been evacuated. We fell in with various convoys of wounded in the dark, who were lost, and directed them to our Field Ambulance. The latter eventually lit a beacon fire to show everyone its whereabouts. On arrival we found the C.O. out, superintending the collection of wounded ; the two officers in charge were in rather a quandary, as an A.D.C. from the G.O.C. Desert Column had just told them to move the whole unit to Sheikh Zowaid as quickly as possible, because 4,000 Turkish reinforcements were advancing on Rafa. This was the reason why the garrison of Rafa had held out so long, knowing that this force was advancing from Beersheba ; as a matter of fact the enemy, on approaching Rafa, had been heavily attacked by an Australian Light Horse Brigade, and learning that the garrison had capitulated, had retired eastwards. The Field Ambulance officers did not know the latter part of this story (we heard it next day), and it looked as if they might be captured, as the Brigadier had previously ordered all ambulance waggons to return to the battle-field. At 8 p.m. we left for Sheikh Zowaid and arrived at 10.30, rejoining the regiment after watering our horses. Prisoners were handed over to the A.P.M. and the remaining wounded were taken to the Corps Collecting Station. There was plenty of water for the horses, as the R.E. troops attached to Brigades had been at work all day. The rations and drinking water brought up from El Arish by our camel convoy were much appreciated. It appeared that Fritz, who had not done much during the battle, had bombed the R.E. parties heavily while they were developing the water supply. Our aeroplanes were wonderful during the whole day, continually spotting for the batteries by dropping smoke-balls over the enemy and bringing in fresh news of the Turkish dispositions and reinforcements.

January 10*th.*

At 1 a.m., in the rain, the Brigade started on its return journey to El Arish. We were all very drowsy, not having rested for two nights, and were continually falling asleep in our saddles. This 20-mile ride seemed endless, and in our tired state the shadows on the desert caused the most extraordinary hallucination of vision, which differed according to the individual concerned. Our C.O. told me that he seemed to be passing a continual succession of cafés, each with a large number of tables apparently in the roadway ; my impression was that we were passing many rows of tents, and every few minutes we seemed to be riding over the edge of a precipice, although we were really riding on a level track. At dawn we met a large ambulance column coming out to clear our wounded from Sheikh Zowaid. On reaching our own camp at El Arish, our horses were watered and everyone immediately fell asleep. Our Field Ambulance and many of the wounded came in during the day, one Brigade Australian Light Horse having been temporarily left near Rafa as a rear-guard. The following letter picked up in a captured Turkish trench, and marked outside " Passed by Censor," is typical of the simple Turkish soldier :

(*Translation.*)

My LIFE-GIVING AND REVERED FATHER, ABDULLAH AGHA,

I am awfully worried at not having received any letters from you for more than a year to tell me whether you are quite well. I think that it is hardly fair of you to let your son worry like this, when he has joined the army to serve his Fatherland and fellow-countrymen. I can only attribute this to the fact that you must be very busy in your office. By the grace of God, my health is quite good. May it please Providence to grant my mother, yourself, and all my relations the best of health. Under the auspices of our Government and nation I am quite well, and you need not worry about me at all. I beg to kiss both my little gracious mother's hands, and am always in need of her dear prayers. Trusting you are quite well, my dearest father, I kiss your two holy hands, and anxiously await the answer to my letter.

(Signed) CORPORAL ——,
Regiment No. 8,
2nd Battalion,
No. 3 Company.

January 11th.

We moved our camp further up the Wadi El Arish and spread out the squadrons more, on account of enemy aircraft. Orders were issued that everyone should dig himself a deep dugout in the sand : this was not easy, as we had no revetting material. We could get no head-cover, as timber was not available, but a hole was better than nothing. In the afternoon the regiment was paraded and the C.O. made a speech about the recent operations ; he also read a letter from the G.O.C. Desert Column and the Inspector-General of Cavalry, congratulating the Fifth Mounted Brigade on their behaviour. Afterwards some of us rode up to the 3rd Australian Light Horse Field Ambulance, and the 2nd Lowland Field Ambulances, which were situated between railhead and the Fifty-second Division, and visited some of our wounded. It appeared that our Brigade had sustained the heaviest casualties in the recent fighting. Near the new pier, where steamers were lying, we saw some guns which were trained on the sea, and whose crews were keeping a sharp look-out for submarines, which might shell the supply depot and railhead at this point. On the way back to camp we passed the prisoners' cages, where the Turks and Germans were in separate enclosures ; the latter were clothed in their European grey field uniforms and were mostly machine gunners. A German officer told us that they had held out so long on the 9th because they knew that their reinforcements were close at hand ; he also told us that the war would last another two years ! Together in killed, wounded and captured, the Turko-German force had lost over 2,000 men, with a large number of rifles, field guns and machine guns. Our successful cavalry raid had been purely a mounted affair, and not a single infantry battalion had taken part in it. The light cars armed with machine guns, which were manned by details from some Scottish regiments, were of great value. The successful issue had been mainly due to our mobility, moving out 30 miles, fighting a strenuous battle, and starting back to our advance base the same night. In the evening we had a Brigade Memorial Service for the Dead and the Brigadier made a touching speech.

January 12th.

During the morning two "aviatiks" bombed us as usual, but without our regiment sustaining any casualties. Our machines bombed Beersheba at midday and again by moonlight at night, and dropped a message saying that for every bomb dropped on El Arish, five would be dropped on Beersheba.

January 14th.

We heard that Rafa had been reoccupied by the Turks after our raid—Intelligence stated that a very large force of the enemy had concentrated at a point midway between Gaza and Beersheba, but much nearer to the Turko-Egyptian frontier than these two towns. Our squadrons were now doing advance patrols on the desert tracks east of El Arish.

January 15th.

Another 30 miles of railway material arrived at railhead, also a large supply of aeroplane bombs; the latter was to us particularly pleasing.

January 16th.

After being bombed as usual in the morning, we heard a very loud explosion near the pier, which turned out to be a mine captured and exploded by two of our mine-sweepers. It had probably been laid by a submarine which was reported to be in the vicinity.

January 18th.

During the next ten days the regiment remained in bivouac outside El Arish, and with the exception of daily bombing by Fritz, nothing of interest occurred. The bombing was always accompanied by a good deal of shrapnel from our own guns, which fell in our lines. The unit had its first experience of the " delousing train," the first that had been seen on this front. Universal anti-cholera and anti-typhoid inoculation was carried out, as these were now due; the order was that every man should receive two anti-cholera inoculations four times and two anti-typhoid twice a year. In addition to this, whenever a case of smallpox occurred in the vicinity every one in the regiment was vaccinated.

February 1st.

The regiment marched to El Burj, where part of the brigade was already bivouacked. This place, which consisted of a few tamarisk-trees and an old well, was half-way between El Arish and Rafa, being situate on the wooded sandhills overlooking the caravan route, about a mile from the sea and 10 miles ahead of the railway line. We rode by the seaside route, and on arrival found that excellent drinking water had been developed on the shore by our R.E. It was a curious fact that the whole way up the Sinai Peninsula, although the water was brackish inland, it always had a very low degree of salinity when obtained near the coast. In this case the degree of salinity was 14 : 100,000. It was possible to drink water of a salinity represented by 150 : 100,000, but it ought to be under 100 : 100,000. This water was so free from bacterial contamination that it only required one measure (about 30 grains) of chloride of lime to sterilize 200 gallons. This sterilization of drinking water was one of the most important functions performed by R.M.O.'s, and guards were always posted over all water-tanks in order to prevent unauthorized persons from interfering with the water supply. As we rode up from the beach into our camp in the moonlight, the sand was so white in colour and the tamarisk-trees were so large that in our somewhat sleepy condition the scene reminded one of an English park covered with snow. Our outposts received a warning that there would be a flight of our aeroplanes low over the camp at midnight *en route* to Jerusalem and Ramleh; the latter had just been discovered to be the new enemy aerodrome between Jerusalem and the coast.

February 2nd.

Three of our aeroplanes were hidden on a small Sabkhet (dried lake) amongst the sandhills near our camp in order to attack Fritz when he returned to his base after his daily bombing of El Arish, it being necessary for him to pass over El Burj on his return journey. During our stay in this place our patrols brought in prisoners daily. I interrogated a Turkish soldier, who turned out to be a Syrian and could speak French ; he stated that he originally came from Beyrout, where he was formerly employed as an engine-driver by a French railway company—he told me that the Turks used wood fuel for their engines, a fact which we also discovered later on, when we found enormous stacks of wood at every railway station. He also said that the new Turkish aerodrome was at Ramleh, and that the Turks had recently built a railway from Beersheba to El Auja due south, but that it was not completed to Kossaima ; the latter was situate on the Maghara hills, which we had been watching a few months ago. The Arab irregulars said that they had deserted because they did not wish to fight against the Sheriff of Mecca.

February 4th.

Some of us went out to the secret aerodrome, where we watched our planes ascend and attack Fritz on his return from El Arish. We found quite a number of animals which we had not seen before, such as tortoises, small snakes, tarantulas and iguanas : the latter are a species of lizard about twenty-four inches long, resembling a tiny crocodile.

February 5th.

I interrogated some more prisoners during the day, and one of them told me (in French) that he was a chemist from Constantinople who had served at Gallipoli ; he had deserted on account of shortage of food, and said that the 31st, 32nd and 170th Regiments were at Shellal, accompanied by Austrian batteries. Many of the deserters who came in had been plundered and ill-treated by the Arab irregulars who operated in the neutral area near Rafa ; one caused a certain amount of amusement to our men, as he came in dressed only in a pair of shorts. At this period our rations were augmented by small fish caught by the natives, which were a very welcome addition to our diet. A camel-load of oranges passed through our camp in the afternoon, and in a few seconds were distributed amongst the men. They turned out to be a supply which had been ordered through our native interpreter for Brigade Head-quarters ! At this period the wire road which was being laid down on the soft sand by the infantry reached our camp. This road consisted of four widths of rabbit wire pegged down on to the ground, and was of great value to enable the infantry to march easily. All sorts of dire penalties were enforced if a mounted man was found to be riding on this road, or if any car, other than a General's, was seen driving on it. The infantry also invented a form of snow-shoe, consisting of a wire frame attached to their boots, which prevented them from sinking into the heavy sand when marching where no wire road was available.

February 6th.

We were interested to hear that a new Cavalry Division was to be formed which would consist of two Australian Light Horse Brigades, our Fifth Mounted Brigade and the Sixth Mounted Brigade ; the latter Brigade, consisting of the Berks, Bucks and Dorset Yeomanry, had been recently transferred from the western frontier of Egypt. In the evening, while a regimental football match was in progress on the El Burj Sabkhet, a troop of Warwickshire Yeo-manry caused some amusement by suddenly appearing over the crest of the hill, driving before them a herd of about 300 camels, which they had captured while grazing in charge of a few armed Bedouin, 10 miles south-east of our camp. These camels, which were in excellent condition, were eventually handed over to the Camel Transport Corps.

February 10th.

At this time we used to receive two messages a day by aeroplane with reports of the nearest enemy dispositions. At 8.30 a.m. the regiment accompanied a detachment of R.E. to Sheikh Zowaid, where wells were being developed, and on arrival threw out patrols towards Rafa ; the latter got into touch with the enemy, and captured a few prisoners who said they came from Shellal. We found that the Turks had erected some useful concrete tanks, but that they had destroyed the pumping machinery before retiring. The tomb from which the village took its name was the most marked feature of the surroundings and contained an interesting old sarcophagus.

February 11th.

An interesting and useful discovery was made by some of the men, namely, that the numerous ants in our camp were rapidly clearing the regiment of lice ! These little insects, when allowed to run over a man's clothing, appeared to be much more efficacious than any insect powder. Fritz paid his usual visit in the afternoon, and we began to feel that we should quite miss him if he failed to appear.

February 13th.

At 7.30 a.m. the regiment marched to Sheikh Zowaid again for general reconnaissance, and in order to protect some Staff officers of the Fifty-second and Fifty-third Divisions who were studying the neighbourhood. Our patrols were thrown out to within 2 miles of Rafa, and we could see the Turks plainly through our glasses. The whole time we were in helio, flag and telephone communication with Sheikh Zowaid, and were under orders to fall back on the infantry before Burj if attacked by numbers. We noticed a large number of Bedouin with their flocks before Rafa, and came to the conclusion that the Turks could not be so very short of food, as they had apparently not interfered with the cattle. Deserters told us, through our interpreter, that these Bedouin were all friendly to the enemy and informed them daily of our whereabouts ; they belonged to the hostile tribe already referred to, and in accordance with orders from the G.O.C. Desert Column we captured half a dozen for Intelligence purposes. These Bedouin, when pursued, habitually conceal their arms when they see that there is no escape possible—on these occasions, after following their track for a short distance, one could usually find some newly turned earth where arms and ammunition had been concealed. On leaving the outpost line in order to return to camp a voluble old Arab patriarch rushed up and insisted on accompanying us ; we could not understand a word he said, so he was placed on a pack-horse and taken 15 miles back to camp. It appeared that he came from Beersheba and that he claimed some Turkish ponies which one of our sergeants had rounded up with great difficulty and brought back to camp ; the latter was very crestfallen when the old patriarch proved his case and returned in the evening with his ponies to his native village.

February 14th.

Railhead continued to move very quickly, and during the afternoon the Sikh Pioneers and their railway embankment appeared opposite our camp. These troops were now doing all the advance railway work, and provided their own protection by digging trenches just in front of railhead every night. During the next few days the regiment did daily patrols to Rafa, and in places got in touch with the enemy. Intelligence stated that a new Turkish Division — the Fifty-third — had reinforced the Third Division at Shellal. This Fifty-third Division had been withdrawn from the Caucasus front and had been recently stationed at Aleppo. The Turks were evidently getting anxious about the Beersheba front.

February 19th.

In the afternoon our Machine Gun Detachment captured the first Turkish cavalryman whom we had seen for nine months. He was evidently a patrol who had got lost south of our camp. The machine gunners were practising at a target which consisted of two palm-trees when, much to everyone's surprise, he calmly rode out from behind them. He was mounted on a sturdy Arab pony and was wearing a medal, which caused some amusement when our interpreter explained to us that it was the Suez Canal medal ; he informed us that there were three cavalry regiments at Shellal.

February 22nd.

It appeared that about 1,000 Turks had been located at Khan Yunus, and that they were to be rounded up by the New Zealand and Australian Light Horse Brigades, our Brigade being left in reserve together with two batteries and an Infantry Brigade at Sheikh Zowaid. At 2 p.m. the Fifth Mounted Brigade left Burj, proceeding south of the usual route to Sheikh Zowaid. Recent rain had brought on the barley, which our horses enjoyed immensely. The idea of the concentration of troops at this place was in order to prevent the Turks from Shellal from attacking our communications, while our two Mounted Brigades were in touch with the enemy at Khan Yunus. We captured two deserters, who turned out to be Algerian soldiers who had been made prisoner by the Germans in Belgium in 1914 ; they were very pleased at having escaped from the Turks, which they did on the pretext of foraging for food.

February 23rd.

At dawn the two Australian Light Horse Brigades advanced on Khan Yunus, and a few hours later an aeroplane reported that the enemy had vanished, and it was decided that the Australians should round up some hostile Bedouin tribes instead. At about 10 a.m., however, a message came through that the Australians had fallen in with a very strong Turkish force and were retiring, after taking the Turkish first-line trenches between Khan Yunus and Rafa. At midday our Brigade started to return to Burj, on the way passing the Twenty-second Mounted Brigade (Stafford, Lincoln and West Riding Yeomanry) who were on their way to take their place in the Anzac Mounted Division; this Division consisted of the above-mentioned Yeomanry Brigades, with three Australian Light Horse Brigades, and the Imperial Mounted Division consisted of two Australian Light Horse Brigades and the Fifth and Sixth Mounted Yeomanry Brigades.

February 24th.

We were astonished during the morning to hear an anti-aircraft gun firing at Fritz from only a few hundred yards away. The former had been established in the valley beneath our camp, and as we were on the hill immediately above the gun, the shells seemed to skim our camp and some prematures burst in our kitchen.

February 28th.

It appeared that our big offensive was expected during the coming full moon, and many were the conjectures as to where our Brigade would attack. It was stated that we were opposed by some 30,000 Turks in the vicinity of Shellal and Beersheba.

March 1st.

The railway had now reached Sheikh Zowaid, and our mounted patrols had been in touch with the Turkish cavalry to the south of Shellal.

March 4th.

Our C.O., who had been away for a few days on patrol with the Staffordshire Yeomanry, told us that the Turks (30,000) held a very strong position at Weli Sheikh Nuran, where our cavalry had come in contact with their outposts, also in the neighbourhood of Abasan El Kebir, Abu Khatli and El Abreish.

March 10th.

The Brigade marched along the shore to Bir El Amafidi and Thamila, about a mile distant from Sheikh Zowaid, and bivouacked with the rest of the Imperial Mounted Division.

March 12th.

Sheikh Zowaid had now become an important railway station, and a large number of infantry regiments and batteries were bivouacked in the vicinity. During the next few days Fritz attacked us regularly, but did not cause many casualties in our area. Maps of Kosseima, Beersheba and Jerusalem were issued, which evidently meant that we should be soon advancing over new country ; but before this occurred G.O.C. Desert Column gave permission for the Imperial Mounted Division, the Anzac Mounted Division, the Fifty-second, Fifty-third and Fifty-fourth Divisions to hold a steeplechase meeting on the fine grass country outside Rafa. On March 16th we were joined by the Sixth Mounted Brigade, and heard that we should soon be attacking Gaza.

CHAPTER IV

PALESTINE

March 21st.

Owing to impending operations, Desert Column races were held near Rafa during the day ; it had been intended to hold them a week later. The Fifth and Sixth Mounted Brigades left their camps at 8 a.m. and proceeded to the northern side of Rafa, where they bivouacked just across the frontier in Palestine. Our Brigade was now ready to move " light " at a moment's notice, three days' rations being carried by every man and an extra two days' rations for each being carried by pack-horses. We were given full instructions as to the areas in which we might expect to find water during our advance, and we were told that the Fifty-third and Fifty-fourth Divisions would probably attack Gaza, aided by the Anzac Mounted Division on their right flank and by the Imperial Mounted Division on the Beersheba side.

March 22nd.

Our " A " and " C " Squadrons proceeded to the Goz El Taire Ridge, 3½ miles east of Khan Yunus, where they assisted and provided protection for the R.E., who were developing wells. Fritz was over during the afternoon, and appeared to be very curious about the concentration of troops in the Rafa area. Orders were received for the Imperial Mounted Division to make a reconnaissance in force towards Gaza.

Orders for March 23rd.

Objective of the Worcester Yeomanry is Sheikh Nebhan, on the Wadi El Ghuzze. First bound, Gloucester and Worcester Yeomanry proceed to Beni Sela, east of Khan Yunus. Second bound, Worcester Yeomanry proceed to 320 (In Seirat), and then move to 310 at 8 a.m. Warwick Yeomanry and Field Ambulance proceed to 340, whence Warwick Yeomanry will take up a position on Tel El Jemmi. R.E. field troop and the Worcester Yeomanry will look for wells near Seirat. Divisional Headquarters at 330. B.H.Q. at Abu Teibig. Fifth Mounted Brigade holds the line Sheikh Nebhan to Abu Bakra (both on the Wadi). Third Light Horse Brigade on the left holds the line Sheikh Nebhan to the sea. Sixth Mounted Brigade will be in Divisional Reserve behind Seirat, and camels and tent subdivision of Field Ambulance remain at Khan Yunus. All ranks will carry six days' rations with them and on pack-horses.

Before going to sleep we worked out the bearings of these various positions in order to be able to find our way back if we should be isolated from the main body.

March 23rd.

At 5 a.m. our Brigade left camp, according to orders ; as we passed over the hill and descended into the Khan Yunus valley, a veritable Promised Land met our view—below us lay a flourishing village, dominated by the ruins of an ancient Crusader castle and surrounded by tall trees and green fields, which were irrigated by running water and plentifully dotted with bright-coloured flowers ; and stretching away in the distance were the golden cornfields of southern Palestine ; on the rolling downs towards the sea many cattle and sheep were grazing. It was a scene of peace and plenty, and was a great contrast to the sandy wastes of the Sinai Peninsula. It must be remembered that at this time the country was still flourishing from the effects of the recent winter rains ; a month or so later the same country-side presented a very different picture. We arrived at the village of Beni Sela about 7 a.m., and after a halt proceeded along the 300 contour-line on the Goz El Taire Ridge and halted at 320, near the hamlet of In Seirat. Here we found the Sixth Mounted Brigade in Divisional Reserve and some curious " aviatiks " buzzing overhead ; we rode on over very rough ground, intersected by numerous small Wadis, which were tributaries of the Wadi El Ghuzze, until we reached 310, and took up our line according to orders.   We could see the bearer section of our Field Ambulance at 340, and to the south-east the Warwickshire Yeomanry on that very marked feature Tel El Jemmi, on the western bank of the big Wadi.   From our position we obtained a view of Gaza and could hear the 3rd Australian Light Horse in action on our left ; meanwhile the Turks were shelling our patrols with their mountain guns.   While this was in progress, those of us who were in reserve grazed our horses on the green barley and watered them in the numerous water-holes.   While this reconnaissance was in progress the Staff officers of various Divisions obtained a good view of their future objectives.   The flowers on the Goz El Taire Ridge made a beautiful picture, and in some places the poppies gave colour to the whole hill-side.   The tent subdivision of our Field Ambulance, which had been ordered to move to Abasan El Kebir, was attacked by some Turkish patrols and had to withdraw to Beni Sela.   At 3 p.m., the reconnaissance having been completed, we were ordered to retire.   A little later some " aviatiks " attacked us with their machine gun, causing some casualties amongst the Warwick Yeomanry ; the rear-guard squadron of the latter regiment were attacked near Tel El Jemmi, when retiring, by a squadron of Turkish cavalry, who fired from their horses as they trotted through the standing corn—needless to say, without causing any serious casualties.   After spending some time in assisting to extricate one of our men from a ditch, who was in difficulties owing to his horse lying on the top of him, I caught up the main body and returned with them to camp at sunset.

March 24th.

All day long Infantry Brigades marched in, and by the end of the day the railway extended 3½ miles into Palestine.

March 25th.

The Brigade marched out at 8 a.m., and proceeding along the beach, halted midday amongst the sand-dunes at Tel El Marakeb, where they fell in with the Sixth Mounted Brigade. In the afternoon the two Brigades marched to Deir El Belah, where they arrived at sunset. We bivouacked near the shore of a pretty lake, which was surrounded by vegetation and palm-trees, and at one end of which a European house had been built ; the latter was evidently the summer residence of some Gaza merchant. We were given a very rough idea of the dispositions of the enemy forces :

The enemy are in force at Huj, Abu Hareira, Tel El Sheria, and Gaza. The Imperial Mounted Division will hold the line from Abu Teibig to Huj—facing south. Anzac Mounted Division will hold the line from Huj to the sea—facing north. The Fifty-third Division will be on the Gaza road, and the Fifty-fourth Division will be in the vicinity of Sheikh Abbas.

In other words, our force on the morrow was to completely surround Gaza.

We off-saddled for a few hours after watering at the lake, and an officer was sent out to reconnoitre the position of the great tree at El Demeita, where we were to rendezvous on the morrow. We were in good spirits, as from all accounts there was not a very formidable foe before us.

March 26th.

At 1 a.m. the Brigade left its bivouac, less the Gloucestershire Yeomanry, who had been detached in order to act on the left of the Fifty-third Division on ,he sea-coast. The distance from Belah to Demeita was about 2 miles, but owing to the head of our column taking a most serpentine course, it was dawn before we reached our rendezvous, and saw what a short distance we had come after riding for many hours. While *en route* I had to stop to attend to a man who had just been extricated from under his horse in a ditch, and, after making sure that his leg was not broken, discovered that our column had completely disappeared in the inky darkness. However, after waiting about five minutes we heard mounted troops approaching, and were delighted to find that it was the

head of our column ; the latter had evidently described
a complete circle, luckily for us ! And so we struggled
on through the night, alternately walking, trotting and
galloping until certain landmarks became quite familiar—
in the dim dawn we fell in with the Sixth Mounted Brigade,
and proceeded with them over the In Seirat Ridge to the
Wadi Ghuzze, the precipitous banks of which were crossed
north of Tel El Jemmi, and reached the Divisional rendezvous at El Mendur about 7.30 a.m. The Anzac Mounted
Division had crossed the Wadi an hour previously and
were proceeding in a north-easterly direction for Beit
Durdis, about 5 miles east of Gaza. Our (Imperial
Mounted) Division now rode north-east, making for
Khirbit Sihan. The rôle of the cavalry and Imperial
Camel Corps was apparently to keep off the enemy reinforcements which were approaching from the north and
east. We were informed that the enemy had 48 guns, of
which 24 were in Gaza, and that the disposition of his
troops was roughly as follows : Gaza 4,000, Huj-Sihan
5,000, Beersheba 5,000, and Nejile 7,000. As the sun
appeared, the heavy fog which had enveloped us gradually
disappeared, and we noticed that the landscape had now
changed, and that instead of the rough and stony country
intersected by Wadis, whose banks were so steep that they
could only be crossed at certain points, we were now
riding over grassy, down-like country, actually intersected
by English-looking brooks fringed with kingcups ; in
the neighbourhood of Khirbit Sihan we were able to water
the whole regiment in one of these refreshing-looking
streams. Our Brigade, after crossing some old Turkish
trenches, reached the Gaza–Beersheba road, at that time
not yet menaced from the east, and passing under the telegraph wire which connected these two towns, our C.O.
sent a man up to cut the line, and one thought for a
moment that Gaza was isolated from Beersheba ; however, the passage of Fritz overhead, who was following
the road, soon reminded one that the Turks would throughout the day be able to communicate with their reserves.
Divisional Headquarters were located at Khirbit El

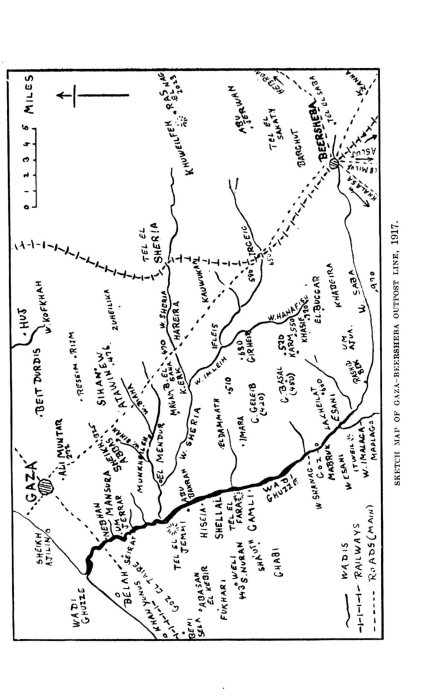

SKETCH MAP OF GAZA—BEERSHEBA OUTPOST LINE, 1917.

Reseim, where also the Divisional Dressing Station was established. Our Brigade Headquarters were established at 457, facing south-east, with the Worcester Yeomanry on the left and the Warwick Yeomanry astride the Beersheba road on the right. Our " C " Squadron reconnoitred towards Hareira, where they came into action. " D " Squadron were held in reserve, and " A " proceeded towards Khirbit Zuheilika ; at the latter place a camp was surprised and surrounded, the occupants of which surrendered as the squadron galloped up. Our post corporal, who had taken a particular liking to a German officer's sword, galloped the owner down until he eventually possessed himself of the weapon. Half an hour later the squadron returned over the hill to Regimental Headquarters with about 100 prisoners, most of whom presented a rather ridiculous appearance, as they had been surprised while being disinfected and were very scantily clothed. Some German officers who escaped had left all their kit behind, and for weeks afterwards " A " Squadron were to be seen wearing the latest thing in silk shirts straight from Berlin. While this little comedy was in progress, the great tragedy of the first Battle of Gaza had already commenced. We heard heavy firing to the west before Gaza, and a little later became ourselves involved with the enemy reinforcements, who were approaching from the east. A big gun from Hareira began to bother us, one shell taking heavy toll of the Warwicks near Brigade Headquarters. During the morning " aviatiks " flew backwards and forwards continuously over our heads between Gaza and Beersheba, generously peppering us with their machine guns *en route*. Some patrols of Turkish lancers were encountered, but did not show much initiative. The early morning fog was followed at midday by a " Khampsine," and the heat became very great. The action now became general, the Fifty-third and Fifty-fourth Divisions making great progress south of Gaza, while the two Cavalry Divisions, being in action with the enemy reinforcement, completed the investment east and north. We heard afterwards that the Anzac Mounted

Division had actually got into Gaza from behind and had captured the G.O.C. and Staff of the Turkish Fifty-third Division, who were leaving the town in cabs. On our left (looking east) towards Huj, the Sixth Mounted Brigade were in action on the hills, and at 5 p.m. our "D" Squadron were sent over the Wadi Kofkhah to reinforce them; the former, with the Berkshire R.H.A., appeared to be heavily engaged with the force advancing from Huj. At 5.15 p.m. we received a message that our Brigade Headquarters was being heavily attacked from the Beersheba road by a Turkish infantry battalion, and a squadron was accordingly sent to reinforce the Warwickshire Yeomanry. Our patrols reported that the enemy were advancing in considerable numbers from the east and south-east, but we appeared to be in a good position, with a fine field of fire towards the enemy. About 6 p.m. our Brigade, which was rather scattered, received orders to rendezvous at Beit Durdis, after all wounded had been evacuated to Khirbit El Reseim. As I had little to do I was dispatched to call in our "D" Squadron, who had been sent up to the Sixth Brigade, and was told that a bearing of 315° would bring us to the point near Beit Durdis where the Brigade would rendezvous. Dusk was falling, and after crossing the Wadi Kofkhah and riding up a hill our "D" Squadron was discovered. We set out according to orders, but could find no one at the appointed rendezvous; we rode on for hours in the darkness, falling in with detachments of various units, but no one seemed to know whether Gaza had been captured or not. At one place we came across one of our own batteries, which seemed very vague as to what had happened; at another we found the remnants of our Divisional Headquarters, who could give us no information as to the whereabouts of our regiment or our Brigade— the situation was obscure. Should we chance it and make for Gaza ? Not a single Staff officer we encountered that night could tell us anything. As we crossed the Beersheba road in the darkness, a motor dispatch rider rode by, saying that Gaza had fallen and that he was taking in dispatches. About 11.80 p.m., when the squadron horses were getting exhausted, by the greatest luck we fell in with our regiment, which we found resting by the roadside between Khirbit Sihan and Ali Muntar. Here we rested for about an hour, our C.O. receiving no orders ; various units rode by, last of all the Imperial Camel Corps. " Who is following behind you ? " called our C.O. " The Turks," was the laconic answer, which it appeared was perfectly true ! And now we began to realize the ghastly fiasco that had been enacted. We knew that we had surrounded Gaza, and that our Division had not been heavily engaged (our own Brigade had had few casualties), that the Infantry Divisions had got into Gaza and had captured Ali Muntar, and that the Anzacs had entered the town from behind—and in spite of this we were retiring !

March 27th.

At 1 a.m. our own regiment commenced to retire, and riding through the night over very broken ground, often held up by retreating transport columns and guns and by precipitous ravines, we reached a crossing of the Wadi Ghuzze near Sheikh Nebhan at dawn. Just before descending from the higher ground into the valley, we had a last view of Gaza with its stately minarets, which we had thought the day before was already ours. Some armoured cars passed us which had narrowly escaped capture, having found themselves surrounded by the Turks in the dim dawn. Everywhere one saw evidence of our hurried retreat, every unit striving to cross the Wadi as quickly as possible. Endless strings of camels bore our swaying wounded westwards, and as the sun rose and the last mounted units began to ride through the Wadi, the Turkish gunners commenced to shell the crossing. Some of our transport had to be abandoned, owing to the nature of the ground and broken axles. Within a short time the whole of the force had retired by various crossings west of the Wadi Ghuzze, and by 9.80 a.m. our Division was back in its original bivouac at Deir El Belah. After watering our horses in the lake, we had just off-saddled and were beginning to light our fires, in the hope of getting some food and rest after two nights without any sleep, when orders were received that, on account of an expected offensive by the enemy, our Division was to take up a defensive position on the In Seirat Ridge. The clear morning had been followed by another torrid day, and as we rode out through the native village we were almost choked by the clouds of fine white dust. The two Cavalry Divisions halted near El Demeita and remained there in reserve until dusk. We heard that the Turks were threatening our right flank and that they would try to reoccupy the Sheikh Nuran positions which they had evacuated in January after the Battle of Rafa. The enemy had evidently "got their tails up," after driving us back from Gaza, and were intending to press home their advantage. We were to hold the Abasan El Kebir positions. At dusk the Brigade moved up to In Seirat and deployed on the Goz El Taire outpost line, with the Third Australian Light Horse Brigade on its left and the Sixth Mounted Brigade on the right. That night, to our great relief, we had our first tea for three days. So ended the first Battle for Gaza, and the following extracts, taken from *The Times* (weekly edition) of April 6, 1917, which we received about a month later, are of interest :

1. *British Report.*

FIGHT FOR THE HOLY LAND.

SIR A. MURRAY'S VICTORY.

20,000 *Turks Defeated.*

8,000 *Casualties.*

Telegraphing on March 28th, the G.O.C.-in-Chief, Egypt, reported : We advanced our troops a distance of 15 miles from Rafa to the Wadi Ghuzze, 5 miles south of Gaza, to cover construction of the railway. On the 26th and 27th we were heavily engaged in this neighbourhood with a force of about 20,000 of the enemy. We inflicted very heavy losses on him, and have taken 900 prisoners, including G.O.C. and whole Divisional Staff of Fifty-third Turkish

Division. . . . The operation was most successful, and owing to the fog and waterless nature of the country round Gaza just fell short of a complete disaster to the enemy. . . .

2. Turkish Report.

A BRILLIANT VICTORY.

Turkish Report, March 28th.

Sinai Front.—The long-awaited attack, which had been so carefully prepared by the enemy, began on March 26th. The fight developed in the neighbourhood of Gaza on the afternoon of March 27th, and terminated in a brilliant victory.

The British forces were composed of about four divisions. Numerous heavy guns and several armoured motor-cars of the enemy also participated in the action.

During the course of the battle, which lasted two days, the enemy suffered heavy losses, leaving numbers of dead on the ground. Two hundred, including one officer, were made prisoners. One armoured motor-car and two other motor-cars were also captured.

The enemy retired in a south-westerly direction, pursued by our troops.

In this fight our 125th Infantry Regiment particularly distinguished itself. In spite of the extreme violence with which the fight was contested, our losses were quite small.—*Reuter.*

March 28th.

When the sun rose we found ourselves on the edge of the standing corn on the Goz El Taire Ridge, and sent patrols to Abasan El Kebir and Weli Sheikh Nuran ; we were soon aware that the Turks had followed up our retreat to the Wadi banks and had even crossed it in places, as our patrols came in contact with the enemy and sustained casualties at El Imaan. During the morning we were reinforced by the One Hundred and Fifty-sixth Brigade of the Fifty-second Division ; this Division had been in reserve during the Gaza fighting ; and at night, after being relieved, our Brigade came down to the Wadi Selka, near Belah, for a well-merited rest.

March 29th.

The bivouac at Selka was a fairly good one, and a plentiful supply of fresh water was discovered near the beach. It can be well imagined how the bathing was appreciated after our experience of the last few days. Rumour had it that another attack was to be launched on Gaza during the next few days, assisted by tanks and gunboats ; we, who knew the very large number of casualties our force had sustained, could hardly imagine that the idea of an attack could be entertained before large reinforcements arrived ; it seemed to us that there was a very good chance of the Turks, who were now in large numbers on this front, cutting our long line of communication near Rafa. The scene presented quite an animated appearance as several small gunboats and an old French battleship appeared off the coast. In the evening the Sixth Mounted Brigade joined us, and we heard what very heavy casualties the Fifty-third Division had sustained.

March 30th.

At midday our Brigade marched to the Goz El Taire line, and took up the outpost line west of the Wadi from El Breij-Seirat to Abasan El Kebir, relieving the Third Australian Light Horse Brigade. The weather was much cooler, and there was a pleasant breeze on the top of the ridge from the sea. In the afternoon, we could see Fritz bombing railhead about 8 miles away, the latter being now 2½ miles beyond Khan Yunus. More entrenching tools were sent out to us, and the Fifty-second Division held the line on our right.

March 31st.

Most of the day was spent in digging trenches, and there was a little desultory rifle fire at our patrols near the Wadi. In the evening the Brigade returned to the Selka bivouac, near Belah, after being relieved by an Australian Brigade. All night long our big guns were busy shelling Gaza.

April 1st.

A rumour was current that Enver Pasha had arrived near Gaza with large reinforcements. A message was

read from General Sir Philip Chetwode saying that the
harder the work he gave our Division, the better it was
done, and that we had held up a very much superior
number of Turks near Gaza on a 12-mile front. In the
evening we heard that eight tanks had arrived, which we
had never seen before on this front.

April 2nd.

Fritz was very busy in the morning, as he found the
two Cavalry Divisions an easy mark for his bombs. We
heard that the Seventy-fourth Division (Dismounted
Yeomanry) was about to join our force and that the
Turks had received large reinforcements, now amounting
to six Divisions, and that Enver Pasha had been down
and told them to hold on at all costs. During the last
few weeks we had seen no Turkish deserters, probably on
account of troops with better moral being employed on
this front. In the cool of the evening some of the newly
arrived tanks caused much amusement by going through
the enormous cactus hedges, which in some places were
at least ten feet high and ten feet thick, with the greatest
ease.

April 3rd.

Half the regiment marched out at 5 a.m. to dig fresh
trenches along the outpost line on the Wadi, where they
were shelled by Turkish mountain guns. Orders were
received to make a new type of cavalry stretcher, and the
regimental saddlers got to work immediately. These
stretchers consisted of two light bamboo poles four feet
long, joined by a piece of canvas three feet by nineteen
inches ; they were ultimately carried attached to the
sword, and proved invaluable when full-size stretchers
were not obtainable. Owing to native spies having cut
the air line between Belah and Khan Yunus, we were
ordered to send out a patrol every night between these
places. In the evening an Armenian M.O., who had
deserted from the Turkish battalion to which he was
attached, crossed the Wadi and joined us. He had taken

a degree at Harvard, and told us in good English that the Turks had a large force at Jaffa, where they feared a landing with a view to an attack on Jerusalem ; he also told us that the enemy had 50 guns round Gaza, two of which were 15-inch, but that at present they feared to take the latter off the railway.

April 4th.

On account of the very precipitous Wadi banks, which in some places constituted a sheer drop of from 50 to 100 feet, it was considered essential that crossings should be made by which guns and transport could traverse the river-bed. At present there were only a few places where this was possible, and these were well registered by the Turkish guns. These proposed new crossings were to be utilized in the coming attack on Gaza. At 5 a.m. our regiment, with many others, moved out to the Wadi Ghuzze and commenced to dig an artillery crossing over the Wadi near Tel El Jemmi, one squadron being sent on to the further side for protection. Fritz was very inquisitive and tried to disturb us while at work, but by 5 p.m. the regiment had completed a cutting and a ramp down to the river-bed capable of taking two lines of transport abreast. The men returned to camp thoroughly tired out, as they had been working very hard in order to get the work done before dark.

April 5th.

In the early morning the Brigade took over twenty-four hours' outpost duty again. The line was advanced a mile beyond the I in Taire. Fritz came over at nine o'clock and again at two, when he was shot down between us and the sea. We found that quite a considerable trench system now existed on the outpost line, of which our Brigade held the portion between the I in Taire and Abasan El Kebir. The Worcester Yeomanry were in the centre, with the Warwicks on the left and the Gloucesters on the right, while the Fifty-fourth Division were on the left of the Fifth Mounted Brigade and the Seventy-fourth

Division and Imperial Camel Corps were on the right. On the whole it was a quiet night, with a little sniping in the morning.

April 6th.

After a cold night we ·came down from the outpost line to our horses, which were grazing a few hundred yards below ; this valley, with its waving corn and beautiful grass fields studded with marguerites, cuckoo flowers, poppies and cornflowers, was most beautiful, and a most remarkable contrast to the terrain which existed on the other side of the Goz El Taire Ridge. We were very short of firewood, but luckily several evacuated native houses were found, consisting of mud and wooden beams, which disappeared remarkably quickly when our men got to work on them. It was an extraordinary fact, which we learnt to our cost, that these old Bedouin houses, though not lived in for months, were absolutely infested with the most vicious type of flea. In the afternoon we were relieved as usual by another Brigade, and returned to the sea-shore.

April 7th.

At this time, owing to the large number of troops congregated round Belah, the dust was becoming intolerable, and we decided to move our camp further away. A pleasant site accordingly was selected between the fig groves and the sea. Fritz saw us move and bombed us at 9.30 p.m. and 6 p.m. Gas-masks were issued to us during the day, and we began to wonder how long we could exist in them during the heat of the day. During the night a large number of our aeroplanes flew over us and bombed Gaza by moonlight. The jackals, no doubt attracted by the numbers of horses and camels killed in the vicinity, became very noisy at night.

April 9th.

In the evening the Brigade moved out to be in reserve to the Sixth Mounted Brigade, as there was some idea that

9

the Turks might attack ; this, however, did not mature, and we spent rather a cold night standing to.

April 10*th.*

The Brigade returned to Selka, and with great regret we said good-bye to our General, who had commanded us in the field for nearly three years. During the next few days hundreds of camels were employed to carry water in fanatis, in order to fill the large native cisterns which existed between Um Jerrar and Tel El Jemmi. A reference to the Bible showed us that these wells had originally been dug by Abraham.

April 11*th.*

Information was received that the enemy had altered their dispositions, and that Gaza was now only held by three Brigades, while a great concentration of troops had taken place round Beersheba. It was said that on this account all our plans of attack would have to be altered. At midday our Brigade moved out for its usual twenty-four hours on the outpost line, one of our squadrons holding an advanced post on Tel El Jemmi. To the north of the latter place the infantry advanced and seized some ground which was required.

April 12*th.*

During the morning we heard loud explosions at Rafa and Belah, and later some Taubes returned over us after their bombing raids. It appeared that they had bombed our aerodromes at both these places. A little later our planes ascended, and passing over us, visited Beersheba, making three journeys, each time returning for a fresh supply of bombs. In the evening, on returning to camp, we received a warning not to bathe far from the shore, as sharks had been seen in the vicinity. At this period the bathing was very enjoyable, especially after sleeping one or two nights in one's clothes. At camp there was still a great shortage of firewood in order to cook the evening meal, and the former had to be brought long distances on camels after the demolition of deserted native huts.

April 13th.

During the morning we could see our outpost line being shelled by the Turks, but the shells did not fall beyond the ridge. Rumour had it that in addition to the Fifty-second, Fifty-third, Fifty-fourth, Seventy-fourth, the two Mounted Divisions and the Camel Corps, other Divisions from India and East Africa were going to reinforce us in the next attack on Gaza ; we also heard that a composite Franco-Italian Division was on its way up. The Turks had now been reinforced by two more Divisions from the Caucasus. During the afternoon an enemy aeroplane flew over and dropped the identification discs of the killed and a list of the captured at the Battle of Gaza. Fritz was somewhat troublesome in the evening, and we suffered somewhat from our own shrapnel, my own helmet, which was lying by my side, being pierced by a piece of one of our own shell-cases.

April 14th.

We were awakened early by the Turkish big gun, which had now got the range of the Belah camp. The supply dump by the railway had a particularly hot time. During sick parade Fritz dropped some " eggs " as usual, and we suffered some casualties to men and horses.

Intelligence.—The Turks now have 25,000 troops opposite us, including their Third and Fifth Division, and some seventy guns. The forces are grouped chiefly at Gaza, Sheria and Hareira. Beersheba has been evacuated,[1] and the line torn up between it and Sheria in several places. There is a big supply dump at Dhaheriyeh, near Hebron, where also is a cavalry regiment, 6,000 strong.

Our battery commander told us that the big gun which had been shelling us in the morning was 8 miles away, and that none of our Belah guns had got that range.

[1] This information proved to be false.

April 16th.

During the day the Warwick Yeomanry reconnoitred before El Mendur, accompanied by some of our officers, one of whom had his horse shot. The land batteries near Gaza shelled our ships in the roadstead, but without doing any damage. We were informed that our dispositions on the morrow, preparatory to the second Battle of Gaza, would be as follows : " Our Brigade was to take up the line at Asseiferia to Khirbit Erk, with its centre at the junction of the Wadis Sheria and Imlieh, and with the rest of our Division was to hold the Turkish Sheria force. The Anzac Mounted Division was to go to Shellal and hold the Hareira force. The Fifty-fourth Division was to attack the Sheikh Abbas position at dawn with the Fifty-second Division on its left and the Fifty-third Division on the sea sector. Every mounted man was to carry five days' rations for himself and his horse. On the second day there was to be a general advance, our Division attacking the Atewinieh trench system with the Fifty-fourth Division on its left, who were to be supported by the Seventy-fourth Division, after a general bombardment at dawn. Before dawn on the first day the Worcester Yeomanry were to send out two officers' patrols, who were to gallop through the Turkish outposts and cut the telegraph wire on the Gaza–Beersheba road in front of El Munkheileh." At 6 p.m. the whole Division rode out to Tel El Jemmi, where we bivouacked for the night.

April 17th.

At 1 a.m. two of our " D " Squadron officers, each accompanied by five picked and well-mounted men, left on their adventurous expedition ; in order to make certain of success, it was decided that they should attempt to get through the Turkish outpost in two places. An hour later our Brigade trotted out in the dark over the Wadi Ghuzze, and after about an hour reached the S in the Wadi Sheria, where Brigade Headquarters was established. It was now getting light, and as the regiment trotted on to the plain we came under rifle fire, and dismounting, took up the line Zummara–Magam. At 8.45 our officers' patrols returned, having accomplished their object with only one casualty and one horse shot. It was a fine piece of work, as, although they got through the line unobserved, on their return journey in the dim dawn they came into close contact with the Turks, and it was only the pace of their horses which enabled them to escape, followed by a shower of bullets. Meanwhile, we had entrenched our line and the Turks had advanced in one place, but were easily repulsed. We heard the bombardment of Sheikh Abbas going on on our left, and later heard that the Fifty-fourth Division had captured their objective. As a considerable number of the enemy appeared on a ridge on our left, south of the Wadi Baha, the C.O. asked for a battery, which came into action east of Khirbit Um Rijl and effectually dispersed the force. At midday we watered our horses at the well near the El Magam mosque, a few at a time, owing to our being directly under hostile artillery fire. At 2 p.m. the Sixth Mounted Brigade, which had been in divisional reserve at Jemmi and had watered at Abu Hiseia, crossed the Wadi Sheria at 280 and relieved us ; the enemy's guns now registered this crossing, but with a certain amount of luck we managed to get the whole unit across without any casualties, and proceeded over a grassy plain some 3½ miles to Karim Abu El Hiseia. Here we passed through a regular mountain gorge before reaching this part of the Wadi Ghuzze, which lies just north of Shellal. Excellent watering arrangements had been made by the R.E. for men and horses, which were much appreciated by both. It appeared that Fritz had been over a few hours previously and caused serious casualties to an Australian Light Horse Brigade which was watering at this spot. After watering, the regiment proceeded along the left bank of the Wadi and reached the bivouac at Jemmi at nightfall.

April 18*th.*

During the day we were held in reserve at Tel El Jemmi and heard the French and British battleships bombarding Gaza from the sea. In the afternoon our C.O. gave us orders for the morrow.

The infantry will hold the line from Khirbit Sihan to the sea, and together with the cavalry on their right will attack soon after dawn after two hours' bombardment, provided there is no fog. The Imperial Mounted Division will operate on the right of Sihan with the Fourth Australian Light Horse Brigade on the left, the Third Australian Light Horse Brigade in the centre (Directing Brigade), and the Fifth Mounted Brigade on the right, the Sixth Mounted Brigade being in support ; the Anzac Mounted Division will operate on the right of the Imperial Mounted Division. The direction of our attack will be 60°, and our objective is the Atewinieh Redoubt on the Beersheba road. " C " Squadron Worcester Yeomanry will advance before dawn and dig a special trench in front of the Wadi Baha on a ridge facing 60°. All ranks will carry gas-masks. When the attack commences the regiment will advance on foot out of the Wadi in front of Munkheileh, the front of the attack for the Fifth Mounted Brigade being from the H of Munkheileh on the left to the R in Rijl on the right. To commence with, the Gloucester Yeomanry will be on the left, the Worcesters on the right, and the Warwicks in support. The Anzac Division on our right has for its objective Baiket El Sana. All horses will be left in the Wadi, with the exception of those belonging to squadron leaders and pack-horses carrying ammunition.

The following medical orders were received the same evening :

A Divisional Dressing Station will be established at a point half a mile west of Asseiferia by 6 a.m. on April 19th. Six waggons from the Fifth Mounted Brigade Field Ambulance will be attached to the Divisional Dressing Station to evacuate wounded to the Collecting Station at Jemmi. The remaining eight carts with mounted bearers will be available to collect wounded from the regimental aid posts and will be at El Mendur by dawn on April 19th.

Each regimental Medical Officer was also supplied with one or two sledges, drawn by a single horse and led by a mounted man, which proved most useful where the ground was suitable.

THE SECOND BATTLE OF GAZA.

April 19*th.*

At 2 a.m. our Brigade left the bivouac at Tel El Jemmi and arrived south of the first H in Munkheileh at 5 a.m. All the horses were left in the Wadi behind Munkheileh Manor Farm, and at the latter place our first dressing station was established. At 5.30 our general artillery preparation commenced, but only lasted until about seven o'clock ; during this period the enemy were silent, but directly it was over they responded vigorously with shrapnel and H.E. Meanwhile the Brigade moved out of the Wadi to commence a dismounted attack towards the Gaza–Beersheba road. There was no cover and casualties from our own and an Australian Brigade on our left quickly accumulated, so in order to keep up with the regiment my dressing station, with personnel, pack-horses and sledges, etc., was quickly advanced to the Wadi Munkheileh, to the west of the Wadi Baha, and we started to collect casualties from the Fifth Mounted Brigade and the Third Australian Light Horse Brigade. As the ground was of a sandy nature our sledges proved most useful, and it was possible in some places to bring them back almost at a gallop ; but in several instances they became involved with the field-telephone wires, and in this way seriously affected communication with Brigade Headquarters. As we advanced the fire became heavier, and after pushing our dressing station into the open we were able to get a view of our Divisional Dressing Station at Asseiferia, away on our left ; the latter appeared to be in an awkward position, as wounded had apparently to be evacuated parallel to the firing-line, over a route which was being continuously shelled, as along it were located our divisional reserves. Our Field Ambulance, with its carts, now moved up to the Wadi Munkheileh, in part of which was also located Brigade Headquarters ; we evacuated our cases to the former, whence they were passed through the Divisional Dressing Station at Asseiferia to the Collecting Station at

Tel El Jemmi, for ultimate transference over rough country
to the railhead Casualty Clearing Stations at Deir El Belah.
By midday the enemy's shelling became worse, and
every minute we expected to see our Field Ambulance in
the Wadi annihilated, as H.E. was apparently falling all
round it. Our led horses, nearly all of which we had left
behind us, and the H.A.C. battery also had a hot time,
one of the guns of the latter receiving a direct hit. Meanwhile our Brigade had advanced to within a short distance of the Atewinieh Redoubt, and were lining a short
depression on the ridge before it. This redoubt was
situated on the Beersheba road and was the objective
of our regiment. Our Regimental Dressing Station was
moved forward behind this ridge, luckily escaping the
shrapnel which was falling round it. The Field Ambulance
now moved up to the commencement of the Wadi Baha,
where also Brigade Headquarters was established. As
it was now impossible to get wounded out of the firing-
line on this ridge from behind, as we had been previously
doing, I decided to work up the Wadi Baha towards the
Beersheba road and remove them through a cleft in the
rocks which led up into the firing-line ; accordingly we
rode back to our Field Ambulance to secure sand-carts,
my sergeant having his horse shot under him *en route*,
an accident which was quickly remedied by catching a
loose horse. We found our Field Ambulance crowded
with wounded and enveloped in clouds of acrid smoke
from the enemy's aircraft bombs and H.E. shells, the
latter being probably intended for our battery, which was
situated a few hundred yards behind it. After securing
the carts we took them up to the Wadi Baha, towards
the firing-line ; this Wadi was the usual dried watercourse
with sandy bottom, flanked by cliffs some twenty feet high,
and here and there intersected by small confluent Wadis
which led up into the plain. After proceeding a short
distance we soon realized that the Turks, aware of the
route by which our reinforcements were being brought
up, had registered this Wadi, as the cliffs began to fall in
here and there, owing to the enemy's shelling. The

road was littered with casualties, but our duty was to bring the carts as near as possible to the firing-line, so we pushed on. Leaving our horses near the Gloucester Yeomanry Headquarters (this regiment and the Warwicks were holding the line on the right of the Wadi), we proceeded on foot, followed by our carts, as far as the ground was practicable. While resting for a few minutes with the Medical Officers of the other two regiments, the enemy again commenced to search the Wadi methodically with his guns from below upwards. We could see the shells gradually exploding nearer and nearer to us. Should we run on 50 yards to the next bend, or stay where we were ? We decided to remain, and the next shell exploded at the very spot to which we had intended to run, bringing down tons of cliff at the same time. We now established another dressing station and collected casualties from both sides of the Wadi, which at this point were sloping, not precipitous, and constituted part of our front line. It was difficult work for our stretcher-bearers to carry the wounded down from the banks of the Wadi at its extreme end, as at that point they were in close contact with the enemy. Finding a narrow cleft in the rocks on our left, we were able to reach our regiment and evacuate our wounded to the carts which were waiting below. Our dressing station was next established in a slight depression on the ridge which we were holding before the Atewinieh Redoubt. It was a strange experience, as being on a slight eminence, about 200 yards directly in front of the enemy's batteries, his shells meant for our batteries behind the Wadi Munkheileh just skimmed our heads at the commencement of their journey, then exploded about 2 miles in our rear. Meanwhile our own shells also passed immediately over us, exploding just in front on the Atewinieh Redoubt. About 3 p.m., owing to our losing touch with the regiment on our left, a large gap appeared in the line, and we could see the Turkish infantry advancing through the standing corn on our flank ; they enfiladed us, and our left being now completely in the air, the situation looked serious. Our " A " Squadron leader was killed, several officers were wounded, and many casualties occurred amongst the other ranks ; our ammunition was running low and the enemy was steadily closing in. A message was sent for help, and within a short space the G.O.C. Sixth Mounted Brigade dispatched the Berks and Bucks Regiments to our aid. These units, which had been in divisional reserve behind the Wadi Munkheileh, responded gallantly, and galloping across the plain under heavy fire, dismounted and came quickly into action. The situation was saved, but at a price, amongst the killed being one of the most popular and brave officers who ever commanded a squadron of the Berkshire Yeomanry, and amongst the wounded the C.O. of the same regiment, shot through both legs—many others fell that day, including some of the finest yeomen from the South Midlands and West of England. We found our short cavalry stretchers most useful, as they could be easily carried through the narrow clefts in the rocks. At 6 p.m. orders were received to retire, and soon afterwards we commenced to withdraw to Munkheileh. At the latter place one could be of some assistance, as several carts of seriously wounded had just arrived, and needed immediate attention before being dispatched to the Jemmi Collecting Station. After procuring two men for the C.O. of our Field Ambulance to act as ground scouts for his column of waggons, which was about to proceed over very broken country in the dark, I discovered that our regiment had completely disappeared in the night. Having previously taken the bearings from Munkheileh on several landmarks, our little party rode by my compass across the Wadi Sheria and the Wadi Ghuzze, eventually falling in with the regiment at Tel El Jemmi at midnight. A curious accident occurred just before reaching the latter place, a yeoman and his horse disappearing into one of the large native cisterns ; on calling to the man below, he answered that he was all right, and after giving his horse a feed, clambered on to his back and was pulled out of the well by his friends ; on the next day a working party got to work and successfully dug the horse out. So ended, as

far as we were concerned, the second Battle of Gaza—
we did not know whether Gaza had fallen or not, but we
knew that our Division had lost heavily and had failed
to pierce the enemy's line in the direction of Sheria,
chiefly on account of the lack of artillery ; the two hours'
artillery preparation which we had witnessed in the
morning now seemed pathetically short, considering the
volume of the enemy's artillery fire which we encountered
later in the day.

April 20th.

At 2 a.m. we reached El Mendur, dead beat, and heard
the news that Gaza had not fallen. Horse lines were put
down, and every one, except the unfortunate line pickets
and sentries, immediately fell asleep on the stony ground.
At 6 a.m. we were up again, and received orders that a new
outpost line was to be entrenched, our Brigade extending
from Tel El Jemmi to El Mendur. The regiment accordingly commenced to dig trenches on the hills overlooking
the Munkheileh district, while Fritz amused himself by
dropping a few bombs on us and also some smoke-balls,
the latter, however, failing to attract the Turkish gunners'
attention. During the afternoon orders were suddenly
received to stop digging, and on scanning the plain below
us with our glasses, we could see the enemy's cavalry and
infantry advancing. The Brigade immediately mounted
and galloped some 4 miles across the plain, and took over
the line Munkheileh–Erk from the Berks Yeomanry, who
had been holding it since the previous night. The C.O.
of this unit told us that the enemy infantry had been
strongly reinforced in our front, and that some cavalry
were threatening his left flank. It was said that the
enemy, strongly reinforced since April 19th, were assuming
the offensive all along the line. We found that the
trenches which we had made on April 17th had been much
improved during their occupation by the Sixth Mounted
Brigade. Our Brigade Headquarters was established at
280, near the crossing over the Wadi Sheria, where also
the horses of the three regiments were located for the

night. The expected attack did not, however, mature, and we passed a quiet but wakeful night.

April 21st.

At dawn " C " Squadron sent back for their horses and patrolled in the vicinity of Erk. We had considerable difficulty in watering our horses, as it was a question of either riding all the way back to Jemmi or else watering at the wells near the white mosque at El Magam ; the latter course was followed, although watering parties were shelled every time they approached the wells. Rations now reached us regularly, and were dumped in Wadi Sheria.

April 22nd.

In the morning our patrols were in touch with the enemy infantry and cavalry, but with the exception of our watering parties being shelled there was very little going on. We heard that it was proposed that our regiment should gallop the Baiket El Sana position, which had been the objective of the Anzac Mounted Division on the 19th, after dark. To attack at the gallop a strongly entrenched and wired position in the dark appeared to us to be a mad idea. One could not help remembering that if this idea materialized, the attack and probable debacle would take place on April 23rd, a date of ill omen. Fritz appeared as usual at midday, and later we heard how our planes had retaliated for the bombing of our Brigade a few days ago. Finding a Turkish Cavalry Brigade massing for a counter-attack in the Wadi Imlieh, forty-eight bombs were dropped on the regiments, which were closely packed between the steep banks. Needless to say, no counter-attack materialized. Later we heard that the attack on the Baiket El Sana position had been cancelled, and that our Brigade would withdraw to Abasan El Kebir at nightfall. Naturally this gave rise to a good deal of surmise as to why our present line was being abandoned, especially as the enemy did not appear to be assuming the offensive. We heard for the first time of

the very heavy losses sustained by the Fifty-fourth
Division on April 19th, and how the Norfolks had suffered
on rushing in to capture a redoubt which was supposed
to have been successfully gas-shelled ; we also heard how
some of our tanks had been lost, and of the changes
which had taken place in the Higher Command. These
facts, coupled with the news that the Turks had received
another 14,000 reinforcements and the total number of
casualties which our whole force had sustained, had rather
a depressing effect on some of us. We had had practically
a complete week's fighting and digging, with little sleep
and scarcity of water, and had apparently little to show
for it except a retirement as far as our Brigade was
concerned. At 6.45 p.m. our rear-guard squadron was
withdrawn from the front of the white mosque at El
Magam, where it was patrolling, and by 7.30 the whole
Brigade was carefully withdrawn over the Wadi Sheria,
with scarcely a shot being fired. In absolute silence the
Brigade rode to Abu Bakra, where the twelve mounted
regiments of the Imperial Mounted Division assembled.

April 23rd.

At 2 a.m. the Brigade arrived at the native village of
Abasan El Kebir, after riding over precipitous banks
in the darkness. At one time two Brigades were retiring
in parallel lines close to one another, and now and then
one found oneself riding with a strange regiment, and
a good deal of confusion prevailed amongst the various
units. As there was no drinking water available at
this bivouac, it had to be fetched all the way from
Khan Yunus, which entailed the strictest economy in
water consumption. We received orders to remain in
this camp for four days in order to dig trenches (officially
designated a rest) and then return to a new outpost line.
We heard that two enemy aeroplanes had alighted two
days ago close to the railway on the Sabkhet at Salmana
in the Sinai Peninsula, some 60 miles in our rear, and
while one of the Germans got a machine gun into action,
the other proceeded to blow up the railway line and the

pipe line. Both these aeroplanes managed to escape unharmed, as our lines of communication were so thinly guarded ; the damage which had been done was, however, quickly repaired, and the amount of water which had been lost was not sufficient to seriously hamper the front-line supply.

April 24th.

In the morning the regiment rode down to Deir El Belah and much appreciated a bathe in the sea, which was the first wash we had had for about ten days. The heat was terrific, as a Khampsine wind was blowing. We visited the railhead Casualty Clearing Stations at Belah and saw many of our wounded, returning to Beni Sela at night after watering at Khan Yunus.

April 25th.

More English newspapers were received, with accounts of the first Battle of Gaza. In the evening we came across some of the new Seventy-fifth Division, who were doing outpost duty in our vicinity. The view from Beni Sela towards Khan Yunus, with the old Crusader castle and other buildings surrounded by masses of trees and vegetation, set in the midst of sandy country and backed by the brilliantly blue Mediterranean, was very fine.

April 26th.

At 4 a.m. the Brigade marched to Sha'uth, formerly one of the Turkish strong posts south of the eminence known as Weli Sheikh Nuran, which had been evacuated by the enemy after the Battle of Rafa. Some of us left later, at 8 a.m., and rode with a convoy of carts and pack-horses to El Gamli, where the Nuran–Beersheba road crossed the Wadi Ghuzze. A wild gorge led down into the Wadi, the banks of which were rugged and mountainous. We found excellent standing water in the pools which had been left behind after the river had ceased to flow a few weeks ago. We ate our lunch sitting on a rocky shelf overhanging one of these pools, which was delightfully cool and shady in the heat of the day. After resting and watering we joined our regiment some 4 miles from the Wadi, where they were encamped amongst the defences of Sha'uth.

April 27th.

Our camp at Sha'uth was on the 500 contour-line 2 miles south-east of Weli Sheikh Nuran ; the Turks, according to prisoners captured at the Battle of Rafa, had spent many months in 1916 in fortifying the former two places, and when one saw the magnitude of the work undertaken and the commanding positions, it was hard to understand why they had been evacuated. There were literally miles of well-made trenches in the Sha'uth system ; these had been dug when the clay was soft and were now baked hard by the sun; the dugouts were wonderfully made, and underground stables existed for the cavalry. Our regiment was bivouacked in an apricot orchard to the west of the chief redoubt, and at night the Turkish trenches were manned ; unfortunately, these faced the wrong way, i.e. west, consequently a lot of work had to be put in, in order to convert the former reserve trenches into front-line trenches looking east. In front of their trench system the enemy had constructed many rows of pot-holes, in order to hold up advancing cavalry. These holes were perfectly round, about six feet in diameter and four feet deep, and it was evident that they had been made in the wet weather, when the clay was soft, with some special instrument, as they were all perfectly symmetrical. Sign-boards were still up in the trenches, being written in Turkish and German, and it was apparent from the inscriptions in the battery positions that most of the howitzers had been Austrian. About 3 miles to the north-east of our camp was that very prominent feature Tel El Fara, a hill with precipitous sides which rose abruptly from the plain on the west bank of the Wadi Ghuzze, somewhat resembling in outline Tel El Jemmi. As only our three regiments were at Sha'uth, it devolved on the senior Regimental Medical Officer, in conjunction with the R.E. officer, to arrange for the Brigade's water supply. Accordingly, two 2,000-gallon canvas tanks were erected at Gamli (some 3 miles from our camp), into which water was pumped from the pools in the Wadi; here the water was chlorinated in bulk and the usual precautions were taken against Bilharzia, as the standing water in the green pools suggested the possibility of such an infection. Guards were placed on the water supply, and a way down the steep Wadi banks was eventually discovered by which it was possible for water-carts to descend. It was arranged that the three Medical Officers should take it in turns to be responsible for the purity of the day's water supply, and be present at its distribution. While this water supply and also the horse watering arrangements were being developed, a squadron was sent over the Wadi for protection and came in contact with a few patrols. We arranged for the transference of possible casualties by sand-cart to Weli Sheikh Nuran, whence they could be fetched by motor-ambulance or camel convoy to our Field Ambulance at Beni Sela. One realized at this time that any morning we might find our watering area in the hands of the Turks, in which case we should have to fall back on the water from Khan Yunus, which was 12 miles in our rear. We heard that the Turks had got several new Divisions and might try to turn the flank on which we were. A good deal of time was taken up in watering the horses, as twice a day 6 miles had to be covered in order to water them. As the men were digging when they were not watering their horses, it will be understood that they were having a pretty strenuous time.

April 28th.

During the morning our Field Ambulance arrived, and we worked out the best line of evacuation should the Sha'uth position be attacked. Some Turkish cavalry captured on patrol stated that they were part of 3,000 who had been sent down from the Caucasus; they were well equipped with lance, sword and rifle, and were mounted on stalwart ponies. Our battery arrived in the afternoon and was parked near the Brigade. During the evening, watering at Gamli, we saw numbers of very fine storks, which were probably on the way to Central Europe. On the way back to camp we passed through orchards of pear and apricot and almond trees, the blossom of which made a beautiful picture. There was a thin crop of grass on the light sandy soil of the Fara plain, over which our horses, on the way to water, very soon developed marked tracks; and within a week or so, when other cavalry brigades had arrived, not a single blade of grass or wheat could be seen, and the terrain resembled a desert scene.

April 29th.

After dawn one squadron reconnoitred down the Wadi Shanag by Goz Mabruk to Bir Esani, where some enemy camps were seen. On account of the precarious position of our water supply, which, being 3 miles from camp, might be seized any night, a reserve of water was collected by day and stored in canvas tanks in the trenches; a reserve ration dump was also developed by means of camel transport from Khan Yunus, so that in the event of our being surrounded we should be able to hold out for some days. An officer deserter told us that the enemy would attack Sha'uth on May 1st, and at the same time would cut our communications at El Arish.

April 30th.

A Brigade of the Anzac Mounted Division arrived and bivouacked on the plain between Sha'uth and Fara. It was my day on water duty, and one could not help thinking that the M.O. who was down in the Wadi at dawn on the morning on which the Turks attacked might have an exciting time in getting back to our camp.

May 1st.

After standing to all night, the Turkish attack did not mature; Fritz merely came over and dropped a few bombs.

10

At midday we were joined by an Indian Imperial Service cavalry regiment.

May 2nd.

Intelligence stated that the enemy were in large numbers at Beersheba, Hareira and Sheria, and that he had received large artillery reinforcements. We were now joined by the Seventy-fourth (Dismounted Yeomanry) Division on our left, a regiment of the latter sending a double company to occupy Tel El Fara ; this position covered the Wadi crossing, and it was considered that if the garrison could prevent the enemy from watering for twelve hours, the latter would have to return to Beersheba for watering purposes. These yeomen, on their lofty position at Tel El Fara, were known as the Die-hards, although the place was subsequently never attacked.

May 3rd.

Our Brigade left Sha'uth during the morning, after being relieved by the Fourth Australian Light Horse Brigade, and rode via Weli Sheikh Nuran to Abasan Kebir.

May 4th.

In the early morning we heard the heavy bombardment of Gaza going on, assisted by our ships from the sea. In the afternoon our horses were inspected by the Divisional General.

May 5th.

One of our officers, returning from Deir El Belah, told us how Fritz had dropped thirty-five bombs on the 53rd and 54th Casualty Clearing Stations at railhead, causing some hundred casualties amongst patients and R.A.M.C. personnel. We heard that we were to go to Tel El Marakeb, on the sea-shore, for a rest in a few days' time, when the Sixth Brigade would take our place in the reserve line. We needed a rest badly, as the Brigade had been hard at work continuously since the first Battle of Gaza, and most of the men were wearing bandages on account of septic sores, partly caused by lack of washing facilities. The slightest abrasion would cause a sore, which was quickly followed by the inflammation of the nearest lymphatic glands. At this period some hundred men attended sick parade daily, in order to have their sores dressed ; but owing to recent casualties, and lack of reinforcements, most of these men had to be kept on full duty. Pediculosis was also rampant, as the officers and men had seldom had an opportunity of getting their shirts washed. We had been sleeping in our clothes for over six weeks, and merely had the change which we were able to carry on our horses, so looked forward with considerable pleasure to seeing our valises again ; we had endured all this discomfort owing to all our Brigade transport being taken away and used by the Divisional Ammunition Column.

May 6th.

Fritz dropped a message in the morning, saying that he had bombed our hospitals as a reprisal for our shelling a mosque in Gaza and for bombing a convoy of his wounded. As a matter of fact, the mosque contained an enormous ammunition dump, which we saw subsequently, after the fall of Gaza six months later. It was said that the convoy of wounded, having no distinctive marks on its waggon, was mistaken for a transport column. Fritz also added in his message that he would bomb the hospitals again at 8 p.m. on the same day. It was a moonlight night and he kept his promise, but this time only causing about thirteen casualties.

May 8th.

The Brigade marched to Tel El Marakeb, where we rested for a week—it was a pleasant bivouac on the beach, and plenty of bathing was indulged in both for men and horses. We began to feel the want of tents, as the sun was getting hot, but on account of aeroplane observation none were allowed.

May 15th.

Our rest having come to an end, the Brigade moved into reserve, bivouacking at El Fukhari in the Abasan watering area.

May 18th.

During the next two days a Khampsine blew, accompanied by appalling dust-storms. The heat was tremendous from this hot wind, and we had several cases of heat-exhaustion. The temporary dugouts in which we lived became quickly filled with sand, and this percolated into all our food.

May 21st.

The authorities appeared at last to be alarmed at the sick-rate in our Brigade, which at this time amounted to 10 per cent. hospital admissions daily, on account of septic sores ; everyone was thoroughly stale and listless, and it appeared that we were the only Mounted Brigade which had been continually on service east of the Canal since February 1916 without any rest other than an occasional few days. A rumour had it that we might get a protracted rest, and in any case, if the latter did not mature, it was evident that the Brigade, which was already far below strength, owing to casualties, sickness and lack of reinforcements, would rapidly dwindle away.

May 22nd.

In the morning operation orders were received for a raid on a Turkish railway on May 23rd.

General Idea.—To destroy the railway line between Asluj and El Auja (this was the line which the Turks had built southwards from Beersheba in 1915 for their attack on the Canal. From its termination at El Auja a good road led to the Maghara hills, and an enemy force in this district, although separated from our railway line by some 20 miles of desert, might threaten our lines of communication south of El Arish, via the Hod Bayud. In November 1916 our Brigade had been watching the Maghara hills for this reason.) The enemy hold the line Bir Imleih–810–El Hathira.

The Imperial Camel Corps, one squadron from the Imperial Mounted Division, and two squadrons R.E. will destroy the railway. The Anzac Mounted Division will proceed at 4 a.m. on the 23rd towards Khalassa, via Esani, and thence to Goz Sheihili, to watch the approaches from Beersheba.

The Imperial Mounted Division will attract the enemy at Beersheba from the raid on the railway, and at 4 a.m. Divisional Headquarters will be at Goz Lakheilat. The Sixth, Fourth, and Third Mounted Brigades, in the above order, will hold the line 550–Imsiri–El Buggar–Rashid Bek, joining the left of the Mounted Anzac Division. The Fifth Mounted Brigade will be in reserve at a point 1 mile south of Khasif at 4 a.m. on the 23rd. The Imperial Mounted Division will advance against the line Bir Imleih 810, El Hathira, Abu Yaia, the Sixth and Fourth Brigades being north of the Fara–Beersheba road and the Third Brigade south of it. Divisional Dressing Stations will be established on the east bank of the Wadi at Gamli and Fara.

At 7 p.m. the Brigade left its bivouac and marched 9 miles to Gamli, where we bivouacked west of the Wadi with numerous other Brigades.

May 23rd.

At 2 a.m. we crossed the Wadi Ghuzze and proceeded to our rendezvous 1 mile south of Khasif, two troops leaving our regiment to act as escort to a heavy battery at Karm. At 7 a.m. we heard the railway demolition party at work in the direction of Asluj. A little desultory shelling went on through the day, our Division getting within 3 miles of Beersheba with practically no opposition. About midday our heavy battery at Karm opened fire on the railway embankment north of Beersheba. Karm appeared to consist of a few white houses, one of which was of considerable size, and later became known as Karm Tower House, being surrounded by some fine orchards ; at a later date this place became a sort of No Man's Land, and was usually held through the day either by British or Turkish cavalry patrols, whoever happened to seize it first in the morning. There was a particularly venturesome Turkish squadron leader, who rode a white Arab pony and was well known to all the Yeomanry and Australian Light Horse regiments as the Squire of Karm.

There being no water at this place, owing to the cisterns having been pumped dry, we watered at the wells at Khasif. In the afternoon the Anzac Mounted Division covered the retreat of the railway raiding party, and later the Imperial Mounted Division covered the Anzacs. At 6 p.m., the Third, Fourth and Sixth Brigades of our Division having retired, our Brigade acted as rear-guard, a few shots being exchanged and a few Turkish cavalry following us in the dark. We passed through the wire before the Wadi at 10 p.m., and bivouacked on the western bank at midnight.

May 24*th.*

While watering in the Wadi during the morning, together with the Bucks Yeomanry, Fritz came over and caused some casualties. At midday we returned to Abasan El Kebir, and noticed that the branch railway from Rafa had reached Weli Sheikh Nuran. During the next two days we remained in reserve, and received orders that the Imperial Mounted Division would take over from the Anzacs on the 28th.

May 28*th.*

The Division moved to the Fara plain, where they disposed of themselves between the Tel and Sha'uth. We all received orders to dig dugouts in the sand at least six feet deep, as it was realized that we should be a very good mark for enemy aeroplanes ; we were bombed three times during the day, and our anti-aircraft guns seemed to have no luck. It appeared that at this time our own aeroplanes were not of the newest variety, and were quite unable to cope with the new " Halberstadts," which had recently arrived on this front from Germany. In the evening orders were received for our Brigade and its battery to cross the Wadi and proceed along the Beersheba road to Karm, on the morrow, where we were to take up an. advanced outpost line from the El Buggar Ridge to the Wadi Um Sirr, while some Staff officers studied the surrounding country.

May 29*th.*

The Brigade, less the Warwicks, who were out at Ghabi digging trenches, left its bivouac at 3 a.m. and proceeded along the Beersheba road to Karm. Here we left Brigade Headquarters with our " D " Squadron in reserve. The Gloucester Yeomanry proceeded towards Um Sirr, while we went on to Khasif, below the El Buggar Ridge. It was now light, and we could see parties of Turkish cavalry and infantry appearing over the ridge about a mile and a half to the east. As we advanced, brisk rifle fire broke out, and we had an excellent view of the enemy running in and out of cover. We gradually forced the Turks over the ridge, which we held while the reconnaissance by the Staff officers proceeded. Meanwhile the Gloucester Yeomanry were advancing the same way on our left, and the Fourth Australian Light Horse Brigade on our right. During the morning the Brigade had a few casualties and lost a few horses. While the action was progressing, the led horses were watered below the ridge at the Khasif wells. These " wells " were wonderfully made, and were really large cisterns which had been filled with water during the rainy season by means of converging trenches from the hills around. On letting a bucket down one could see the blue water some twenty feet below in an enormous cave, the surface of the former being brightly illuminated ; on going down the side of the hill one could see the reason for this, a large arched window having been cut in the rocks, through which one could see a vast cave of white chalk stone, the roof of which was supported by pillars, whose reflection was continued into the bright blue water ; the light streaming in from above caused the interior of the cave to be brightly illuminated. This cave, with its carved pillars, had possibly been a retreat or a place of worship in ancient times, which the Turks had at some time converted into a reservoir, by making a hole in the roof and diverting the surface water from the hills into it. Close to this cave was a large cup-shaped depression, surrounded by rising ground, around the circumference of which was a large system of caves, all connected with one another, their roofs being supported by carved stone pillars. These caves had evidently been recently used by the Turks as underground stables, and we estimated that one cave alone would conceal a whole squadron. In one place there was a carved niche in the wall, where evidently some image or altar had formerly been. One could not help wondering whether these caves might not have been a retreat of the early Christians, or some temple of the Philistines. Before midday we retired " by bounds," occupying ridge after ridge, the Turks following for a short distance. After riding about 10 miles we reached the Gamli crossing, and reached our camp as Fritz left it. As moonlight nights were coming on, we deepened our dug-outs, as we knew that night air-raids would be regular. At this time we were getting very tired of Fritz's attentions, as he used to come with absolute regularity at 8 a.m., 4 p.m., and sometimes again at 6 p.m. ; it was particularly annoying, as he practically always left unscathed.

May 31st.

The Sikh Pioneers had at this time started a railway cutting down to the Wadi between Fara and Gamli, and the Egyptian Labour Corps had laid the railway to within a mile of our camp. " A " Squadron was sent out to Ghabi to assist the Warwicks in digging trenches and putting up wire. This position was on our right flank, and somewhat exposed to a flank attack. In the evening orders were received that the Brigade would assemble at Gamli at 7 p.m. and move to Esani, which was said to be occupied by the Turks. Our Brigade was to take up a line north to south through Rashid Bek, the Sixth Brigade continuing it northwards to El Buggar. Brigade Headquarters was to be at Tel El Itweil and Divisional Headquarters near Esani at 7 a.m. The Worcester Yeomanry were to reconnoitre the Wadi Imalaga from Bir El Esani to Maalaga. The Brigade marched out at 7 p.m., after digging trenches all day, and halted at Goz Mabruk, the

Worcester Yeomanry providing advanced guards and outposts. Tel El Itweil was reached at midnight.

June 1st.

At 2 a.m. we forded the Wadi Shanag and negotiated its precipitous banks with the Gloucesters, the battery and Brigade Headquarters remaining at Esani. The country on the eastern bank at first was wild and broken, but after proceeding for about a mile we found ourselves riding through undulating barley fields. We reached Rashid Bek, a large stone farm-house overlooking the Wadi, soon after dawn. The Sixth Brigade could be heard in action on our right, and a little later our outposts opened fire on the enemy, who were on the Khabeira and Um Ajua hills. Whilst this was going on a reconnaissance by the G.O.C. East Force and his Staff was proceeding. The enemy did not seem to be very enterprising, but a few were disposed of and some prisoners taken. At midday the Warwicks, who had arrived from Ghabi, took over our line, and we recrossed the Wadi at Esani. As the Gloucesters retired they were followed by the enemy, who did not, however, cross the Wadi. The Brigade then assembled at Itweil and escorted the guns back to Gamli. We heard on arrival that Fritz at his usual visit had inflicted very heavy losses on the Bucks Yeomanry while watering at Shellal. It was a very unfortunate thing that when regiments were watering at the troughs in the Wadi they were absolutely at the mercy of enemy aircraft, and the latter knew from observation exactly when and where the various Brigades watered.

June 2nd.

Daily working parties were sent out to dig trenches at Ghabi, which was very strenuous work in the hot weather. We found that the slightest scratch from the barbed wire caused septic sores, which were often followed by serious inflammation. During the next ten days we remained at Fara, alternately digging and doing outpost duty.

June 13th.

At this time energetic measures were taken to prevent the breeding of the mosquitoes in the pools of the Wadi Ghuzze. A certain number of men were taken from every regiment to work with the Divisional Sanitary Section for this purpose. A French " 75 " battery joined us at Sha'uth. In the morning Fritz dropped a note offering to fight any five of our aeroplanes, and later on he dropped another message saying good-bye, and adding that he had come down to the Palestine front for a rest cure and was now returning to France. We heard that the Turks had been reinforced again, chiefly on account of the Russian inactivity in the Caucasus. About this date " B " Battery H.A.C. were detached from our Brigade, and their place was taken by the Ayrshire R.H.A. We were told that our big advance would not take place until ten Divisions had been collected on this front. At night a concert was given at Divisional Headquarters, a good band being supplied by the Fifty-third Division ; this was the first band that we had heard in Palestine.

June 14th.

Although Fritz had said good-bye on the previous day, plenty of his associates continued to pay us daily attention at 8 a.m. and 4 p.m. In the evening some of our officers returned from a reconnaissance in connection with future operations, and told us that they had seen the Squire of Karm at the head of his troop, and had obtained a good view of the Beersheba railway viaduct ; it was always considered important by Divisional Headquarters that reports of trains passing over this viaduct should be made, and we did our best to see the trains as often as possible.

June 15th.

We heard to-day for the first time that General Allenby had taken over the E.E.F. More French troops arrived, and also the Sixtieth Infantry Division, which had come from Salonika.

June 16th.

It was said that the "man-power" General had arrived, and that after combing out the "indispensables" in Cairo and Alexandria, he was about to do the same at the base at Kantara; it was considered by some that he should be able to collect at least a Division from that place! The Turks held the Khasif wells during the day, and prevented our troops from watering there. It was said that the enemy had built a loop line east of the Beersheba viaduct, as we threatened the latter. A Turkish cavalryman captured in the afternoon was well equipped, and told us that the three Turkish Cavalry Brigades with which we came in daily contact had their headquarters at Hareira, north of Beersheba, and at Khalassa.

June 17th.

At 4 p.m. some of us rode out to see the new observation line which we were going to hold during the coming week. After crossing at Fara and calling on the Headquarters of the three infantry regiments (Fifty-third Division) who were holding the line behind the wire east of the Wadi, we rode out over the plain towards Goz El Geleib. It was decided that our day observation line would be El Dammath, Abu Shawish, Goz El Geleib, Goz El Basal, and Goz Mabruk. At night, with the exception of a few Cossack posts, we would retire behind the wire and then seize the observation post at 3 a.m., displacing any Turks who might have arrived there first. In the distance we could see the Bedouin getting in their harvest at Ifleis, with Turkish patrols guarding them. At dusk we returned through the wire and over the Wadi to our camp.

June 18th.

Arrangements were made with our Field Ambulance by which we could have some sand-carts just outside the wire during the day and behind it at night. The Wadi at this time was strongly fortified, and we had a number of guns in position on both banks. Some anti-aircraft guns were also established just behind our camp. In the evening " D " Squadron left to take up the night outpost line.

June 19th.

At 3 a.m. we crossed the Wadi and proceeded to Goz El Geleib, the Headquarters of the outpost line. We saw our Verey lights go up from Basal and Shawish, showing that all was clear at these posts. Reports were then received from the other posts on our extended 9-mile front ; a little opposition was encountered at El Dammath, but no casualties were reported during the night. One prisoner, on being captured, said : " Oh, you are the Worcesters ; I know you well by your flash, and fought against you at the first Battle of Gaza, when I was wounded." At this time we were leaving leaflets on the outpost line written in Turkish, asking the enemy to surrender, and saying what a good time they would have if they did so, etc. It seemed rather a degrading thing to do, and one was reminded of some of the answers which we had received on similar occasions at Gallipoli. The prisoner who was captured stated that the enemy expected us to attack any day.

June 20th.

We rode out as usual at 3 a.m., and on arrival at Headquarters on the outpost line heard that one of our posts had been rushed on the previous night, when the troop was being withdrawn at dusk. Before it was light two officers' patrols managed to get down into the Wadi Imleih amongst the Turks and collected valuable information. While waiting at Goz Geleib we watched one of our troops drive the Turks off " tree-post " (Dammath) and finally occupy it ; the other posts were easily seized. We were warned to look out for a French Spahi deserter who had left Khan Yunus and was supposed to have been making his way through our lines to the enemy.

June 21*st.*

Before dawn the Turks were observed on all our posts, and a number of small actions took place in order to disperse them. One of our patrols from Basal advanced to Karm, but at Kasif came in contact with strong cavalry and infantry detachments and had to withdraw again. In the afternoon two sections of our battery were escorted to Hill 510, whence the Turks were shelled at 680 and at the Wadi Imleih crossing. The officer who went to Karm found many messages written in charcoal on the walls of the White Tower House ; they were all written in perfect English, and told us that if we would surrender we would be well looked after, and that their hospitals were good ; the messages also stated the number of our Gaza casualties, and contained some taunts about our Generals. From Goz Geleib we had a good view of the Turkish camps north of Beersheba and of the trains passing over the viaduct. It was arranged that three parties, each consisting of one officer and ten other ranks, should make their way after dark to the Wadi Imleih and " scupper " three outposts some 7 miles from our wire. Soft shoes would be worn, and only bayonets and entrenching tools were to be taken. At six o'clock our guns were escorted back to camp, and a little later the regiment withdrew. I remained out on the wire, with some sand-carts, in order to look after our raiding party if they required my assistance. A light was to be shown on Fara in order to guide us back through the Cheshire infantry to the Wadi.

June 22*nd.*

At 2 a.m. we received a message that two parties had returned safely, and we fell in with the third a little later on. The raid had proved fruitless, as the enemy outposts had been withdrawn, probably on account of our shelling on the previous day. Patrols, however, could not get beyond the enemy's front-line wire, but a valuable reconnaissance had been made to Hill 680, which was an impossibility during the daylight. Everyone was very tired, as we had had three days and three nights practically without any sleep, especially the signallers, who had kept up intercommunication the whole time by helio, lamp, flag and telephone, between the various posts. It was said that the Turks had dropped a message saying that they would cease to bomb us if we would also desist, as the war was going to end soon !

June 23rd.

Our General conceived an idea that by carefully throwing out a net composed of his Brigade, by night, the former might be drawn in at dawn, containing the Turkish patrols which were doing the same work as ourselves on their outpost line. Accordingly, orders were received for the Worcester, Warwick, Gloucester and Bucks Yeomanry to take part in this operation on June 25th.

June 24th.

Orders were received for the drive on the morrow. The Worcester Yeomanry were to spend the night near Maalaga, and then move to Rashid Bek at dawn between the Khabeira tracks, proceeding with Bucks Yeomanry on the left and the Warwick on the right to the Taweil cross-roads. A halt of ten minutes was to be made on the Buggar Ridge, and then the force was to sweep on towards Karm, joining the Gloucester Yeomanry and the light armoured cars, who had been holding the line 550 at El Geheir, Imleih, and 720. Brigade Headquarters was to be Lakheilat, and prisoners were to be sorted out into their respective regiments at Karm at 10 a.m.

We left camp at 8.30 and rode through Tel El Itweil to Imalaga, where we arrived at midnight. On the way we saw some large bonfires which the Bedouin had lit in order to warn the Turks of our approach.

June 25th.

Soon after dawn our force moved north-east, a Dorset squadron proceeding to Esani, while we were accom-

TURKISH CAVALRY ON THE WADI IMLEIH.

(Turkish photograph.)

panied by the Bucks and the Warwicks. As we crossed the Wadi Imalaga our right flank was attacked from Um Ajua, and we could see a troop of enemy cavalry retreating over the sky-line above Rashid Bek. After crossing the Wadi Esani and leaving Rashid Bek on our left, we ascended through Khabeira through most desolate country, our rear-guard being engaged from the east and using its Hotchkiss guns with some effect. On reaching the Buggar Ridge the whole force left-wheeled and advanced at a trot with drawn swords, the Warwicks on the right having joined up with the armoured cars and the Gloucesters, whose left had been resting on 720 ; the latter had joined up with the 4th Australian Light Horse about Abu Shawish, and the " net " was thus complete. It appeared that the Gloucesters, before joining hands with us, had sustained considerable casualties, together with the 4th Australian Light Horse, from the Turkish guns across the Wadi Hanafish. As we advanced our trot became a gallop, and we would no doubt have been an inspiring spectacle to any of the enemy who might have been caught in our net. When the " net " was closed up it was found to contain not a single Turkish soldier, as the enemy had evidently got wind of our proceedings in the night and had retired on Beersheba before the cordon had been completed. One Bedouin boy, apparently of very low intellect, was, however, " captured," and was handed over with some ceremony by two yeomen with drawn swords to Brigade Headquarters at Karm ; it was here that we had had orders that the prisoners should be sorted out into their respective regiments. The day's work was a complete fiasco, but it proved to us that the Turk was wide awake, and that on account of friendly Bedouin assistance it was difficult to catch him napping. On return to camp we said good-bye to the Sixth Mounted Brigade, who were leaving our Division in order to join the new Yeomanry Mounted Division. Our own Division, which up till now had been called the Imperial Mounted Division (containing two Yeomanry and two Australian Light Horse Brigades), was in future to be called the

Australian Mounted Division (containing our Yeomanr:
Brigade and two Australian Brigades).

June 26th.

In the afternoon one of our aeroplanes dropped a
message saying that three of ours had been shot down or
forced to descend in No Man's Land, west of Khalassa
and near Naga El Asseisi, and that they were in need of
immediate protection, as hostile Bedouin and Turkish
patrols were approaching them ; we were informed that
their pilots had made good their escape to one of our
advanced posts at Basal. The regiment left at 6 p.m.
and rode 12 miles, as quickly as possible, across country,
the Bedouin lighting the usual fires on the way, and
arriving at Asseisi before midnight. Our advance guard
was fired on, and one of our men had the, up till then,
unique experience of thrusting his sword through one
of the enemy at the gallop.

June 27th.

We discovered two of our aeroplanes just before dawn,
and had a fracas with some Bedouin who had already
partially stripped one of them. At eight o'clock we were
relieved by some Australian Light Horse regiments, who
had brought transport in order to remove the remains.
On our way back we burnt some Bedouin houses and also
some of their stocks of corn and tibbin, which had been
placed there for the use of enemy cavalry patrols. We
much appreciated some large melon gardens which we
traversed, and everyone tried to balance two or three
melons, the size of footballs, on the front of their saddles
and bring them back to camp.

June 29th.

During Fritz's usual evening constitutional three of our
planes attacked him, and it was said that the latter were
all shot down. It must have been heart-breaking work
at that time for our aviators to have to fly in such inferior
machines.

PALESTINE 161

June 30th.

About this time some tents were issued to the A.M.D.,[1] but the Yeomanry Brigade got very few. We heard that of the seven aeroplanes which went on the Jerusalem raid only two had returned safely, and it was said that we had lost nine during the last week.

July 1st.

In the morning the 4th Australian Light Horse Regiment brought off a very successful ambush. A squadron had proceeded at night to Karm. One troop dismounted, and leaving their horses at the latter place, advanced about 3 miles on foot and hid themselves in one of the ruined houses overlooking the Khasif wells before dawn. Soon after dawn the Australians noticed two squadrons of enemy cavalry crossing the Buggar Ridge and advancing towards the Khasif wells. Some Turkish scouts were thrown out ahead to make the ground good ; this they did in a somewhat perfunctory manner, as they had apparently been doing it daily. One Turkish trooper rode up to the house in which the Australians were hidden, but did not trouble to enter it, and gave the signal " All clear." Thereupon the Turkish squadron proceeded to water at the wells ; the Australians, in addition to their rifles, had two Hotchkiss guns, and at about 100 yards' range caused heavy casualties amongst the Turks. Directly the firing opened the Australian squadron at Karm galloped up with the led horses and joined battle. The Turks, however, immediately mounted, and those who were left galloped away. As a retaliation, a few hours later they attacked one of our outposts, but were repulsed. That evening we took over the night outpost line again, standing to every morning at 3 a.m.

July 3rd.

While the Gloucesters were holding the outpost line the Worcesters and Warwicks suddenly received orders

1 Australian Mounted Division.

11

to rendezvous at Gamli at 6 p.m. Destination unknown.
On arrival we received the following orders :

> Proceed swiftly and silently across country 135° to Khalassa,
> about 16 miles distant. In this place lives a man called Luftie,
> who runs a Turkish Intelligence Bureau, whose agents operate
> between Khalassa and Khan Yunus ; in this way the Turks in
> Beersheba are kept informed of our movements and reinforcements,
> which pass through Khan Yunus station. On arrival a cordon
> will be formed round the village, the Worcesters approaching
> from the west and the Warwicks from the east ; anyone trying
> to escape to be shot, and all males to be taken prisoners. Luftie's
> house is to be demolished by our field troop R.E.

It was a bright moonlight night, and we were accompanied by one or two Staff officers and an Intelligence officer, some native Sinai police, a few " doubtful " Bedouin and an interpreter.

July 4th.

After riding over some very rough country our column struck the Khalassa–Auja road and telegraph at 1 a.m. After about an hour we discovered Khalassa and surrounded it. A few shots were exchanged as we approached the village, and I had one mule shot. The village, however, was found to contain only women and children ; squadrons were therefore sent out to scour the neighbouring hills, and brought in some thirty Bedouin at dawn. Luftie was not amongst the prisoners, and it was probable that he succeeded in escaping when we reached the Khalassa road ; however quietly a Brigade of cavalry advances by night, the native Bedouin knows of the enemy's approach long before he arrives. At 6 a.m. we left with our prisoners and rode to Esani in order to water, burning the Bedouin tibbin which had been stored for the Turks *en route*. After leaving Esani we rode back to camp, passing through some excellent pomegranate and melon fields which were much appreciated. On arrival at Fara we heard the Beersheba and Hareira guns very active, as four Mounted Brigades were

July 20*th*.

In spite of uncomfortable rumours during the night, we were not called out of reserve. It appeared that on the day before three Turkish cavalry regiments had advanced over the Buggar Ridge towards the Wadi and had then withdrawn, leaving some 5,000 infantry and guns in position; the latter had shelled the Wadi and the Gamli railway. It was apparently merely an enemy reconnaissance in force. This accounted for the alarm and our Brigade's being disturbed from its rest. By midday we were allowed to return to Marakeb.

August 14*th*.

The Brigade started on its march to El Arish, and proceeding by the shore route over the ruins of Anthadon, reached Rafa at dusk. Here we found a number of Indian regiments and also some Italian Bersaglieri.

August 16*th*.

After bivouacking the preceding night at El Burj, the Brigade arrived at El Arish, where we camped about 3 miles up the Wadi. At this time the heat was very great. During the next three and a half weeks we remained at El Arish, and occupied a camp vacated by the Seventy-fifth Division under the palm-trees on the coast. Leave was given to Egypt, and a new rest camp was established at Port Said. More remounts were received, and the condition of the men and horses continued to improve. The rations were much better, being on the railway, and we obtained a very plentiful supply of quails (caught by the natives in nets), dates, figs and fish. Although we were now on the lines of communication, we noticed that our right flank was well protected by several forts, garrisoned by British West Indian troops and some regiments of the Egyptian Army. One day we received a warning that a German spy had penetrated our line near Jemmi, and was now amongst us, masquerading alternately as an Australian, a member of the Egyptian Labour Corps and a Camel Transport driver.

September 14*th–October* 13*th.*

As the Seventh Mounted Brigade, which had lately
been in Salonika, was moving up to the front line, less
one regiment, the Derbyshire Yeomanry, the Worcesters
were temporarily taken out of the Fifth Mounted Brigade
and were attached to the Seventh. Accordingly, we left
El Arish at midday and proceeded along the well-known
route, bivouacking for the night at the usual places.
The salt lake at Sheikh Zowaid at this time presented
rather an extraordinary appearance. The surface was
covered with a sheet of white salt, here and there shaded
brown, red, pink and yellow, probably on account of
the presence of iron in the water below ; in some places
the latter could be seen bright blue in colour, showing
between the cracks in the salt ice. While walking round
the lake we put up two foxes, and saw a number of quail
and duck amongst the green vegetation on its banks.
It seemed extraordinary that productive fig-trees and
vines should grow on the very edge of the salt. On
September 16th we reached Amr and joined the South
Notts and Sherwood Rangers Yeomanry. On arrival at
Gamli, two days later, we camped at Jezaiye, and found
that many more infantry battalions had arrived during
our absence at El Arish. We noticed also that Fritz
was no longer so impudent, and that he respected our
aeroplanes and anti-aircraft guns. We received a number
of maps showing the latest Turkish defences of Sheria,
Hareira and Beersheba, almost entirely produced from
aeroplane photographs, and inferred that another attack
on the enemy was impending. It was said that Enver
Pasha had now arrived on the Palestine front. On
September 23rd, together with the Essex R.H.A., our
Brigade took part in one of the usual Divisional recon-
naissances. On the second day the regiment was in
reserve at Rashid Bek, and in the morning some of our
officers reconnoitred the road to Khalassa with a view
to future operations. In the evening our Brigade rode
out to cover the retirement of the rest of the Division,

our own regiment holding the line Wadi Bir Saba–Um
Ajua–780–Ghalyon with the Essex Battery; the latter
shelled the Turks, who reoccupied 970 after the Third and
Fourth Brigades had retired. We had a fine view of the
Turkish camps and their trenches before Beersheba, and
eventually retired with the rest of our Brigade and
reached Gamli at midnight. For the next few days we
were holding the usual outpost line, which we now knew
so well; the latter was rather unpleasant in certain
places, on account of the number of horses which had
been killed, chiefly by Fritz, during the past month. On
one occasion a troop was holding an outpost beyond
Basal, when our regimental dog, " Warpaint," ran out
in front into No Man's Land and was shot at by the
Turks. Although he was not hit he seemed aware of
his danger, and made the best of his way back to us as
quickly as possible; from that day he became a most
arrant coward, and absolutely refused to accompany the
regiment when it was going into action. On September
29th the regiment on duty for the day was heavily
attacked at 680 and Khasif, and we, with the Sherwood
Rangers and the battery, were ordered out to reinforce
them. The enemy was eventually successfully dispersed,
but owing to their having moved some of their guns
further forward, their H.E. was rather unpleasant. It
appeared that they had got a new Cavalry Brigade
opposite us who wore a green uniform. Accordingly,
orders were received to capture a specimen, alive or dead,
for identification purposes; the Intelligence people were
anxious to know whence this Brigade had arrived. The
following day we saw 200 of these horsemen on the
Buggar Ridge, but were unable to capture any. On
October 2nd another large Divisional reconnaissance
was carried out, and it was evident that the Higher Command were personally seeing as much as they could of
the country around Beersheba before the coming attack.
During this reconnaissance one squadron reached Itwail
Semin, a place actually south-east of Beersheba. On
the following day we left the Seventh Mounted Brigade

and were joined again by the Warwicks and Gloucesters. We received a new interpreter, who did not appear to be very much use, as he knew no Turkish, merely Arabic. At this time we used to leave more pamphlets on the outpost line for the Turks to pick up ; these contained pictures of (1) three Turks surrendering to a British soldier ; (2) Turks eating bully beef and bread and jam ; (3) Turks being offered cigarettes by a smiling Tommy ; and (4) living in comfort in the P. of W. Camp at Cairo. Each of these pictures had an appropriate explanation underneath, written in Turkish. One evening we practised with the new red flares in order to be able to communicate with aeroplanes at night. On October 8th we saw a particularly good fight between two of our and two enemy aeroplanes. One Fritz was disabled and came down between the Wadi and Basal. On bringing him in, he told us that he had been in Palestine and Mesopotamia for three years, without any leave, and was the following week to have gone on leave to Berlin. Apparently he was taken unawares, and did not know that we now had first-class aeroplanes on this front. At this time dust-storms, which used to get up every afternoon, were very trying. During this period we received many warnings about spies, especially regarding one individual who had successfully posed as an inspector of Army and Navy canteens, dressed as an officer, riding a bay horse (without brand) and calling himself Schofield. On October 11th two officers made their way through our Brigade outpost line at dawn, telling the officer in charge that they came from the Fifty-third Division and were arranging about artillery practice ; it eventually turned out that the " officers " were not known to the Division and had probably got through some nights before, and used this ruse in order to return to the Turkish lines.

October 14th.

In the morning, while on the outpost line, a corporal and two men were captured by the enemy on Hill 720, who put out a cavalryman as a bait and then ambushed our yeomen. The regiment concerned determined to get their own back when the opportunity should occur.

October 15th.

The enemy were now getting more active on the outpost line, and evidently resented the way our railway from Weli Sheikh Nuran, which had now crossed the Wadi at Shellal, was progressing across the plain towards Karm. Our regiment experienced some difficulty in dislodging them from the heights above the Wadi Imleih, on account of their artillery fire, and in the afternoon it was necessary to call on our battery, machine-gun squadron and four armoured cars to assist us ; the cars, moving swiftly over down-like terrain, returned undamaged after doing a valuable reconnaissance ; we had a few horses hit, but no serious casualties.

October 16th.

At dawn the regiment which had had three men captured two days previously got their own back on the Turks. At 2 a.m. an officer and ten men, under cover of darkness, occupied the stone hut on Hill 720, having previously left their horses some 3 miles away at Karm. At 7 a.m. an enemy troop rode up the hill, and the yeomen, opening fire, accounted for some and took a few prisoners. One of the latter, a squadron-sergeant-major, stated that they knew exactly where and when we should attack, and also told us that the famous " Thunder Division " had been moved down from Aleppo in order to prevent us getting through on the Beersheba sector.

October 18th.

Soon after dawn another reconnaissance in force by our Division took place, our line being advanced beyond Ifleis and El Gehier, in order that the Staff might obtain a nearer view of the Beersheba defences. Again we experienced considerable difficulty in dislodging the enemy from various points, and our battery had to be called on to drive them out of the Ifleis chapel. The Turkish guns from the neighbourhood of Irgeig, near the railway viaduct, were particularly troublesome. On returning to camp we received some preliminary instructions with respect to " Z " day, and realized that our big attack would not be long delayed.

October 23rd–27th.

At dawn, owing to the pertinacity of the enemy, the section of the outpost line usually held by the Worcester Yeomanry was held by the whole Fifth Mounted Brigade. Our railway, which was being built and protected by the Sikh Pioneers, had now reached Karm, to which place the pipe and telegraph wire had also been brought. At midday the Gloucester Yeomanry were attacked on 620 by four squadrons of Turks with motor-cars ; the enemy were, however, driven off after they had inflicted a certain number of casualties. In the afternoon our battery was called on again, and, galloping into action, drove the Turks across the Wadi Ifleis. On returning to camp we received the latest Intelligence in the form of a small pamphlet on Napoleon's Syrian Campaign ! During the next few days the enemy became more and more aggressive, and on October 27th attacked our new railway from the Buggar Ridge to Hill 510 ; they were eventually driven back by a brigade from the Yeomanry Division, assisted by an Australian Light Horse Brigade. One squadron of a London yeomanry regiment behaved most heroically, defending a hill until they were relieved, after they had been almost wiped out, the Major commanding eventually receiving a posthumous V.C. While this fighting was in progress, our Brigade, with the rest of the Australian Mounted Division and the Anzac Mounted Division, was preparing to march south, the Fifty-third Infantry Division marching out to re-inforce the mounted troops on the outpost line. Medical Corps orders were received for the approaching operations, and amongst other things we learnt that the Desert

Mounted Corps "receiving stations" would on the morrow be as follows:

Anzac Mounted Division—Rashid Bek.
Australian Mounted Division—Asluj.
Yeomanry Division—Shellal.

In the evening our Brigade marched out, picketing the road north of Esani, to Ghalyun, via Maalaga.

October 28th.

At dawn our three regiments relieved the Imperial Camel Corps on the sector Khalassa–Ghalyun–Maalaga–Abushar, the enemy being in considerable force opposite us at Ibn Said. Water was developed at Bir Abu Ghalyun and Brigade Headquarters was established outside Khalassa. At sunset we were joined by a battalion from the Sixtieth Infantry Division, and a Brigade-Major from the Anzac Mounted Division told us that the water at Asluj had given out—we realized that if this could not be remedied, the attack of the two Mounted Divisions would be jeopardized, as it was essential that we should have a good watering area at Asluj for the six Brigades of cavalry before the attack on Beersheba from the south-east, east and north-east could mature. The Turks, by destroying the water supply at Asluj, thought that an attack by us on Beersheba from the east was impossible.

October 29th.

The Brigade rode to Khalassa at dawn, leaving a squadron at Hill 970 in order to watch Ibn Said; the former, said to have been an ancient Christian town of some importance, was now a mass of ruins. At night we held the heights to the north-east without anything of importance occurring; it was brilliant moonlight, and a number of tumuli, which had evidently never been opened, made one long for a stay of a few days in this locality in order to excavate their interiors.

October 30*th*.

There was a good deal of aerial activity during the day, and as soon as darkness came on our Division, preceded by the Anzac Mounted Division, commenced to march to Asluj. *En route* we passed the ruins of Khalassa and the Turkish wells in that place, which our R.E. had just opened up again. After a monotonous ride over very rough and stony ground, we entered the large defile which led into the Wadi Asluj. Asluj was reached at midnight ; this place was situated on level hard ground in a very wide part of the Wadi, flanked on either side by precipitous cliffs. It consisted of a number of houses with barracks, officers' mess, store-houses, bakeries, cavalry stables, waterworks and stone watering troughs half a mile in length. There was also a picturesque mosque which, with the other snow-white buildings, looked very striking in the brilliant full moonlight. The whole impression was somewhat artificial, and reminded one of the stage or an exhibition. Asluj in peace-time evidently maintained a small garrison, since increased during the attack on the Sinai Peninsula. One large building was taken over for the Australian Mounted Division Receiving Station, and another contained a detachment of the Sheriff of Mecca's soldiers, who had apparently brought their women and children with them. The waterworks, although entirely destroyed by Turkish high explosives, were through the indomitable perseverance of our engineers put in order sufficiently to water the two Divisions.

BATTLE OF BEERSHEBA.

October 31*st*.

At 1 a.m. we heard our infantry attacking Beersheba north of Khalassa, and an hour later we rode out, passing the railway station and the remains of the viaduct which we had destroyed last June. This was the railway which used to run from Beersheba to Auja, whence a motor road led to the Maghara hills. A very long march, ascending the whole way over moor-like country east of Itwail El Semin and Ras Ghannam, brought us to the heights of Iswaiwin (1450), which overlooked the Beersheba plain. The distance we had come from Khalassa, including an hour's halt at Asluj, was 33 miles. The battle had now commenced: the Twentieth Infantry Corps attacked Beersheba from the west, while the Anzac Mounted Division and Australian Mounted Division, together with the Camel Corps, attacked from the east, with the Seventh Brigade communicating to the south. Collecting Stations had been established at El Semin and Iswaiwin, with Receiving Stations at Asluj and Rashid Bek. Our Brigade was in Corps reserve behind Iswaiwin, and during the day only suffered casualties from aeroplane attacks. From Brigade Headquarters a wonderful panoramic view of the battle lay beneath us : a few miles away lay the picturesque town of Beersheba, the most striking feature of which was its large mosque, surrounded by cypress-trees ; we could see the Wadi Saba spanned by a fine viaduct and the continuation of the railway to the north-west. It seemed strange that we could now obtain such a fine view of this town, which for the last six months we had been trying to see from the west. We could see the explosions caused by our guns from Karm and the Buggar Ridge occurring on the outskirts of Beersheba on the west. The batteries of Desert Mounted Corps were active from the east, south-east and north-east. At midday the New Zealand Mounted Brigade had captured the important height of Tel El Saba, to our north, and the various mounted units were gradually advancing on the town. A little later, the Seventh Mounted Brigade, advancing from the south, galloped the trenches at Ras Ghannam and thus opened up the road from Khalassa to Beersheba. Although the infantry were now closing in from the west and the cavalry from the east, the garrison of Beersheba, which had remained after the last train had left for the north, appeared to be going to make a very stubborn resistance ; however, about 5 p.m. the 4th Australian Light Horse, in the fading light, galloped the trenches just outside the town and broke the resistance of the enemy. This was a brilliant piece of work, and the Australians had heavy casualties, as some of the trenches were too broad to jump, many being killed in this way ; however, the rest swept on and finished up with a successful dismounted bayonet attack. Unfortunately, some of our batteries were not aware that the Australians had entered the town, and continued to shell it for a time. At dusk the last two enemy aeroplanes left Beersheba, and flying so low that we thought they must almost touch us, dropped bombs and caused many casualties to our Fifth Mounted Brigade Transport Column. Meanwhile the Twentieth Infantry Corps from the west had consolidated and captured many more prisoners, including one trainful which was about to start. The Australians in their charge were said to have captured a large number of men and field guns. It was now dark, and after watering in some muddy pools at Hamam, we rode down to Beersheba and bivouacked just outside the town, after passing our newly established Collecting Station at Khashim Zanna.

November 1st.

After a cold night we woke up outside the town and moved down to the Wadi Saba in order to avoid the enemy's guns from the north. On the opposite side of the Wadi we found the Turkish cavalry stables, which contained useful fodder and equipment. A little water was found in the Wadi, but there was some shortage, owing to the fact that Abraham's original seven wells (Bir Saba), in the centre of the town, after having been blown in by the departing Turks, had not yet been repaired. During the morning the Fifty-third Division, an Anzac Brigade and the Imperial Camel Corps took the enemy's positions at Abu Irgeig, where a large railway viaduct had been demolished, Muweileh and Makruneh, with many more prisoners, rolling stock and guns. We rode into the town and saw the railway station and one railway train which had been unable to escape. The hospital, Governor's house and chief mosque were imposing buildings. Some of the houses and factories, and especially the waterworks, had been blown up by the Turks, and the ground was strewn with corpses and dead horses. A few of the usual traps had been laid, but our men were by this time on the look-out for this sort of thing. The honour of the Battle of Beersheba evidently lay with the 4th Australian Light Horse, as after the Desert Mounted Corps and Twentieth Corps had subdued the outer defences of the town, the garrison might have held out for some time, had not the 4th galloped the town in the evening. We saw evidence of the bitter fighting they had had before they eventually succeeded in gaining an entrance. In the evening some enemy aeroplanes hovered over their former home and dropped the usual bombs.

November 2nd.

In the morning an officers' reconnaissance took place to Barghut, in which direction we expected shortly to advance. We began to wish that our anti-aircraft guns would arrive soon, as Fritz was again very spiteful. Transport now began to arrive from the south, as the Khalassa road was now open. We also received supplies from railhead, as the Fara–Beersheba road over the Buggar Ridge was now practicable. In the afternoon many more prisoners were rounded up and brought into camp. When night fell we had a very bad doing from Fritz, who dropped a hundred bombs and caused a large number of casualties in our Field Ambulances. We were informed that two Brigades of the Anzac Division were holding the line Bir Arara, Wadi Malah, and Wadi Hora east of Beersheba, that the Imperial Camel Corps were near Tel El Khuweilfeh, and that the Seventh Mounted Brigade were at Towal Abu Jerwal, the two last-named places being 10 and 8 miles north-east of Beersheba. The Fifth Mounted Brigade was taken out of its own Division and placed at the disposal of the G.O.C. Anzac

Mounted Division, and warned to be ready to move any time after midnight.

THE BATTLE OF RAS EL NAG.

November 3rd.

At 8 a.m. our Brigade marched out from Beersheba (suffering the usual casualties from enemy aircraft), and crossed the Hebron road near Tel El Saba, arriving at Rjm Abu Jerwan at 10.30 a.m. The road was a fair one, and the ground rose the whole way. We passed numerous ammunition columns and infantry on the march. It was evident that we were in for some new adventure. To the north we could hear heavy firing and could see the shells exploding ; we received orders to trot on for 2 miles, and then came across battalions of infantry in reserve and four field batteries in line, hard at work. The objective appeared to be Tel El Khuweilfeh, a high and strong position, jealously guarded by the Turks, as it commanded the water supply of the region and also the road to Hebron. Any force operating against this place from the south was forced to water at Beersheba, some 10 miles away. An Infantry Division was attacking Khuweilfeh from the south-west, while the First and Second Australian Light Horse Brigades were holding the salient to the east, which ended in a hill called Ras El Nag (2023). We halted near Mikreh and were ordered to gallop 2½ miles along the front of the Turkish position in order to reach the two narrow defiles which led up to Ras El Nag. The Brigade started at a trot and then broke into a gallop as the Turkish fire became severe. We could see the enemy snipers lying out in the open a few hundred yards away on our left. Here and there a man or a horse was hit and came down. The bullets churned up the ground under our horses' feet and continually sang in our ears. We had to stop two or three times in the middle of this gallop, and taking cover behind some rocks, picked up the wounded and then followed the

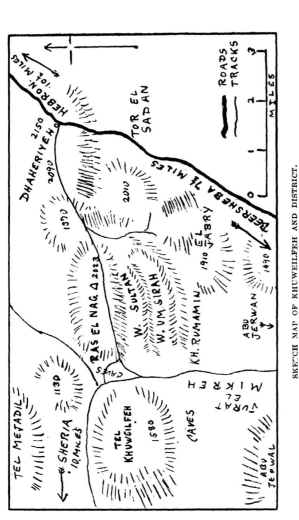

SKETCH MAP OF KHUWEILFEH AND DISTRICT.

regiment. Eventually the entrance to the Wadi Um Sirah was reached, where it was possible to give more attention to our casualties; here, however, we were followed by the fire from the enemy's guns as we ascended the valley. At the end of this valley Brigade Headquarters was established, and crossing to the next valley, that of the Wadi El Sultan, we established a dressing station for those wounded who had arrived by a different route. These two Wadis, both of which debouched into the plain opposite the Turkish main position, were separated by a precipitous ridge and met towards the summit of Ras El Nag. Our Brigade now relieved the 1st Australian Light Horse, who it appeared had suffered considerably, while the 2nd Australian Light Horse continued to hold the hills to the east of our position. While we were busy attending to cases in the Wadi El Sultan we suffered from well-directed shelling, which accounted for both men and horses. Leaving the latter in the Wadi, the regiment now disposed itself on the heights and displaced the Turks from the Nag road; here we found the remains of a small Turkish ammunition column, several mountain gun positions, a few dead Turks and a Red Crescent ambulance waggon; the latter we made use of, and, with the aid of some ponies, managed to transfer our wounded from the higher ground to the head of the valley in which was established our dressing station. It struck me as extraordinary that in one of the evacuated enemy gun positions I should find Dickens's *Dombey and Son* lying open on the ground; one somehow could not associate a Turkish gunner with Dickens, but of course one knew that a large number of Turks had been in America and could speak English. It seemed, however, a curious book to be reading during such exciting times; possibly the reader had been one of the dead Turks lying near. The enemy shelling from the south-west, west and north was very troublesome during the afternoon, but ceased at dusk. At 11 p.m. one of our R.A.M.C. corporals managed to bring the water-cart in the dark from Mikreh

along the front of the Turkish positions into the Wadi
Sultan. It was a great performance, as the country
was very difficult to cross in the dark and the entrance
to our Wadi was only a few hundred yards from the
Turkish trenches. We issued the water to the men, who
had had none since dawn, and who had been in the saddle
or fighting all day. Meanwhile our wounded, which
included a number of Australians, had accumulated.
We could not evacuate them down the Wadi, as this at
one spot was too narrow to admit our Field Ambulance
carts. After a consultation we decided that the only
way was to carry the stretchers up the precipitous rocky
hill and down again into the Wadi Um Sirah, which
admitted wheeled transport at its lower end. Calling
for a party of forty-eight bearers from the regiment, we
commenced, by means of relays, to carry the wounded
over the ridge and down into the second Wadi. It was
essential to complete the work before dawn, as no man
could have lived on the top of the ridge by daylight, as
the latter was in full view of the Turks a few hundred
yards away.

November 4th.

Our men worked hard, but it was killing work, owing
to the steep ascent and descent. However, the task was
completed before 6 a.m., and the cases were evacuated
by Field Ambulance carts to the New Zealand Field
Ambulance at Mikreh, six mules being killed *en route*
and one ambulance completely smashed by a shell.
During the morning the Regimental Dressing Station was
established under some Turkish waggons just below the
summit of Ras El Nag, and we were kept busy. The
regiment were holding the crest of the hill, taking cover
behind the very large boulders which abounded. The
enemy rifle fire and shelling never ceased all day, and
the men suffered terribly from thirst, especially those
who had had their water-bottles pierced by bullets. At
midday an enemy cavalry regiment was seen to be
advancing on us from the north-west under cover of

their own guns—the whole Brigade was ordered up at once and repelled the advance. During the afternoon things quietened down for a time, but at 4 p.m. Turkish infantry (with reserves from Hareira, whose dust we had seen approaching for some time) counter-attacked in force, getting up under cover of the boulders to within 80 yards of our front line; they fixed bayonets with a shout and came on with a rush—it was an exciting moment. Our fire, however, from rifle, machine gun and Hotchkiss checked them just in time and rolled them back. It was evident after this that the enemy had been again reinforced, as attacks were made all along our line. They evidently considered the salient of Ras El Nag of vital importance to themselves, as it commanded their left flank and also the road from Khuweilfeh to Hebron via Dhaheriyeh, where they had large depots. At 9 p.m. a New Zealand Brigade arrived, having left their horses with ours in the Wadi, in order to relieve us. Our C.O. explained the situation to them, and warned them that another counter-attack was probably maturing. (This proved true, as a few hours after we had left the Turks attacked in force, but were repulsed after a New Zealand regiment had suffered 100 casualties.) We now had a large number of wounded, and the question arose as to how they should be carried down into the plain. After burying our dead, we organized a bearer party of eighty men, and with the C.O. leading, carried the wounded in blankets over ground in some places almost precipitous, a distance of 3 miles to a point in the Wadi Sultan where carts could penetrate. The lightly wounded men we mounted on horses, and all the stretcher cases were left in charge of a few orderlies at the mouth of the valley, to be picked up by an officer with a section of the Field Ambulance during the night. Our C.O. then led the Brigade out into the plain across which we had galloped the day before; although it was dark, the enemy on Khuweilfeh learned of our approach and sent up star-shells, which were immediately followed by rifle fire. Luckily, the dust which we raised obscured us to a certain extent, but we could see the sparks flying as the bullets struck the stones in our vicinity. A little further on a battery " reached " for us, but we managed to escape with little harm to the Brigade. On leaving this danger zone, we dropped into a walk after reaching Mikreh. About 4 miles down the Hebron–Beersheba road we came across the Australian Mounted Division Collecting Station, where we deposited the wounded we had been carrying with us on our horses. In conversation with some Australians, we heard that the Ras El Nag position was a regular trap, as, in order to enter the Wadis which approached it or leave them, one was exposed to Turkish fire from three directions for about 3 miles ; however, this salient had to be held by a Mounted Brigade, as it commanded the enemy's main communications.

November 5th.

At 4 a.m. we reached our camp at Beersheba, the horses having been without water for about forty-eight hours and the men having had almost forty hours' continuous fighting and the rest of the time in the saddle. The horses, on scenting the water, although tired out, made a rush for the troughs, and many of the men, oblivious of previous orders, could not resist plunging their heads into the horse-troughs. Our wounded were evacuated from the Collecting Station on the Hebron road to the Australian Mounted Division Receiving Station in the German hospital at Beersheba, whence they were conveyed by motor-ambulance to Karm and subsequently to railhead. In the afternoon we visited our wounded in the town hospital, and met the Yeomanry Division, which had just entered the town from the west and were about to move out at midnight.

November 6th.

We heard that the Twentieth Corps had attacked and taken Khuweilfeh, but that the Ras El Nag position was held on one side by the enemy. The New Zealand

Brigade, which had relieved us, was heavily attacked after we left and had sustained numerous casualties. We were kept in readiness all day to move up again at an hour's notice. In the afternoon the Turks counter-attacked the Imperial Camel Corps, who had relieved the New Zealanders at Ras El Nag, three times, but were driven back after bitter fighting at the point of the bayonet. It was evident that the enemy still considered this position of vital importance, although the main position at Khuweilfeh had already fallen. In the evening our Machine Gun Squadron and a squadron of the Warwick-shire Yeomanry were sent up to assist the Imperial Camel Corps. The Turks, it was stated, had received large reinforcements on their right, which had previously been waiting at Aleppo, destined for either Palestine or Meso-potamia. Late at night we heard the good news that the Sixtieth and Seventy-fourth Divisions had captured all their objectives, and that the enemy had evacuated Tel El Sheria and Hareira. Our regiment was warned to be ready to move between midnight and dawn.

November 7th.

At 2 a.m. the whole Brigade marched out along the Beersheba railway line to Abu Irgeig, and thence on to Tel El Sheria, where we saw the works and camps cap-tured by the infantry on the previous day. Numerous wounded were still being evacuated towards Karm. When day broke, we rode through many infantry bat-talions and trotted down to the Wadi Sheria ; here we took cover while the Turkish guns were shelling us, one of our batteries in the Wadi on our left suffering severely and losing fifteen horses at one moment. Later, we advanced, now again over down-like country, to Khirbit Barata, where the shelling got rather worse but ceased at dusk. It appeared that a number of enemy batteries after the fall of Sheria and Hareira had retreated northwards, and being mobile, were endeavouring to hold up the advance of the Infantry Divisions. After dusk we were told that what appeared to us a mad scheme had been for-

mulated, namely, that we should ascertain the position
of these batteries and charge them in the pitch darkness.
For two hours we wandered about, probably at one time
behind the enemy's outposts, but luckily for all concerned we did not bump into the batteries. At ten
o'clock we were ordered to withdraw back to the infantry
line and water at Sheria near the demolished railway
viaduct, which was surrounded by dead horses from
our batteries which had been in action there. We were
now in the positions which we had often looked at from
the old outpost line before Fara, but unfortunately, on
account of the darkness, we were unable to satisfy our
curiosity. We did, however, come across the light railway which carried the big gun which used to shell us as
far back as the first Battle of Gaza.

THE CHARGE AT HUJ.

November 8th.

At 6 a.m., after a very short and cold night's rest, we
left Sheria and rode through Barata in order to attack the
Turks, who were fighting a rear-guard action, with the
Sixtieth Division on our left and the Third Australian Light
Horse Brigade on our right. We learned later that a new
Brigadier had been appointed to command us, but at the
time we appeared to be without a Brigade Commander.
Our first objective was Zuheilika, which we had attacked
during the first Battle of Gaza. The batteries from which
the Sixtieth Division and ourselves had suffered on the
previous day retired, covered by about 2,000 infantry,
and shelled us heavily again. At Juaithim we came
across much abandoned material and many wounded
Turks. For some reason or other we were not supported
by our own artillery, and the enemy gunners, although
retiring, had it pretty well their own way ; their infantry,
however, who were covering the retreating batteries,
for the time being engaged all our attention. After
advancing about 4 miles, our " D " Squadron and a
squadron of the Warwicks were dispatched to the Sixtieth

Division on our left. The Gloucestershire Yeomanry were now on our right, and we kept advancing by " bounds," galloping from one ridge to another, each of which we held successively, and gradually forced the enemy back ; they made determined stands at the above-mentioned places and also at Baghl. We had now advanced about 10 miles, and could hear from the explosions of the shells that we were rapidly gaining on the guns. The Sixtieth Division, on slightly lower ground, we could see advancing in extended order and suffering very much from the enemy's shelling. An urgent request was sent for our Ambulance, as we recognized that in a short time we should be having heavy casualties ; as it was, we left our wounded, if unable to ride, here and there in charge of one man, as it was known that the rest of our Brigade and other regiments were following in our tracks. The ground was strewn with dead Turks and the material they had abandoned in their haste— shells, gun limbers, equipment, ammunition waggons, etc. It was noticeable how during this retreat they had commenced by throwing away merely the old shell-cases, and gradually, as time went on and they were more pressed, more and more important equipment was abandoned in order to make their retreat easier. As we had had no water since the previous night the men were parched, but some of the small water-barrels usually carried by Turkish transport, which were found abandoned, were a Godsend. Meanwhile, we were getting nearer and nearer to the enemy's guns, and as our advance over the dry turf caused clouds of dust, his gunners paid us more attention. We noticed an explosion taking place a couple of miles away on our right, which was followed by tremendous clouds of smoke ; this turned out to be due to the destruction of the enemy's ammunition dumps at Jemmamah. Soon after midday we found ourselves east of Huj, and a message was sent to the Third Australian Light Horse Brigade asking them to co-operate with us in charging the guns. While this message was being taken, our two squadrons of Worcesters and one of Warwicks (the whole only ten troops strong), who were now in advance of the Gloucester Yeomanry, Third Australian Light Horse Brigade and the Sixtieth Division (who were on our left), received orders from the G.O.C. of the latter division to charge. At the moment we were dismounted, giving our horses a breather and attending to some of our recently wounded behind a slight ridge. Our Second-in-Command gave the order to mount, and called out, "Now then, boys, for the guns!" Away they galloped, and the moment they appeared over the crest of the ridge, 200 yards from the batteries, the gun fire became terrific, accompanied by rifle and machine gun fire from some 2,000 Turkish infantry who were protecting the guns. My orderlies and I followed in the rear, almost unconscious of what was happening, on account of the deafening noise as we galloped down the grassy slope ; the enemy gunners had shortened their fuses as the yeomanry came in sight, and were now banging away as fast as they could, the shrapnel apparently bursting on the ground instead of some thirty feet above it. The Worcester and Warwick squadrons, already thinned out by casualties, swept on, and topping a rise, charged through the infantry screen and were lost to view. Suddenly the terrific din of shrieking and exploding shells ceased, and we knew that the end had come. A wonderful and terrible sight met our view : in addition to the casualties which had already occurred, the ground was strewn with horses and fallen yeomen, many of whom were lying close to, and some beyond, the batteries. Twelve guns, three 5·9's and nine field guns, were in various positions, surrounded by Austrian and German gunners, many of whom were dead or wounded. About 300 yards behind the rearmost battery a mass of enemy infantry were retreating, a few of whom were still firing occasional shots from various directions. Our squadrons had not fired a shot, and every single casualty we inflicted was caused by our sword-thrusts. Our Second-in-Command had fallen wounded under a gun, and was on the point of being dispatched by a gunner with his saw-bayonet, when a yeoman from the former's old squadron killed the Austrian. The German and Austrian gunners fought gamely round their guns when cornered, for a few moments, although the mass of the Turkish infantry had broken. Some enemy machine guns were seized and turned on the latter. Of the three squadron leaders (two Worcesters and one Warwick) in the charge, one was killed and two died of wounds. On that day there fell, amongst others, an officer of the Worcester Yeomanry who was most dearly loved by us all, and his death, together with the loss of so many gallant comrades, cast a gloom on the regiment, in spite of the everlasting laurels it had won. The Warwickshire Yeomanry also, amongst their killed, lost some of their best.

We commenced to dress the wounded at once, and found them scattered in all directions. Wounded Turks came crawling in, and one could not help contrasting their clean wounds, caused by our sword-thrusts, with the ghastly wounds sustained by our men from shell fire and saw-bayonet. Part of a Turko-German Field Ambulance, which had been unable to escape, was found in a hollow behind the batteries, and their equipment was invaluable to us, as our dressings soon ran out and our Field Ambulance had not yet arrived ; the Turkish orderlies were put to work amongst their own men, and the intelligent German sergeants proved quite useful. Our little force, after the charge was now scattered and very weak, on account of the heavy losses it had sustained, and one could not help wondering whether the Turkish infantry, who had retired only a short distance, would not counter-attack when they saw that we had no supports. However, the enemy had apparently had enough of it, but one was relieved when the first regiment of the Sixtieth Division joined us ; the latter were quickly followed by an infantry Field Ambulance from the same Division, a few of whose bearers had been already on the scene. Our new General, only appointed that morning to command our Brigade, rode up and congratulated it. It seemed an auspicious occasion to take over a new command, with the twelve guns captured by his regiments in the background as a recommendation of their prowess. When night fell we bivouacked near the batteries and ate our evening meal, there being only eight officers left in the regiment—some were killed, some wounded, and others had been casualties during the last ten days. Late at night we received a message saying that the Worcesters and Warwicks had received the personal congratulations from the Commander-in-Chief on their brilliant action, and stating that they had upheld the best traditions of the British cavalry.

November 9th.

During the previous night our " A " echelon transport arrived, together with a welcome supply of drinking water. At dawn some of the oxen which had been drawing the German 5·9's were slaughtered, and we looked forward to some fresh but tough meat. News arrived that Gaza had really fallen, and that the Fifty-second Division were advancing along the sea-coast. From the débris left round the Huj guns we were able to collect some useful equipment, especially Turkish leather saddle-bags and water-barrels. Our horses, which had had no water since the evening of November 7th at Sheria, now had to go 10 miles to reach a suitable watering place, and did not return till 5 p.m., as the whole of the horses of the Australian Mounted Division had been taken to the same spot. At sunset thirty-one of our aeroplanes flew over, all loaded with bombs, evidently about to harass the retreating enemy. Just before midnight the Brigade marched, passing Huj station in the dark. We were glad to be on the move, as one did not relish another day in the proximity of so many dead horses.

November 10th.

As dawn began to break, we found ourselves riding over undulating country, which supported large flocks of sheep and goats. Here and there were to be seen

the low black tents of the nomad Bedouin ; the latter
did not appear to be in the least disconcerted by our
presence, although some of us enjoyed roast lamb the
following night. The Wadi Hesi, fringed by rushes
beneath Tel El Hesi, proved a good watering place.
After a cold night in the saddle our fires had just been
lit, and everyone was looking forward to some tea, when
the usual order to move at once was received. We rode
out with our battery to Munteret El Kaneitera, our
objective being the village of Arak El Menshiye and its
railway station ; the latter was occupied after some
shelling on both sides by midday, and a certain amount
of rolling-stock was captured. While this was going on,
the Third and Fourth Australian Light Horse Brigades
had seized Faluja on our left. After dusk we made a
night attack on Summeil from the south, the Third and
Fourth Australian Light Horse Brigades co-operating
from the north and north-west ; our shelling was somewhat erratic in the dark, and we were lucky to escape
casualties from our own guns from the west. At midnight our three regiments returned to Arak, and were
relieved to find that water had arrived from Hesi. The
wells in this district were very few and very deep, which
made the drawing of water a tedious process. The
horses, however, had to be sent back all the way to Hesi
in order to be watered.

November 11th.

During the morning a large number of sick men and
horses were evacuated. The strain was beginning to tell ;
We had now been on the move for fourteen days, and
the horses had on more than one occasion been forty-
eight hours without water and often twenty-four ; on
many occasions the latter had been equally long without
having their saddles off—the men were badly in want
of sleep, and many had broken out again with septic
sores, chiefly on account of their inability to wash or
take off their clothes for the past two weeks. A certain
amount of dysentery also began to develop again. How-

ever, the advance had got to go on, however great the wastage in men and horseflesh might be. It appeared that the motor-ambulance convoys had broken down, and that there was a great accumulation of wounded and sick at Hesi and Faluja. Our regimental transport arrived during the day with rations, but as the other two regiments were without the latter, our food had to be distributed amongst the whole Brigade, with corresponding shortage to ourselves. However, as one or two " accidents " occurred to some sheep in the vicinity, we did not go to sleep so hungry after all.

THE BATTLE OF BALIN.

November 12*th.*

The Brigade marched out soon after dawn, a good many horses being led, on account of sore backs. Soon after starting we fell in with some wandering horses who attached themselves to our Brigade for the sake of company, and many of whom proved quite useful. On the aerodrome near Arak station we found five burnt aeroplanes. The station buildings, which we had left after they had been captured on the previous day, were being freely pillaged by the Bedouin. Summeil was reached again at 9 a.m. and was found to be evacuated, but a few shells were falling to the north of the village from the direction of Berkusie. We were told that the Anzac and Yeomanry Divisions had advanced their line on our left from Burka to El Mesmye. From the highest part of Summeil village we obtained a view of what, according to the map, must have been the heights of Bethlehem. After a couple of hours' rest, during which several horses died of exhaustion, we commenced our advance on Balin, keeping the Turkish railway on our left. This village was situate on a slight eminence separated by a ridge of hills from El Tine on the north ; the latter was on the same railway, which passed round the left shoulder of the above-mentioned hills. A ride of a few miles brought us within sight of Balin, and under heavy shell fire, my

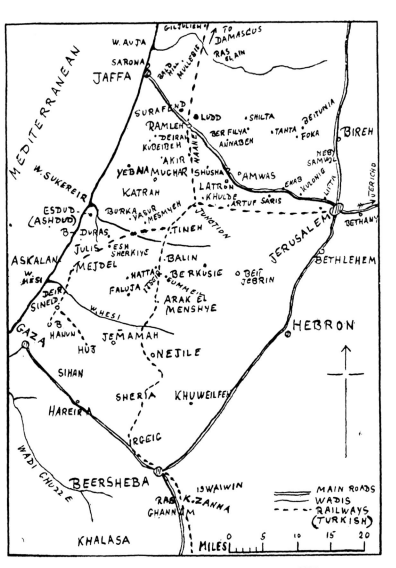

SKETCH MAP OF PALESTINE, OCTOBER–DECEMBER 1917.

(Based on *The Times* map.)

horse being wounded in the head and losing one eye. We galloped round the western slopes of the village and halted below some cactus plantations, shelling becoming worse and numerous casualties resulting. We now had the Fourth Australian Light Horse Brigade on our left, and the Third on our right, the Gloucester Yeomanry seizing the heights on the north of the village, while the Worcesters and Warwicks occupied those to the north-west. Our Regimental Dressing Station was established in a stonewalled camel-yard in the highest part of the village, and soon contained many wounded. After a time we noticed that all troops were coming down from the northern slopes and were streaming away to the north-east. From our position in the village, we at the dressing station could see through our glasses considerable numbers of the enemy detraining at El Tine station, and realized that very strong reinforcements were coming up against us. This seemed to be the great danger, as we, a weak Brigade, were ahead of our main body, while the Turks, with a working railway behind them, could bring up large reinforcements and guns at short notice. Our battery shelled these reinforcements from the south of Balin, but were completely outgunned by the enemy's heavy artillery. On one occasion our H.A.C. battery galloped into the open to the left of the hills, and came into action in full view of the enemy. After being busy in our dressing station for some time, we came out to see how things were going, and were horrified to see strange-looking turbaned troops coming down over the ridge, which a short time ago had been occupied by our yeomen ; in the distance we could see our men retreating on the right. The enemy, who were beginning to descend the steep declivity, were only some 300 yards away. Luckily we had kept the horses on which the wounded had been brought in, so, realizing that escape was a matter of seconds, we hastily mounted all our casualties and galloped them out of the rear of the yard. There were, however, not enough horses to go round, and some of us had to escape on foot. Some horses were relieved by the Seventh, who had just arrived at Ijseir; the relief took a long time, as the troops concerned had to walk a mile in the open, and only groups of two or three were allowed to proceed at one time. Eventually, the whole Brigade was collected in the Wadi behind Ijseir village, and orders were received to move rapidly to Hatte. This ride was an unpleasant experience, as we had to cross an open plain under heavy shell fire from the Turkish guns at Berkusie; however, it was accomplished in very open order. At Hatte, rations and drinking water were issued, but the poor horses still had to go dry. That night, after a weary ride, we eventually reached Es Suafir Esh Sherkiye.

November 14th.

The horses were sent to water early, but did not return until night, most of them having been over sixty hours without any water, and many more succumbed as a result. Our camp lay just west of the railway recently constructed by the Turks from El Tine to Gaza, and during the morning, owing to shortage of firewood, many of the sleepers were torn up. The Australian Mounted Division operating unit was established at Julis, and our Divisional Collecting Station was erected near our bivouac. We heard the news that the Yeomanry Division had been sweeping northwards with some of the Twenty-first Corps and had cut the railway between Ramleh and Jerusalem, thus isolating the latter. All day long reinforcements were marching through and heavy guns were going up. We were informed at night that our Brigade had been taken out of the Australian Mounted Division, and that we were temporarily attached to the Twenty-first Corps. Owing to the number of dead horses in the vicinity, the shrieks of the jackals made it difficult to sleep at night.

November 15th.

During the morning two of us rode over to a Jewish village east of Beit Duras, in order to buy provisions.

we had a superb view of the sea and the maritime plain to the west ; the white towers of Ramleh and Ludd, far below us, seemed to glisten in the brilliant sunshine. A little further on we reached the summit of the pass above Kuryet Enab, which had been captured by the infantry the day before. However, the enemy did not appear to be far away, as their field guns were still shelling the road in the vicinity. We bivouacked amongst the rocks, two of our squadrons proceeding along the road to hold posts at Kustil and Asiati. We were now within 7 miles of Jerusalem. It appeared that the Seventy-fifth Division had had heavy casualties before taking the top of the pass, but the heavy guns of the Twenty-first Corps were now in position and in action. It was a very cold night, and we felt the change in altitude, as we had risen from the level of the plain to 2,500 feet above sea-level. A mountain battery being camped just above us some-what interfered with our sleep, as their wandering mules were very inquisitive about us.

November 22nd.

Having little to do, as the squadrons were out on patrol, some of us walked over to the village of Enab (Biblical Emmaus). It was not a successful visit, as the natives, like ourselves, were short of food. We saw a large Greek convent, later taken over by the Staff, and the house formerly occupied by the German Consul in Jerusalem, which was now inhabited by an infantry Field Ambulance. Two German officers had escaped out of this house on the previous day and had blown up the bridge at Kulonieh, on the Jerusalem road, some 2 miles beyond Enab. From the heights we had a marvellous view of the surrounding country, looking down from some hills 2,000 to 3,000 feet high on the plains and the sea beyond. Two of our squadrons were used in patrol work in con-nection with the Infantry Divisions which were operating west of Jerusalem. The Tenth Australian Light Horse were temporarily attached to our Brigade.

November 23rd.

Intelligence stated that 4,000 Turks with guns were holding up the western approach to Jerusalem, which the Seventy-fifth Division were trying to force ; a new German Division had been located at Nablus, and our attacking infantry were holding the line from Beit Isa to Nebi Samwil. Our rations were rather short, owing to difficulties of transport, and at this time our daily menu consisted of five biscuits (only three inches by three inches), one tin of bully beef and tea ; this did not seem enough in the keen mountain air, and one generally retired to rest very hungry. Occasionally a very small loaf of bread was issued instead of the five biscuits, but the latter were preferable, as the bread was generally mouldy. There was also a tobacco famine, which was very trying for some of us.

November 24th.

In the morning the Sixtieth Division marched up the pass from Latron to Enab, in order to relieve the Seventy-fifth ; the latter, comprising West-Country troops and Indian regiments, had had heavy losses. Owing to the great shortage of water in the mountain, we were ordered to return to Latron. On the way down the pass our Signalling Officer's horse shied at a camel, and man and horse went over the side of the road. Luckily there was not a big drop, and they were merely badly shaken. Half a mile farther down, where the road fell away precipitously on the near side, my horse shied at a mule which had been recently killed by a shell, and it appeared as if both of us were about to fall down the precipitous mountain side to the valley below ; in order to prevent this, I threw myself off on the off side, and my horse recovered himself before he was over. The result was a dislocated shoulder, which caused a certain amount of discomfort, but luckily, after trying various means of transport, I was able to get a motor-ambulance which ran me down to the bottom of the pass, where a hos-

PALESTINE

pitable London Field Ambulance reduced the dislocation. Best of all, this unit, which had recently arrived at Latron, presented me with a pound of tobacco. On regaining my Brigade, it was decided that I should do duty with our Field Ambulance for a time, a substitute from the latter taking my place in the regiment.

November 25th.

Some of our regiment were out clearing the surrounding villages, and we noticed many big guns moving up the pass. One of our dispatch riders had now been missing for two days, and it was thought he must have been either captured by the Turks or fallen over the cliff with his horse. All day long we heard the Yeomanry Division heavily engaged at Tahta, to our north, where they were fighting in the mountain after sending their horses back to Ramleh.

November 26th.

We heard that the attack by the Fifty-second Division on El Gib, near Bire, which commanded the northern approach to Jerusalem, had failed, and that the Sixtieth Division were to attack the former position.

November 27th.

More big guns moved up the pass, accompanied by sausage balloons for spotting purposes, and our Brigade received orders to proceed to Artuf, south of the main road to Jerusalem.

November 28th.

Brigade Headquarters moved to Artuf, but our reconnoitring squadron found that there was no possible track beyond the village for cavalry, so it was decided that we should advance north of that place, probably as infantry. The Seventy-fourth Division marched up the pass during the day to relieve the Sixtieth, as El Gib had not yet fallen and Bire was still occupied by the Turks. From midday we were at short notice to move, but received no orders. It was interesting to note that the Eastern star appeared over the entrance to the pass in a line with Bethlehem every night.

November 29th.

We heard from some friends in the Seventy-fourth Division that two new Infantry Divisions had arrived from the Base and were now at Belah ; a rumour also came from Twentieth Corps' Headquarters that El Gib had been captured. All day long we heard our heavy guns in action, and saw one of our sausage balloons shot down by Fritz, the observer escaping gracefully in a parachute. At this time, owing to the tobacco shortage, the current price for Woodbine cigarettes amongst the men was five a shilling, and one used to see groups of four or five passing a single cigarette from mouth to mouth. Just before sunset Fritz came over, flying low, and caused some casualties amongst us. At dusk the Brigade marched from Latron, passing through Kulde to Junction Station, where we passed the Tenth Irish Division, which had recently arrived from Salonika and which we had not seen since the days of Suvla Bay. Proceeding due west across the plain, we passed the village of El Mughar, where we could see the flash of our monitors' guns firing from the coast, and eventually halted on the sand-dunes south of Yebna.

November 30th.

At daylight we found ourselves on the sand-dunes on the edge of a fertile plain, a few miles north-west of the ancient Gath. We seemed to be out of touch with events here, and were very vague as to what was happening and whither we were about to proceed.

December 1st.

At dawn we were informed that the Brigade would take up a line on the hills, dismounted for a time, until some new Infantry Division arrived from the Base. At 8 a.m. we rode to Akir, where there were good watering

facilities. Here was another of those European Jewish settlements, the village consisting of well-arranged streets and white houses, with picturesque red tiles and green shutters. It seemed strange to see the Jewish population wearing European clothes, particularly old men in frock-coats and seedy-looking top-hats, after being accustomed to nothing but flowing Bedouin robes or Turkish uniforms for the last two years. Jaffa oranges were plentiful, and they were tremendously appreciated. After crossing the railway to Ramleh, at the village of Naane, we fell in with the remains of the Sixth Mounted Brigade Field Ambulance, which had just come down from the hills; the former had had very heavy losses amongst their personnel, and had nothing left of their transport except two mules and a few camels. As we approached that very marked feature, the hill of Abu Shushar (the Biblical Gezer), we were met by the Sixth Mounted Brigade, pitifully reduced in numbers after their recent fighting in the hills. We heard how they had been counter-attacked again and again by first-class troops, and how, after being completely surrounded at Tahta, they had eventually been relieved under cover of darkness by the Seventh Mounted Brigade, after incurring some 500 casualties. We also heard details of the brilliant charge by the Berks, Bucks, and Dorset Yeomanry at El Mughar some weeks ago, when they galloped across from Yebna over 3 miles of open plain, and eventually routed some thousands of Turks with numerous machine guns and some artillery on the opposite hill. After exchanging our experiences with one another, the two Brigades parted, and we received orders to take over the line from Suffa to Tahta, with an advanced dressing station south of Beit Sira. We rode through the native villages of Barriye and El Kubab, and, descending the serpentine road from the latter, halted on the Wadi Neda—orders were then changed, regiments being sent back via Annabeh, Berfilya, and Burj to approach the line from the west, while the guns and the bearer section of the Field Ambulance proceeded up the Amwas track to Beit Sira. As I would not be of much use in rough country with my arm strapped to my side, I was given charge of the remainder of the Field Ambulance, with all transport, horses and camels. Accordingly, together with the rest of the Brigade transport and the horses of the three regiments, we proceeded back to El Kubab in order to bivouac for the night. This place was on a considerable hill on the main road from Jaffa to Jerusalem, and it was interesting to examine the trenches, now two and a half years old, which had been dug by the Turks in 1915, when they feared the possibility of an Allied landing at Jaffa and consequent march on Jerusalem.

December 2nd.

Soon after dawn we were on the move, and descended the road to Ramleh ; the latter appeared to have some fine buildings, particularly the well-known clock-tower, and was known in Biblical times as Arimathea. Leaving this town on our left, we marched across country, through cultivated fields, to the neighbourhood of Ludd, and bivouacked in the adjoining village of Surafend ; however, on account of watering difficulties, as the horses of three Brigades had been congregated at the latter spot, we moved at dusk into the olive grove just outside Ludd itself. Here also there were certain difficulties in connection with the water supply, and being the only M.O. with the Brigade, it fell to me to make arrangements about drinking water, and also to procure water for the horses and camels in the unit, of which I was now in charge. It was always necessary on these occasions to have a totally different watering place for the camels, as horses would never drink from the same source ; the camels, however, were obliging in that they only required a drink once every three days.

During the next two weeks we remained camped in the olive grove outside Ludd with all the horses belonging to our Brigade, while the latter was fighting in the hills to the north. It was hard work for our men in the plain, as each had six horses to groom, water, feed and exercise, and, as usual, the old septic-sore trouble made its appearance again. We sent up supplies daily to our Field Ambulance, and for the time being lived in comparative comfort in the olive grove. At this time railhead was near Gaza, and one had to send a considerable distance in order to fetch remounts, reinforcements or new equipment. In this Palestine campaign it always seemed that the private soldier required a good deal of initiative apart from fighting, owing to the lack of communications and the great area over which at this time our force was spread. I remember sending two A.S.C. drivers with orders to proceed to Gaza, a distance of 42 miles across country, via Yebna, Burka, Beit Duras, Mejdal, and Deir Sineid, in order to bring up some fresh waggons, with remounts and drafts. At that time there was no road properly connecting these places, and the men had instructions to water wherever it was possible and to make their own arrangements *en route*. For some reason or other we suffered very much at this time from a match famine ; the former were not required for smoking, as we had had no tobacco ration for a considerable time, but the question of fire for kindling purposes was becoming acute. When we had had this trouble at Latron there was always the holy fire in the monastery of the Penitent Thief which could be utilized ; this fire was said to have been burning continuously for some thousand or more years, and an Australian Light Horse trooper was heard to remark that it was about time someone blew it out ! We were now well into the rainy season, and our olive grove became a bog, and most of the roads in the vicinity became impassable for wheels, which had a bad effect on the arrival of our rations. We felt this ration shortage particularly at the time, as reinforcements kept arriving from Gaza to be attached to the Field Ambulance without any warning, having expended their own three days' rations *en route*. Owing to the large number of dead horses and camels in the vicinity of Ludd, the jackals, as usual, made the night hideous with their shrieks and laughter. The old town of Ludd was of considerable interest, especially the early Christian church of St. George. On December 10th we heard that Jerusalem had surrendered, and the Jews and Greeks living in Ludd were hilarious in their rejoicings. On the following day the Fifty-fourth Division, who were fighting in the north, to the west of our line, were attacked, but drove the enemy back; this was followed by heavy artillery fire on both sides. During our stay in the olive grove Fritz visited the neighbourhood of Ludd daily, and we witnessed some good air fights. On one occasion a motor-lorry was entering Ludd from Ramleh; the two drivers were buying oranges at a neighbouring stall, and while so doing some natives commenced to loot the contents of the lorry. Fritz came over, dropped his bomb, and killed the natives, obviously a just punishment for the latter. One morning the Third Australian Light Horse Brigade in their camp at Surafend suffered considerably, having eighty horses killed while at water. The Anzac Receiving Station, which had been at Ramleh, was moved at this time, and we now had to send back 42 miles to Deir Sineid for our medical stores. The camels did not do well in the wet weather, and most mornings one was informed by the sergeant in charge of these animals that another one had " passed away " in the night. After being about ten days in this camp we found that a Turkish long-range gun was beginning to drop an occasional shell at the end of our plantation, and therefore we moved to a more salubrious and drier position on the sand, closer to the Ludd road. Reports received from our Brigade in the line stated that things were fairly quiet, except for sniping, and casualties were not numerous. A rumour was current that 40,000 Bulgars were on their way down to our front. On December 13th we received an interesting summary of intelligence compiled by Desert Mounted Corps Headquarters. This told us all about the surrender of Jerusalem, and of the fighting which had recently been going on outside the Holy City. The Turkish newspapers stated that as a result of the Russian peace 40,000 Turkish troops were on their way down to Palestine from the Caucasus. On December 15th the whole of the Brigade led horses and transport, together with a comparatively small number of officers and O.R.'s, left Ludd for Deiran ; as we rode out of the former town we could see the Fifty-fourth Division heavily engaged a few miles to the north. We took the road through Ramleh, crossing the Jaffa–Jerusalem road, and for the first mile or so our route lay amongst wheat and olive groves ; a little later we found ourselves riding through miles and miles of orange groves, heavily laden with fruit. These were the famous Jaffa oranges, and appeared to be cultivated most carefully. There were numerous nurseries where the trees could be seen in various stages, and a wonderful system of irrigation had been installed in the grove, consisting of large reservoirs, pumping engines, iron water-pipes and cement channels, the latter bifurcating in all directions in order to carry the water to every single tree. The earth was of a rich red colour, and the country-side also supported lemon groves, vineyards and almond fields. It seemed to us indeed a land of peace and plenty. Homely looking white farm-houses, with red-tiled roofs, peeped through the foliage, and cleanly dressed, fair-skinned European Jews came out of their houses as we passed. The largest oranges, of superb quality, were being sold at forty for a shilling, but there appeared at that time to be no objection to our men picking as many as they liked without payment. When one looked at these large orange farms and the cheerful well-fed European inhabitants, one could not help thinking with some amazement of the stories which had been circulated in the East, describing how the Turk had maltreated all but the Mohammedan population in Palestine. After riding for miles through these delightful surroundings, through air heavily scented with almond and orange blossom (we noted that the orange-tree flowered and bore fruit at the same time), the lane which we were traversing led out on to some open grassy country about half a mile west of the important Jewish settlement Deiran (Hebrew, Rehoboth). Here we each pitched our camp, and began to hope that the personnel of our various units would soon join us, when they were relieved on the hills, and enjoy the luxuries of this fertile plain. In the distance we could see excellent grazing for our horses, and across the down-like land to the south lay the raised town of Yebna and the villages of new and old Akir. That night several of us walked into Deiran, where we repaired to the " hotel " Kliwitzky, an excellent restaurant, kept by a Russian Jew. We had not sat down to a meal at a table with a tablecloth for many months, and here we enjoyed a most excellent five-course dinner, served up in a spotlessly clean way. Dinner was followed by two sorts of port wine, made by the Jews, which was very much appreciated. The village of Deiran appeared to be populated by Jews from nearly every European country, who controlled the extensive orange, wine and almond trade in this fertile district. The houses were well built and the inhabitants seemed prosperous. There was an excellent water supply and pumping station, the water being laid on to every house, a thing which seemed to us hardly conceivable in Palestine. While at dinner, many Jews came in and were anxious to inquire from us how things were going, especially those whose vine-yards and orange groves were north of Jaffa and still in the hands of the Turks. On the following day we visited the village again, and were very struck, in the daylight, with its picturesque aspect. With its large number of cypress-trees and white houses it reminded one of an Italian scene. We were delighted to find the Field Cashier, generally a very elusive person, whom we had not seen for many months, installed in the town hall. It was quite a strange feeling to be in a place again where money was of some use. We found Desert Mounted Corps Headquarters established in a very fine house, owned by the mayor, in the upper part of the village, and were allowed to study the large flag maps which showed the position of every unit on the Palestine front, including those belonging to the enemy. It seemed wonderful to us how the Intelligence people always managed to know where the various enemy units were situate, including those which were some way behind his front line. Between our camp and the village was a mighty winepress, in the central yard of which we found ample water for our horses. In one of the buildings connected with the winepress it was possible to utilize the numerous vats as baths for the men. During this time we only suffered from one shortage, that of wood. We sent our native camel-drivers out to scour the neighbourhood, but with little success. There were naturally strict orders against cutting down trees, as these were all fruit-bearing. Eventually the only way we could obtain sufficient wood was to steal it from the supplies of wood captured on the railway near Ludd ; these were carefully guarded, but still there were ways of obtaining it. The weather was now very wet, and the mortality amongst the camels and native camel-drivers increased. Although we had no tents, we were able to keep ourselves fairly dry with our bivouac sheets by digging into the side of the hills. South of our camp lay the Yebna–Mughar plain, where the Sixth Mounted Brigade made their famous charge. Standing on the Mughar Ridge and looking down on the plain beneath, it seemed almost inconceivable why the Turkish machine guns on the summit, aided by about 2,000 infantry, were unable to repel the yeomen's charge about a month previously. During these days we used to evacuate our casualties due east cross-country to Junction Station. Owing to the state of the road it became necessary to use eight mules for one light ambulance waggon, and it took them almost a day to complete the journey one way. On December 20th some interesting and amusing Intelligence was published :

An Armenian connected with the Patriarchate in Jerusalem stated that Ali Fuad Pasha, G.O.C. Twentieth Corps, said that he would defend the town to the last. Constantinople, however, thanked him for his patriotism and courage, and told him to evacuate it. A reliable commercial traveller saw Falkenhayn and Von Kress at Nablus. A cabdriver gave valuable information about the roads north and east of Jerusalem. The clerk to a contractor at Rijm Bahr reported great grain transit across the Dead Sea by motor-boats and dhows. There appeared to be great concentration of troops and supplies between Jerusalem and the Dead Sea. From the diary of a Turkish artillery officer, a Divisional Order expressed regret that the O.C.'s 6th and 7th Regiments and their A.D.C.'s had deserted!

The enemy at this time opposite our Brigade were wearing our khaki and helmets.

During our stay near Deiran an order was received that all ponies captured by the various units during the recent advance must be handed over to Divisional Headquarters the excuse being that they might be infected with strangles, or other diseases. Of course, the inference (probably wrong) was that the Staff wished to have the pick of the nice little Arab ponies which some of us now possessed in addition to our chargers ; the former were most useful for carrying spare kit, and also for hacking purposes when we were not on the move. One day we suddenly received orders that the Corps Commander would inspect the horses of our Brigade in an hour's time. Amongst the horses of which I was in charge were some captured ponies, and it became necessary that these should be hidden at once. Our unit happened to be the first to be inspected, so after seeing the horse lines cleaned up, I sent our cooks out of camp with the ponies. Unfortunately, the former took the wrong direction, and met the Staff as they appeared over the hill. However, luck was with us : the ponies were not noticed, and returned to our lines after the inspection.

Railhead had now reached Esdud (Ashdod), and reinforcements and rations were fetched daily from this place. On December 22nd the Sikh Pioneers, followed by the Egyptian Labour Corps, made their appearance in the middle of our camp, and shortly afterwards an embankment appeared, as if by magic, across the valley.

On account of the very wet weather which we were

experiencing, our camels and camel-drivers suffered considerably. When the latter came up for their weekly pay, which they signed for by means of thumbmarks, being unable to write, they looked very wretched, and were continually asking when they would be sent back to Egypt.

The port wine made by the Jews in the neighbourhood was much appreciated in this cold weather, and I managed to secure about fifty litres for the Field Ambulance, of which we dispatched half to the personnel in the hills.

On Christmas Eve the railway had actually appeared in our camp, and it reminded us of Christmas Eve 1916, when we were bivouacked at Bittia, outside El Arish, in the pouring rain, under similar conditions. We had prepared all sorts of Christmas festivities, and were looking forward to a great dinner in one of the Deiran restaurants, when orders were received to proceed to Yebna on the morrow. In the evening the Corps chaplain held a service at Bethlehem, but only the chosen few representing Corps Headquarters were allowed to go up to Jerusalem in order to attend the service. Our reconnoitring party, which had been out to look at the " road " to Yebna, returned with gloomy reports, saying that even then it was almost impassable for wheels, and meanwhile the rain continued to come down in sheets, the lower part of our camping ground being under water. That night I received a stiff letter from our A.D.M.S., who was living some miles away, stating that he had been informed that our Brigade was drinking the water of Deiran unchlorinated—see orders, etc. The reply, however, was easy to formulate, as the water had already been passed by the D.D.M.S. of the Corps, and was being used by everyone, including the Corps Commander.

December 25th.

Many of us will never forget Christmas Day 1917 !

We woke to find the usual inky sky and pouring rain ; the latter had been falling heavily throughout the night, and the plains to the south resembled a great lake, with

the hill village of Yebna apparently rising from the
waters. About 10 a.m. the whole of the horses and
transport belonging to our Brigade left camp and proceeded towards Yebna. I soon found that the waggons
of the Field Ambulance were unable to follow the route
traversed by the rest of the Brigade, so arranged with
my transport sergeant to find an alternative track. We
crossed several small torrents, which appeared suddenly,
while the rain fell in buckets and the streams from the
hills were rapidly inundating the plain. We followed
what in dry weather was called a road, keeping the track
for the railway on our left. After passing through miles
of standing water, at the bad places having to put in
six or eight mules to a light waggon instead of four, the
road became impassable, the mud reaching above the
axles. We determined to turn back and try the sand-
dunes towards the sea, but by this time the water had
risen in that direction and we thought we should never
get out. Eventually, however, it was managed, in one
case it being necessary to use twelve mules at a time
to move a waggon, which was partly submerged, and
unfortunately would not float. We halted our unit about
a mile from Kubeibeh village, the tired horses refusing
to face the stinging rain. On reconnoitring, we found
the Warwicks crossing a swollen Wadi, which had washed
away the railway, and whose presence could not be discovered, as it was part of a great lake, until a horseman,
who was riding through two or three feet of water, became
suddenly submerged. It was an extraordinary sight:
several horses were swimming, and also men, some of
the former disappearing altogether and being drowned
in the swift current. The fact that each man was leading
four horses made things worse. We rode along to look
for a crossing lower down, but the water was rapidly rising,
the stream being now a quarter of a mile across. I
knew that four or five feet of water with an unknown
amount of mud underneath would mean the loss of all
my waggons, which would probably be carried away by
the swiftly flowing stream to the sea. On consulting

my map, it was discovered that the Wadi in question was described as dry! Meanwhile the three regiments, after crossing the first flood, had found another impassable river beyond. They were on an island, and the water was rapidly rising. Accordingly, they recrossed to our side, after several immersions and much swimming, leaving several abandoned limbers in the stream. The large stream which they had encountered appeared to be the Wadi Shellal, also marked as a dry watercourse! At this time one could actually see the water rising as the streams kept roaring down from the hills. Personally I gave it up as a bad job, and pitched our camp on a hill on which was situated the ancient tomb of Neby Kunda, behind Kubeibeh village. The rest of the Brigade rode on and tried a ford below the village—some of the Worcesters got over after swimming their horses, and the rest, realizing the danger of the rising water, remained on our side. Here we were at 7 p.m., Yebna only 2½ miles away, but two rapidly rising rivers between it and us ; food and forage were at Yebna, and there was none behind us. We knew that communication with Deiran was impossible, as by this time the track by which we had come during the day must have been entirely under water. Luckily each man carried two days' rations, but they, of course, were soaked, as most of us had been partly or wholly submerged.

We had several men who were collapsed after prolonged immersion in the water and who had to be resuscitated. Surrounding the tomb of Neby Kunda we found a considerable number of olive-trees, and I committed the unpardonable sin of ordering my men to cut these down for firewood, contrary to all regulations. There were very strict orders against cutting fruit-bearing trees for firewood, but in this case I felt that we were justified. What made my action seem worse was the fact that these trees were growing on holy ground. The rain continued to come down in sheets, but we, although wet through, managed to get some shelter under the waggons. Luckily I had got about thirty litres of the native port wine

which we had bought for our postponed Christmas festivities, and was able to issue it to the men with their
evening meal. The former worked out at half a pint
per man, and in spite of their miserable wet condition
it actually made them break into song as they sat round
the sizzling fire in the pouring rain. At midnight the
deluge still continued, and one began to wonder what
would happen if the floods rose still further on the
morrow.

December 26th.

During the early morning the rain abated, and at
7 a.m. a little blue sky could be seen. One realized
that if it stopped raining for a few hours the floods would
disappear as rapidly as they came. After breakfast, a
friend from the Gloucester Yeomanry came round and
said that the floods had subsided and that it might be
possible for our unit to reach Yebna. We rode out
about 2 miles through water about a foot deep, and
found that the worst crossings were now only about
four feet deep. An hour later we brought all the transport
out, and eventually, with the loss of the contents of one
waggon, successfully negotiated all the crossings and
entered Yebna by the old stone bridge over the Wadi
Katrah. The camels were very awkward, and when
they fell down in about four feet of water we had great
difficulty in preventing them from drowning. The narrow
streets of Yebna were themselves under water and very
congested with transport ; our Maltese cart on one
occasion became completely submerged in what must
have been in summer-time merely a depression of the
road, and it took many teams of mules, after the cart
had been located by feeling for it, to pull it out. About
midday we reached our camping ground, a mile south
of the town, between the Warwicks and the Gloucesters.
Reinforcements had arrived from Esdud (Ashdod), and
we dispatched waggons to draw supplies from that
place.

December 27th.

A considerable number of camels and natives went sick after their recent immersion, and some of them died during the next few days. Our own sick we evacuated to the New Zealand Field Ambulance at the Wadi Sukereir, but as the waggons were unable to cross the Wadi they went to Esdud instead. We found a large Turkish water-tank just outside the town, with a capacity of 30,000 gallons, which proved most useful as a water supply for our Brigade and other troops, as the water could be chlorinated in bulk and drawn off daily. We were warned that owing to several breakdowns on the railway line, on account of the floods, no stores were reaching railhead near Esdud and that we should all be on half rations for the next five days ; that meant a little less than one tin of bully beef and four biscuits a day ; no milk, tea, sugar or jam. On looking at a map of Ancient Palestine that evening, we noticed that we had crossed from Ephraim into Dan.

December 28th.

Owing to the very bad state of the roads and the difficulty in evacuating the sick towards railhead, I sent a mounted man via Mughar and Katrah to Junction Station to report whether that route would be practicable if no more rain fell. This proved possible, and for the next few days we were able to make use of this line of evacuation.

December 29th.

At this time we heard very little of our Brigade, who were still fighting in the hills, but gathered that they also had had a very uncomfortable time during the heavy rain. The Tenth Division had recently made an attack on our left, the Fifth Mounted Brigade advancing their position to Nalim and Shilta.

December 30th.

After dawn the enemy made a determined attack on the Fifty-third Division east of Bethlehem, and at the same time attacked the Sixtieth north of Jerusalem ; both attacks were repulsed, and in the former the enemy lost very heavily. Taking advantage of this, the whole of the western half of our line was advanced, including the part held by the Fifth Mounted Brigade. Now that the floods had gone down, the bodies of many dead Turks were washed down to us from the hills and exposed.

In the afternoon the Yebna Hounds (two and a half couples) met at Brigade Headquarters. A jackal was found in a small olive grove one mile west of the town. Hounds hunted him through several small enclosures separated by low banks and young cactus hedges to the flats near the Wadi Ferhar. The latter was crossed, not without some grief, and then the jackal was viewed making straight for the Wadi Tahranhat, 2 miles below the big stone Jaffa road bridge ; he then doubled back, and was eventually lost amongst the thick vegetation on the banks of the Wadi. On returning to camp we received orders to send up horses to the hills, in order to bring the Brigade down on the following day.

1918.

January 1st.

Unfortunately the rain commenced again, and we feared that the hill party might have our experience over again. A return was asked for as to the amount of transport required by each unit in order to move to Gaza. Everyone was very pleased at the prospect of a rest in moderate comfort.

January 2nd.

Terrific rain fell again during the night, and the whole Brigade rode in looking like drowned rats. As the Colonel of our Field Ambulance was with them, I handed over and returned to the regiment. We heard that all the three Cavalry Divisions were to proceed to Belah in order to re-equip and await reinforcements and remounts. On the following day our advance party went on, and we were joined by a battalion of French Colonial Infantry who were on their way up.

January 4th.

The Brigade marched over heavy going to Esdud, the ancient Ashdod, of which we could see very little. On crossing the Wadi Sukereir we came across part of the Anzac Mounted Division, who were just ahead of us. On the following day our route lay to El Mejdel, where we bivouacked on the sand-dunes near the ancient Askelon. We were getting out of the heavy country, and the roads were now considerably better.

January 6th.

After watering at the lake, we left Mejdel at 8 a.m. in a tremendous downpour. The latter at this time was not intermittent, but when it had once started continued all day. After riding through Burbera to Deir Sineid we halted at midday. Here we saw how our monitors had destroyed the Turkish railway bridge from the sea at an 8-mile range. Some large unexploded naval shells were lying about, also the remains of railway trains and ammunition dumps, which had apparently been very successfully bombed last November. We passed several French camps and French hospitals, crossing our old friend the Wadi Hesi by a big stone bridge.

At night we bivouacked about a mile east of Gaza, behind Ali Muntar, with an Indian Infantry Brigade. The rain continued to fall heavily during the night, and owing to our exposed position everyone was soaked to the skin.

January 7th.

In the morning we were awakened by the storm, and were painfully aware of the large hailstones which were falling. At about seven o'clock we saw a large waterspout coming towards us from the sea; it looked like a column of black smoke surrounded by fog and spray. Luckily, however, it did not burst on us, but dissolved farther inland. As we rode through the fields behind Gaza we noticed the large holes caused by our big guns, where the latter had shelled the roads along which the Turkish transport used to go. The cactus hedges, where not actually destroyed, had been torn to ribbons. The town itself was deserted and mostly in ruins, especially the bazaar quarter. The remains of some fine houses still stood in the upper town. South of Gaza we passed through the Turkish and British trench systems, and eventually reached the mighty Wadi Ghuzze ; the latter, owing to the recent heavy rain, was now a veritable torrent, but luckily we found that the newly erected wooden bridge had not been washed away. After fording what appeared to be another Wadi of considerable size, and rescuing one man who was nearly drowned, Belah was reached in the afternoon. Our advance party had secured a camping area between the lake and the sea, on a slight eminence from which we could see no less than nineteen other cavalry regiments camped around us. Everyone was very happy at being in comparative comfort again, and as we had known the place for over a year, it seemed almost like coming home.

During the next two months the Division remained at Belah, while reinforcements, remounts and equipment were sent up from the Base, and each regiment was brought up to strength again. Salvage parties were sent out to Gaza and worked daily, collecting wood and wire from the old Turkish defences. Every Brigade in the Corps held its own horse show, followed by Divisional horse shows, which caused the keenest competition amongst the various units. On January 20th an impressive Brigade Memorial Service was held for those who had fallen during the recent operations, and was followed by the " Last Post," played by the trumpeters of the Brigade. On the following day the Corps Commander inspected the three regiments and made a speech, thanking us for our work and detailing all the engagements in which we had taken part during the last three months. On one occasion some of us made an expedition to Gaza with the C.O., riding out to the British trenches, where we were met by a gunner officer who had been in charge of a heavy battery during the siege, and who was to show us round the various positions. As our rôle during the first and second Battles of Gaza had been on the right flank, and as we had been engaged at Huj when the third Battle of Gaza was being fought, we had never seen the town at close quarters, and were curious to see the various positions, about which we had heard so much. First we visited one of the tanks which the Turks had captured during the second battle and the various hills where the Fifty-third and Fifty-fourth Divisions had fought so gallantly. Then we rode on to Ali Muntar, the most commanding of the enemy's positions, the top of which had been literally removed by our gun fire. On this hill we noticed that several ancient tombs had been partly opened by the explosions of our shells, and one was very tempted to get to work with a pickaxe and make some wonderful discoveries ; however, the presence of certain unexploded shells, some partly and some completely buried in the ground, finally altered our intentions. We lunched under the hill amongst masses of spring flowers, while our horses grazed on the rich grass, thinking over the many battles which had taken place over these positions during the last three thousand years. The town of Gaza was next visited, which a year ago had been the second largest city in Palestine and was now deserted and mostly in ruins. In the upper town, however, the remains of some very fine buildings were still to be seen. We noticed that where houses still remained not a single door existed, as the timber from the latter had been utilized by the Turks in order to revet their trenches. The large mosque was found in ruins, and still showed signs of the enormous ammunition dump which it had contained.

During this period of rest at Belah, leave was freely given to Cairo, and was much enjoyed. The following story told of an Egyptian Labour Corps native amused us considerably. These natives were always anxious to get leave to return to Egypt, and used to send in applications, often in English, to their C.O.'s. The following is a sample of one of these letters : " Sir, my absence is impossible, some man has uprooted my wife, my God I am annoyed. Yours faithfully." About this time we heard that five Cavalry Divisions, British and Indian, were coming out to Palestine, to be replaced by some of our mounted troops, who would proceed dismounted to France ; consequently the wildest rumours were current as to the future movements of our various Brigades. As a matter of fact, eventually only part of the Indian Cavalry Corps arrived, and a few of our regiments were sent to France as machine gunners.

A two weeks' course for the M.O.'s of the Desert Mounted Corps was held at Moascar, near Ismailia, which many of us attended. We were made the guests of the Second Australian Light Horse Training Regiment, who entertained us most hospitably. The course included signalling, troop and squadron drill, veterinary lectures, reconnaissance, waggon loading, harness fitting, topography, map and compass reading, war diaries, staff organization, etc. ; the lecturer (a Staff officer) on the last named subject prefaced his address somewhat plaintively by saying that the Staff were not really such d——d fools as most people thought. Purely technical subjects, which we doctors were supposed to know about, were dealt with by some of the pupils, sanitation being the lecture which devolved on myself. Though the course was a short one, and rather too many subjects were crammed into it, it was very instructive and a pleasant respite for many of us. The pleasant little town of Ismailia was only a couple of miles distant, with its excellent French club, whose cooking was very much appreciated after the somewhat crude fare we had been accustomed to. While attending the course we had an opportunity of seeing the Duke of Connaught decorating the Seventh (Meerut) Division, which had recently left Mesopotamia and was on its way up to replace the Fifty-second Division before Jaffa, as the latter Division was under orders for France.

On returning to Belah I found that " hunting " was in full swing, the Belah Hounds (Fifth Mounted Brigade) meeting three days a week south of the Wadi, while the Gaza Hounds (Twenty-second Mounted Brigade) hunted the country to the north. The hounds consisted chiefly of terriers and native dogs, but the Sherwood Rangers actually possessed one couple of foxhounds. As a rule the jackal had to be finally dispatched by one of the whips before hounds would break him up, which made the end of the hunt somewhat tame. On one occasion a jackal was hunted from a fig grove outside our camp to Ali Muntar, where he went aground in an old tomb, the distance traversed being about 7 or 8 miles. On March 16th the Seventh Brigade held a most successful steeplechase meeting over the grassy country just outside Gaza, issuing invitations to all the units in the vicinity. Our C.O. drove our H.Q. Mess over in a coach (light ambulance waggon) drawn by four horses, our trumpeter-major tootling the horn. Even at this stage of the war a certain number of horses well known in the Midlands turned out to compete. The course was a good one, and regulation fences had been erected. The race of the day, the Palestine Grand National, which had last year been run just before the Battle of Rafa, was again secured by a horse owned by a Warwickshire squadron leader. On one Sunday several of us rode out to Tel El Jemmi and picnicked at El Mendur, riding on to El Munkeileh, where we had fought the second Battle of Gaza almost a year ago. The place was a mass of beautiful wild flowers, and one could hardly realize the scenes that had been enacted there last April. Near Tel El Jemmi we visited the graveyard where our fallen had been subsequently buried. Riding back through Sheikh Nebhan, some Australians showed us a sixth-century Greek mosaic which had been uncovered at Abu Teibig. There was much talk in these days about the " gap " scheme, as it was rumoured that a Cavalry

Division was to be pushed somewhere through the enemy's line after the infantry had made an opening.

We were now getting excellent rations, being on the railway at Belah, so far behind the line. The natives supplied us with plenty of fish, which they obtained by exploding charges amongst the rocks. Unfortunately, however, the Intelligence people discovered that these Bedouin were using German dynamite, of which they had a large supply, for their fishing operations, and successfully put a stop to this item of our menu. The natives, while being interrogated by our General, were heard by one of our officers, who understood Arabic, to say, pointing to the former : " By Allah ! he must be a great man, for he hath the scissors on his shoulders." On March 26th the Division was warned that it would be moved up shortly, and on the same day two of us M.O.'s received orders to report at Corps Headquarters, Deiran, in order to attend a malaria course at the Anzac Field Laboratory. We left forthwith and travelled by train, accompanied by some French officers, through the country which we had last seen under water and which was now in its normal condition. There being at this time no station at Deiran, we left the train at Bir Salaam, which was the station for G.H.Q., to which place the French officers were proceeding. G.H.Q. was to us regimental officers always a considerable mystery, and one was supposed not to know where it was. However, on this occasion the car which had been sent to fetch us from Desert Corps Headquarters actually drove past the " Holy of Holies," and after traversing devious lanes, up and down hill, through most fragrant orchards of lemon, apricot, fig and orange, growing in the rich red earth which one used to see in this neighbourhood, we emerged eventually at the now well-known village of Deiran and were taken to the Anzac Field Laboratory. This laboratory was a mobile unit, and was at the time situated in a large two-roomed farm-house on the outskirts of the village, and was in charge of an eminent Australian bacteriologist, who, sad to relate, a few months later himself died of malignant malaria, the very disease in which he gave us instruction. At this time the higher medical authorities were alarmed at the prospect of the very malarial country into which we should shortly advance. We were told that the country to the north of Jaffa possessed many malarial patches, and that the Jordan Valley and the neighbourhood of Damascus were very dangerous. In these places the malarial mosquito abounded, and there was a very highly infected native population. For these reasons as many M.O.'s as possible were given a rapid course of instruction at the laboratories of the various Corps, in order that they might be in a position to make a definite diagnosis directly a man fell sick. It was known that in the cerebral type of malignant malaria the first symptom was often loss of consciousness, and a definite diagnosis could only be rapidly established by means of a blood film. About a month later we had a case of this sort, a man previously apparently well suddenly falling off his horse in a state of coma. At this time we heard of the first raid to Es Salt—how the Sixtieth Division and the Anzac Division, after crossing the Jordan, had captured that place and had also partly destroyed the Hedjaz Railway near Ammam.

During our stay at the laboratory we had an opportunity of studying the various sorts of Jews in the village. They apparently spoke all the European languages, except the Yeminite Jews, who were copper-coloured, and were said to have come originally from Aden, and who lived in a little colony outside Deiran. These Yeminites, although of Semitic appearance and professing the Jewish religion, seemed to be of a different caste to the white Jews, and apparently did all the hard labour for the latter in the vineyards and orchards. Towards the end of March the Feast of the Passover commenced, and the inhabitants of the village were all decked out in their best. About April 3rd some of the Anzac Division returned through Deiran, and we heard how they had retired from Ammam after blowing up 4 miles of railway. It appeared that the Circassians in the villages near the latter place were very hostile, and on one occasion had to be almost exterminated by our force, as the former used to fire from their houses on passing troops. These tribes from the Caucasus were very friendly to the Turks because, being Mohammedans, after being badly treated by the Russians in Georgia some years ago, the enemy had allowed them to settle in the fertile district east of the Jordan Valley.

During the Feast of the Passover a considerable number of Jewish volunteers were recruited, and enrolled themselves in the town hall. On the following day there was much weeping and lamentation as they marched away.

On April 7th, although our course was not quite completed, an Australian officer and myself received orders to rejoin our Division, which had recently marched up from Belah to the Jaffa front. Accordingly, at midday we left Deiran in a box car, and driving through Richon, a Jewish village situated in the most famous wine-growing district of Palestine, proceeded along the Jaffa road to Yasur, and thence over the downs to the Selme district, where we found our Division encamped behind the infantry line. The Warwickshire Yeomanry had left for France, and their place was temporarily taken in our Brigade by the Sherwood Rangers. Our Division had apparently been lent to the Twenty-first Infantry Corps for the forthcoming operations. The latter consisted of the Fifty-second (later Seventh), Fifty-fourth, and Seventy-fifth Divisions, and held the line in front of the Auja estuary, north of Jaffa, to within about 10 miles of Bire. Apparently the idea was that the infantry should make a gap in the enemy's line about 8 miles from the sea, and that the Cavalry Division should then be thrown in, gallop about 10 miles, turn left-handed, and attack the enemy force on the sea sector, which they would catch in their rear. It was said that after these operations had been concluded the Fifth Mounted Brigade would be reorganized, and would consist of the Gloucester Yeomanry and two Indian cavalry regiments, and that

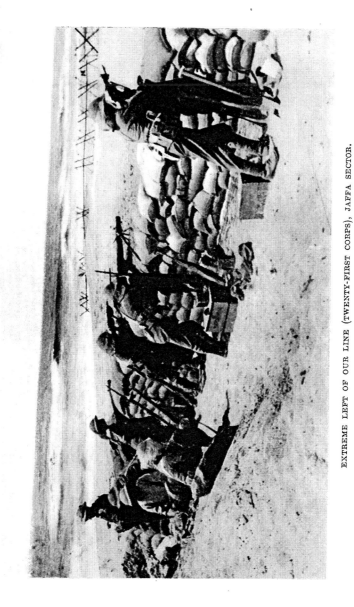

EXTREME LEFT OF OUR LINE (TWENTY-FIRST CORPS), JAFFA SECTOR.

(By permission of the Imperial War Museum.)

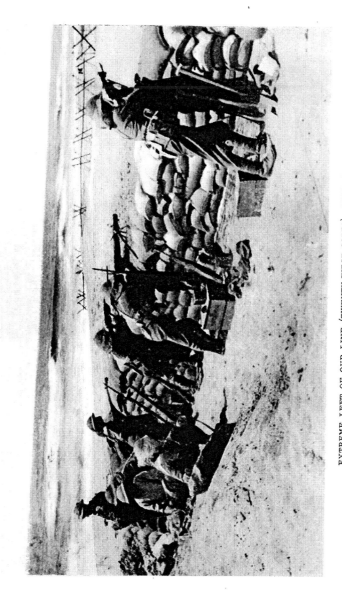

EXTREME LEFT OF OUR LINE (TWENTY-FIRST CORPS), JAFFA SECTOR.

(By permission of the Imperial War Museum.)

the Worcesters would be attached as Corps cavalry to the Twentieth Corps in the Jordan Valley. Our bivouac was a pleasant one, the country being covered with grass, dust being almost completely absent. A Taube was shot down near our camp during the afternoon, and it was said that fifty-seven had been brought down in the last three months. At night the batteries of the Twenty-first Corps were kept busy. On the following morning some of us rode out to a slight eminence known as Bald Hill, which had been the scene of some heavy fighting, as shown by the graves on it, a few months ago, whence we had a fine view of part of the line held by the Twenty-first Corps. Bearings were taken on various points, and landmarks were identified ; below us lay the village of Mulebbis, with its little red-roofed houses, set amongst the trees, and beyond it on the right we could see the old Crusader fortress of Ras El Ain, which at this time constituted part of our front line. The Turkish railway almost up to this point was in our hands. Our shells could be seen exploding in the Turkish lines, and we identified the villages of Jiljulieh and Kalkilieh, with Kefr Kasim and Mejdel Yaba on our right. During the night the right-hand division of the Corps made an advance in the hills after a preliminary bombardment. On the following day the enemy counter-attacked, but were driven back. In the morning two of us rode through miles of beautiful orange and lemon groves and through orchards bordered by eucalyptus and pepper trees into Jaffa. It was an interesting and picturesque town, which had benefited by most of the modern improvements. All the guards of the various public buildings were supplied by French and Egyptian regiments. Just outside the town, along the coast to the north, was the flourishing German colony of Sarona, containing many large houses amongst the orange groves. On the morning of April 10th the " gap " scheme was explained to us, and times and places were noted ; the general idea was not prepossessing, and we were told that no medical arrangements need be made for our regiments by ourselves, as what was left of it was to gallop right through the " gap " and not halt until El Tireh, beyond Tabsor, was reached. We were not to stop for casualties, as they were to be left where they fell, and might be picked up later on if the position was consolidated. A few light ambulance waggons were to gallop through after us, but they also were not to halt until El Tireh was reached; but it seemed highly probable that they would be smashed up long before that, especially as they would have to gallop over the trenches, which our Brigade hoped to jump. On the following morning we lined a ridge with guns, near our camp, while the Gloucester Yeomanry and Sherwood Rangers " discovered " us, and then charged with drawn swords, we opening out at the last moment. Thus the " gap " scheme was practised in a very different way from what we really expected. It was said at midday that operations had been postponed owing to the Seventy-fifth Division meeting with a very stiff resistance. About this time the mounted troops had received their first tin hats, and most of us found them very hot in the heat of the day.

April 12th.

An officer from an observation balloon, who lunched with us, told us that the Turks had some two hundred guns in the vicinity of the position where the gap would be made. That afternoon we M.O.'s received final Medical Corps orders with regard to the attack on Jiljulieh and Kalkilieh. The Divisional Collecting Station was to be at the latter place, the Divisional Receiving Station at K. Hatta, and the Twenty-first Corps Main Dressing Station at Neby Tari; the first two places, it was noted, were well within the enemy's lines. Most people in our Division were very pessimistic about success; the general opinion was that, even if the infantry did make a gap, the greater part of the Third, Fourth and Fifth Mounted Brigades would be sacrificed; if successful, the enemy's right flank might be turned and caught between us and our infantry on the sea

sector. It seemed a needless sacrifice of our troops
at this stage, with so little to gain—even if 7,000
Turks were captured it was estimated that our losses
would be very great, partly owing to the strength of
the enemy's artillery. The Turks had got their tails
up after the recent German advance and their own
advance near Jericho. There were some nasty stories
about the inhabitants of the Arab villages through which
we should gallop ; these people did not love us, as they
had been under our shell fire for some considerable time,
and one could not help thinking that the lot of our
wounded who were left behind might be a very unpleasant
one. On April 13th the attack was again postponed, and
a new " Z " day was fixed, owing to the infantry being held
up again and suffering heavy casualties. Our officers'
patrols rode out to Mejdel Yaba and did some useful
reconnaissance. On the following day we were informed,
much to my personal relief, that the " gap " scheme
was off. It was said that the Higher Command did not
consider that they were justified in incurring so many
casualties, at a time when we were short of troops on
this front, in order to attain such a relatively small
success. This attack had been discussed and rediscussed
for so many days by all ranks, that many of us were getting quite depressed at the idea of it. In the afternoon
several of us indulged in football, feeling that we had
taken a new lease of life, while an air fight went on
overhead, which was not nearly so exciting to us as
the football match. On April 17th our Divisional and
Brigadier Generals said good-bye to the regiment on
parade, as the Division was about to be split up. That
evening we said good-bye to the many good friends we
had been associated with for many years.

April 18th.

The regiment marched from camp at 7 a.m., riding
past the Gloucester Yeomanry and Sherwood Rangers
Yeomanry, who gave us a good-bye cheer. So ended
the old First South Midland Mounted Brigade, which

15

had existed many years prior to the war, of the Gloucester, Warwick and Worcester Yeomanries, the Warwick R.H.A., and the First South Midland Mounted Brigade Field Ambulance ; later, on formation of the old Second Mounted Division in August 1914, the Warwick R.H.A. were replaced by " B " Battery H.A.C., and thenceforward we were known simply as the First Mounted Brigade. After Gallipoli we became the Fifth Mounted Brigade ; after the Battle of Romani our regiment became a kind of Corps cavalry to the Desert Column, when the latter still contained Infantry Divisions. After the Battle of Rafa, on the formation of Desert Mounted Corps, the Brigade was part of the Imperial Mounted Division, which consisted of the Fifth and Sixth Mounted Yeomanry Brigades and the Third and Fourth Australian Light Horse Brigades. Soon after the second Battle of Gaza the Australian Mounted Division came into being, and consisted of the Third and Fourth Australian Light Horse Brigades and the Fifth Mounted Brigade. But to-day the old Brigade had ceased to exist : the Warwicks were at that moment *en route* for France (they were submarined outside Alexandria and suffered heavy losses, including their Commanding Officer, who was formerly one of our majors), the Gloucester Yeomanry were about to be brigaded with two Indian regiments, our Field Ambulance was to be attached to an Indian Brigade, and the Worcester Yeomanry were to become Corps cavalry to General Sir Philip Chetwode, who commanded the Twentieth Corps, with Headquarters at Jerusalem. We all felt the parting very much, as we had many old friends in the other two regiments, with whom we had been in close contact for the last four years.

After watering near Selme, we rode along the dusty Jaffa road to Ramleh, where we met large numbers of British and Indian infantry detraining near Ludd, chiefly units of the Seventh Division, which were taking over from the Fifty-second Division on the sea sector before Jaffa. This was the time of year when the country looked its fairest, as it had benefited by the winter rain and had not yet suffered from the really hot sun. At midday we halted in a small green Wadi full of the most beautiful flowers, those known as the Rose of Sharon predominating ; it was right that we should find these in such profusion, as we were riding along the valley from which the flower takes its name. Passing through El Kubeb, the unit descended to Latron and bivouacked near the old monastery on the road which leads up the pass to Jerusalem ; everything was very peaceful and different to the last time that we had approached this valley, when shells were bursting on the road and the Seventy-fifth Division were scaling the hills on either side. An enormous donkey camp occupied our former site ; these donkeys were at this time used in thousands to supply the Infantry Divisions in the mountains with rations and water.

April 19th to 25th.

The regiment received orders from the Twentieth Corps, under whom we now were, to remain at Latron until further notice. At midday two of us rode out to Abu Shushar (the Biblical Gezer), where the Sixth Brigade had charged and taken 2,000 prisoners last year. Some very interesting cave-dwellings were to be seen, probably relics of the Stone Age. It was near here, so rumour had it, that the prophets had been taken and hidden by fifties in a cave. The whole of one side of the hill was honeycombed with tombs, hewn into the solid rock, the former being approached by narrow passages, often blocked with a large stone, and each containing one or two chambers, with stone coffins ranged round the sides. On another occasion the monastery of St. John of Latron was visited. This was the birthplace of the Penitent Thief. There was a fine monastery garden (which supplied fruit and vegetables to the Twentieth Corps H.Q.), and the cool stone buildings included refectory, chapel, cloisters, cells and library ; in the latter place there were many old books, the best of which had been already looted.

Unfortunately for us, the wine in the extensive cellars had also been looted during the enemy occupation. The French Trappist monks, who had been expelled by the Turks, were now returning to occupy the monastery, which had been used by the Turks as an Agricultural College during the last three years. We arranged for the men to have baths in the enormous wine vats, as a plentiful supply of water was at hand. Later we climbed a hill, on whose summit was an ancient Crusader castle, which guarded the entrance to the Latron Valley, which led up to the Jerusalem pass. During the next few days we improved our camp, and were inspected by our Corps Commander. It was thought that we should now have a " cushy " time, living on the fat of the land, and merely providing a few escorts and patrols asked for by the Twentieth Corps. We were also told that being directly under Corps orders, all our indents for rations, stores and equipment would now be complied with without the slightest delay, as they would not have to pass through so many channels ; this, however, proved to be wrong. On April 24th we suddenly received orders to proceed with the Gloucester Yeomanry and Sherwood Rangers to Jerusalem on the following day. It appeared that two Divisions of cavalry were being hurried across the Jordan on account of certain Arab developments, and it was said that if a considerable number of mounted troops could join the Arabs on the Hedjaz Railway the Composite Force would be joined by all the tribes in the vicinity and would have an open road to Damascus. On the following day the temporarily reformed Fifth Mounted Brigade proceeded up the pass to Kuryat Enab, where we bivouacked just below the village.

April 26th.

Arrangements were made for pack transport for the whole Brigade, as the country through which we were about to traverse would not permit of wheels. At 6 p.m., now four regiments strong, we rode out through Beit Nakaba, Kulonie, and Lifta to Jerusalem. It was a wonderful mountain road, parts of which we had traversed some months ago, and was in some places cut into the side of the mountain, with often a clear drop of hundreds of feet to some little village, whose lights we could see twinkling in the valley below. Convoys of motor-lorries coming down the pass made things rather uncomfortable for us mounted troops, especially when the precipice was on the right side. It was full moon, and the effect, as we climbed higher and higher, with the extraordinary shadows cast on the deep valleys, was very weird and beautiful. Miles ahead we could see our column wending its serpentine or zigzag course as the road steadily mounted to the Jerusalem plateau (2592). Although our patrols last year had been in the vicinity of the Holy City just before its capture, none of us had actually been there, and we were all naturally very anxious to see it. At 9.30 p.m. we reached the outskirts of the city, and, leaving the Jaffa Gate on our right, passed through the modern town just outside the ancient turreted walls. After descending a hill we passed Calvary and the Garden of Gethsemane, and then rode along another mountain road through a couple of small villages until the Mount of Olives was reached. It seemed a pity that we, who had been longing to see Jerusalem for the last three years, at our first visit had to pass through the town at a sharp trot by midnight. We halted for an hour at Bethany, which, owing to its exposed position and altitude, was bitterly cold ; however, fires were lit, tea was made, and we felt ready to continue our journey, many of us walking and leading our horses in order to get warm. The change in the temperature from the orange groves of Jaffa, which we had recently left, to the heights of Jerusalem was very marked. Soon after midnight we commenced our descent towards the Dead Sea Valley, dropping 1,000 feet between 12 and 2 a.m.

April 27th.

We were now on the historic Jericho road, a marvel of ancient engineering—at times cut into the face of the hills, and at others carried by an enormous causeway over a valley. The country grew bleaker and gloomier as we descended ; the mountains appeared in the moonlight to have huge gashes and clefts, as if some giant had deliberately hacked pieces out. We were in a sleepy condition, and had the weirdest impressions ; we seemed to be descending into a sort of Inferno, where nothing grew in the desolate surroundings. At 3 a.m. the ruined caravanserai of Talat El Dumm was reached, known as the inn of the Good Samaritan, as that episode is authentically stated to have occurred here. Talat El Dumm, translated, means " the Hill of Blood." The Brigade bivouacked a little lower down the valley, and everyone fell asleep on the hard rocks. On waking a few hours later we found that our camp was on the sloping rocky ground, just above the Jerusalem–Jericho road, with the frowning bleak mountains in the background. The enormous clefts which we had seen the night before seemed to have disappeared, and they were evidently a delusion caused by the moonlight. At midday the heat became terrific, as our camp was on solid rock surrounded by mountains, and after climbing about 500 feet one had a wonderful view of the Dead Sea, Jordan Valley and Jericho, about 2,800 feet below. An hour later the whole Brigade marched down the road towards the Dead Sea level, dropping from 1,180 feet above sea-level to 1,200 feet below sea-level—a drop of nearly 2,400 feet in eight miles. After proceeding a short distance we took the old Roman, somewhat precipitous, road to the left, while the guns continued by the new Turkish and longer route on the right. The road was rough, and in many cases on the edge of a precipice, at the bottom of which we could see dead camels and transport which had toppled over. Amongst the rocks I noticed a wonderful fossilized tree-trunk, apparently almost complete. At times we saw enormous clefts in the rock which opened into valleys, extending down to the Dead Sea. The remains of a Roman aqueduct, which used to take the water from the mountains to

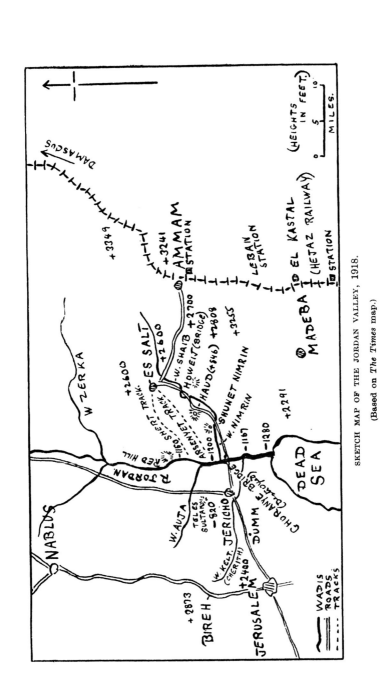

SKETCH MAP OF THE JORDAN VALLEY, 1918.

(Based on *The Times* map.)

the Jericho plain, built into the sides of the valley, was also seen. In one of the above-mentioned clefts, which contained at the bottom the commencement of the Brook Cherith, now called the Wadi Kelt, were two hermits' houses, some 500 feet above the stream, with a giddy path leading down to the plains. Each of these habitations had been made by hewing away the face of the rock and was surmounted by a white cross. They reminded one of the stories in Sir Walter Scott's *Talisman*. At about 5 p.m. we emerged on to the Dead Sea plain, and immediately noticed the great heat after descending from the mountains. We found the Anzac Division Receiving Station on the site of Roman Jericho, close to the remains of Herod's castle : before us lay modern Jericho, now a mere village, and on the right the Dead Sea, as blue as any Italian lake, with frowning mountains to the east and west and the Jordan estuary to the north. We proceeded northwards, raising clouds of the acrid white dust which is one of the curses of the Jordan Valley, over the ruins of pre-Roman Jericho, passing on the left a large Greek monastery, which had been built into the side of the mountain some 500 feet above the track, the former being the Mount of Temptation, on which Our Lord was said to have been tempted by Satan. At first sight the monastery looked inaccessible, but on riding up to it one observed that there was a path up from the plains. This monastery appeared to be the only sign of civilization in this desolate place, and the chapel bell, which at that moment played its chimes, seemed a great contrast to our surroundings. We bivouacked north of the hill known as Tel Es Sultan, some miles west of the Jordan and south of its confluent Wadi Auja. A few small shells greeted us on arrival, but owing to the dusk we were not quite clear whether they came from one of our mountain batteries, which was said to be practising, or from the Turks ; in any case it was not worth while investigating the matter, as we were very tired after our long march, and we knew that there was an outpost line in front of us. The night was a hot one, and one could not help contrasting it with the previous night, when we had been shivering round the fires on the Mount of Olives. It was noticeable that soon after the sun had set a peculiarly unpleasant aroma seemed to be emitted from the ground, apparently due to sulphurous deposits in the latter.

April 28th.

During the morning one began to realize the extreme heat and discomfort of this Jordan Valley in the summer. There appeared to be no breeze until the afternoon, and the atmosphere seemed to weigh heavily upon one. The ground was dry and arid, and seemed to abound in tarantulas and scorpions. One wondered what this district would be like in July and August, when it was already so hot at the end of April. Our horses were taken back twice a day to the spot where the Wadi Kelt (Brook Cherith) emerged into the plains, for watering purposes. Across the Jordan we could occasionally see our shells exploding in the Turkish lines, and our own patrols, who had crossed the river, being shelled. In the evening some of us walked up towards the Imperial Camel Corps trenches to our north, and, climbing some hills near the Wadi Auja, actually found some signs of life, seeing a few hares and some sand-grouse ; the latter evidently were able to exist amongst the vegetation which bordered the banks of the Wadi.

April 29th.

At midday our plan of attack was explained and a conference of M.O.'s was also held. At 8 p.m., completely enveloped in clouds of thick pungent dust, the Brigade left camp and, passing through New Jericho, proceeded down towards the Jordan, making for the El Ghoraniye crossing. The latter was a few miles above the Dead Sea, and at this point the river ran very rapidly in a deep Wadi, bordered at the base of the cliffs by verdant foliage, which was almost tropical in character. As we approached the river-bed our road wound through weirdly shaped

THE JORDAN NEAR EL GHORANYE.

rocks, which had probably at some time been so fashioned when the mighty river was in flood, or possibly they were partly volcanic in origin. After crossing the pontoon bridge, which had been built by our infantry some months ago under heavy fire, we reached the Ghoraniye bridge-head, and, passing through our wire and outposts, halted west of Tel El Nimrim, near the stream of that name. We were told that just before dawn part of the Sixtieth Infantry Division, which held the bridge-head, would attack Nimrim, and while this diversion was in progress our Division would gallop some 6 miles along the east bank of the Jordan, under cover of the hills which the Turks held, and would then bear right-handed up the steep mountains towards the Hedjaz Railway. Perfect silence reigned, as it was hoped that the Turks were not aware of our intentions.

April 30th.

We were moved up closer to the enemy soon after midnight, but luckily were not spotted. At 3 a.m. the Sixtieth Division suddenly attacked Nimrim, and a pandemonium broke out on both sides. The enemy sent up their Verey lights and star-shells, and the crack of the rifles and the explosions of hand grenades added to the din caused by the guns. Just before dawn we were ordered to mount, and then galloped some 4 miles across the enemy's guns, who suddenly became aware of us in the half-light and started to shell the Division, which was galloping by regiments. Luckily, however, we were riding in very extended order and suffered little. As it got light we arrived at the entrance to what was known as the Um Esh Shert–Es Salt track, which was successfully seized. The Divisional Collecting Station was later in the day located at this point, with the Divisional Receiving Station at Ghoraniye. We were now in the foothills, and suffered a little from enemy snipers on the peaks to the north. As we ascended, the track became steeper and steeper, and for several hours everyone had to lead his horse along the narrowest goat-track. This and another track to the south were the only ways of approaching Es Salt, as the Turks held the highroad through Shunet Nimrim to Jericho. Meanwhile the rest of the Division, less one regiment, which was ascending the track on our right, swept on to the north amongst the foothills, whilst the Anzac Mounted Division co-operated on the other side of Shunet Nimrim. After climbing about 3,000 feet we found ourselves in the clear atmosphere again, which was a pleasant change compared with the Jordan Valley, and we were able to see Jerusalem to the west, with the Dead Sea far below us. We had a few casualties, caused by snipers on the opposite heights, and on one occasion I had to make a detour of some miles up and down hill over unrideable country in order to reach one of our men who had ascended by a different path. On arrival we found him dead, but owing to the very rocky nature of the ground it was impossible to bury him. However, his companions covered him with a wealth of the most beautiful flowers, and built a rough tomb with the large rocks which were lying about. A little later I found myself with one of our machine guns, and watched them pick off an enemy machine gun detachment on an opposite hill, some 1,000 yards away, a tremendous valley intervening. We had now lost the rest of the unit, as the latter was very scattered, and as it was impossible to ride by compass bearing upon Es Salt, on account of the very broken ground, we joined the mountain battery which was attached to our Brigade. Our own R.H.A. battery, together with the others belonging to the Division, had remained in the foothills, where they were attacked and lost heavily the following day, as they were unable to get their guns up the goat-tracks. The mountain battery, however, which carried its guns on sturdy little mules, was able to go almost anywhere. One could not help thinking that if we met the enemy with their field guns we should be at a considerable disadvantage with our one little battery. After climbing higher we passed through numerous small valleys, which were

thickly studded with flowers, enormous hollyhocks up to
twelve feet high and large oleander-trees preponderating.
At one moment an ibex flashed across our view, and now
and then a hare was disturbed. At length we reached
a fertile plateau, some 3,000 feet above the Dead Sea.
Here we fell in with the rest of our Brigade, and also
our two Meccan guides, who were supposed to lead us
to the Beni Sakhr tribe, who were in sympathy with the
Arab army from the Hedjaz. It appeared that the
Sherwoods had had the most casualties during our climb,
as they had rather drawn the enemy's fire by going up
the first (Arsenyat) track from the valley. Rumour had
it that Es Salt had fallen to an Australian Brigade, which
had advanced on our left; accordingly, at 1 p.m., after
watering our horses in the abundant streams, orders
were given to march on the town. Before us lay a defile
some miles long, which it was understood led almost
to our goal. Brigade Headquarters and the Gloucester
Yeomanry entered the valley, and we followed a little
later. Unfortunately some enemy machine guns, which
had been bothering us from across a valley during our
ascent, had not been completely disposed of, and as soon
as we had entered the valley we found ourselves under
fire from behind and on our right. For a time the
Sherwood Rangers, who were to follow us, were cut off,
and the head of our column appeared to be hemmed in
by other enemy machine guns. The position seemed
to be distinctly unfortunate, as we were hemmed in in
front and behind, and ascertained that Es Salt had not
fallen after all. It appeared to me that if the enemy
could direct any volume of fire into the defile our small
force might be annihilated. We found a wire running
from Es Salt to Nimrim and cut it, our patrols eventually
dealing with the enemy machine guns in our rear, and
thus allowing the Sherwood Rangers to join up with us.
Some wounded, however, with the bearer party of the
Field Ambulance were cut off, but managed to get down
the Um Shert track when night arrived. After riding
another 2 miles or so our defile opened out into a

considerable valley, and one felt able to breathe again. Strong patrols were put out at night around the sides and ends of the valley, but one still felt that in our packed condition the enemy might, with a few guns, end our existence. No fires were lit, but a comfortable night was spent lying in the luxuriant grass. We had a few prisoners with us, who were very uncommunicative, and it was decided to attack Es Salt, now about 2 miles distant, on foot at dawn.

May 1st.

We advanced to the attack at 5 a.m. in the half-light, climbing up the little terraced gardens which were built on the side of the hill. However, the First Squadron over the final ridge found the town evacuated, consequently the remainder of us rode down the Ammam road and entered Es Salt. It was picturesquely situated in a sort of ravine, and was of considerable size, a fine old arched bridge crossing a mountain torrent which ran through the centre of the town. The houses were well built, and were clustered together on the side of the hill. On arrival we found that there were still ten Germans and a Uhlan captain in a house with a machine gun, who gave considerable trouble until they were eventually subdued by one of our mountain guns. It is probable that these Germans were telephoning final news to their Headquarters at Ammam before surrendering. It was said that our Division had taken about 320 prisoners, and that the remainder of the force had escaped eastwards with Djemal Pasha to Ammam, and westwards to Nimrim, which had not yet fallen. We also captured some lorries full of 5·9 shells, and one or two motor-cars with their German drivers, which were useful to us later on for carrying wounded. We were now on a good road again, but both ends of it were held by the enemy. The inhabitants of Es Salt appeared to view us with suspicion ; they knew that the British had captured the town about two months previously, and then had been forced to evacuate it, and it was highly

probable that those natives who had then openly sided
with us had not been too well treated by the Turk on
his return. The British were now again in possession,
but this time the native was not going to take any risks,
although he was told that he might come under our
protection. After watering just below the town we
moved off down the Jericho road, along which some of
the Turks had escaped a short time before, and who
had now joined their garrison near Shunet Nimrim.
After riding a couple of miles we bivouacked at the side
of the valley overlooking the Wadi Shaib ; the latter was
a little mountain torrent which ran through Es Salt,
and then down along the valley on the left of the Jericho
road, finally joining the Nimrim brook and flowing into
the Jordan. Numerous small tributaries joined it on each
side, and every mile or so one came across a primitive
stone water-mill. The road was in our hands from Es
Salt to the spot where it crossed the Wadi Shaib by an
arched bridge at Howeij, the latter being the name of
a very strong position held by the enemy and successfully
blocking the road at this point. The bridge was mined,
and the hills on both sides of it were held by the Turks.
During the day there was some shelling and a little
sniping near the bridge, as our regiment was on outpost
duty, preventing the enemy from advancing farther up
the Shaib Valley. It was said that the Turks had now
reversed some of their Nimrim guns, and were firing
eastwards instead of westwards. At night-time we became
aware that we were being shelled from the Ammam
direction also.

May 2nd.

The position was now a curious one. We had captured
Es Salt, Divisional Headquarters were in that town, two
Australian and our Yeomanry Brigade were disposed
around it, and the enemy was attacking us from Ammam
and Howeij. The infantry division had, after heavy
casualties, failed to open up the road through Nimrim,
El Haud and Howeij to the Shaib Valley. The track

we had come up by had been closed by the enemy, who had drawn a sort of net round us. It had been hoped that by the time we had captured Es Salt it would have been possible to open up communication with the Jordan Valley by the Jericho road, which was a good one and capable of carrying heavy transport. Our intervening position on this road, between Ammam and Howeij, prevented the enemy to a certain extent from getting supplies and ammunition, although they were able to get a certain amount of both by circumventing us to the south-east. It was evident that the enemy would do his best to join hands with the Ammam force, and by so doing annihilate our Division. At 9 a.m. it was decided by our Divisional General in Es Salt that the Howeij bridge and position must be forced and the road opened to the Jordan Valley. Rations for men and horses were finished, but there was still some grazing, and we had managed to seize a few cattle belonging to the natives. The two Australian Brigades being already busily occupied, one of them holding off the Turkish Ammam force, it fell to our Brigade to attempt the task of taking Howeij hill. On walking a short distance along the road above the Wadi Shaib, one could see a few miles away the position which we were to attack— a steep grassy hill some 300 feet high, with a large open valley before it, lined by a number of guns, whose shells were falling on the road below. Orders were issued to the Gloucester Yeomanry to advance on the right of the road and take up a position a few hundred yards from the bridge. The Sherwood Rangers and the Worcester Yeomanry were ordered to attack the hill on the left of the road and, if successful, open up the latter to Jericho. After leaving our horses in the bivouac in the valley we were a very small force, and taking with us only the Hotchkiss gun pack-horses, we proceeded under the cliffs of the Wadi Shaib for a short distance, but soon discovered that we should be under observation the whole way to our objective. Accordingly, we struck east for some four hours, climbing up and down the mountain

WADI SHAIB AND HOWEIJ HILL (ON EXTREME LEFT)

(By permission of the Imperial War Museum.)

sides, and crossing many beautiful glens and streams,
bordered by masses of giant oleanders, hollyhocks and
roses, until we eventually reached a high position whence
we could see our objective, the guns on which were
shelling the troops on the right-hand side of the valley.
The Turks had several 5·9 guns in action, our only artillery being the little mountain mule battery, which was
in action behind the Gloucesters. One could not help
feeling that our attack was doomed to failure ; we were
two regiments, far below strength, about to cross an open
valley and then ascend a grassy hill, which was so steep
that it would be difficult to obtain a foothold. However, the order had been given and the attack must be
carried out. We had been unable to keep our Hotchkiss
guns with us, as some hours before the ascent had been
so steep that one horse had slipped and gone hurtling
down to the valley below, and the rest were unable to
get any further. As we took a breather for ten minutes
preparatory to the attack, sitting amongst the most
beautiful flowers, under a cloudless blue sky, one realized
what a waste it would be that very soon many of us
would be lying dead in the valley below, never able to
enjoy the beauties of nature again. During this brief
interval the Turkish cavalry were seen on a ridge to
our left, and the order was given to advance. As we
descended the hill in very open order and began to cross
the valley, we were met with very heavy H.E. and shrapnel
fire, which apparently came from behind the Howeij
hill. Every rock, behind which we naturally took cover
as we advanced, seemed to be marked, the second shell
killing two of our officers and casualties resulting in
every part of the field. A little later, rifle fire broke out,
but we were unable to see a single one of the enemy,
and, as one of our men remarked, they could have kept
us off that steep hill simply by rolling stones down on
to us. My first batch of casualties I collected in a cave,
and then with some difficulty slid them down a steep
grassy bank some 100 feet to the stream below ; this
we found was the Wadi Shaib, and we established a

dressing station in a little stone water-mill. Unfortunately, as more wounded were collected there, the Turks noticed the concentration and dropped a shell on to the roof of the mill, and even at this moment a badly wounded man burst out laughing when his companion was covered with flour. Meanwhile our attack was progressing, but it soon became evident that no live man could ever reach the top of Howeij hill. The mill being now untenable as a dressing station, we transferred our wounded with some difficulty through the mill-stream, which was four feet deep, to the opposite side. We had only got our small cavalry stretchers, but these proved invaluable over the rocky ground, and by relays the wounded were carried through some fields to the main road just behind the barricade held by some Gloucester stalwarts. Although we had some more men wounded while our stretcher parties were ascending to the road, as soon as we were identified as stretcher parties the enemy ceased to shell us. The road having been reached, we placed our wounded in some of the German motor-cars, driven by Germans, and evacuated the former to Es Salt. On returning to collect our last wounded from the mill under Howeij hill, we found that the remains of our regiment and the Sherwoods had been forced to retire, as the task before them was absolutely impossible. The whole attack was doomed to failure, and the veriest tyro standing on the opposite hill would have realized that such a small body of men would be unable to take the position, which was so strongly held. We were unable to collect our dead, but managed eventually to bring all the wounded in under cover of the well-grown barley. On returning along the road some 3 miles towards our old bivouac, a few final shells fell amongst us from the Howeij hill as we straggled along. It had been a sad and tiring day, a forlorn hope doomed to failure from the first, and we had nothing to show except casualties. Australian Brigades had co-operated and tried to get through in our vicinity, but we were unable to see them during the day. At night our rations had given out, but we were able to make a fairly decent meal out of goats and green figs. A message was read from an official source saying that Es Salt must be held at all costs, and that reinforcements for the Turks were fast approaching from Ammam.

May 3rd.

It appeared that we were completely cut off, owing to the nature of the ground and the Turkish reinforcements. During the morning, rifle and gun fire seemed to come from all directions, and later on Fritz bombed us up and down the Es Salt–Shaib Valley. An uneasy feeling prevailed, especially as it became known that large reinforcements were on their way from Damascus, via Ammam, and some fighting took place on the Ammam road between an Australian Brigade and Turkish infantry during the afternoon. Our mounted patrols, who were high up on the hill on the opposite side of our valley, reported the presence of some Turkish cavalry regiments on the mountains a few miles away. At 6 p.m. secret orders were issued to each regiment that it was to make the best of its way to the Jordan Valley, which sounded like a general *sauve qui peut*. Our Second-in-Command had a short time before managed to reconnoitre a fresh track towards the west, and it devolved upon him to act as guide to the Brigade. At 6.30 p.m. part of a donkey convoy of biscuits, which had been some days *en route*, managed to get through to us, escorted by a few Indian cavalry and yeomanry, a troop of which had been cut up. The Turkish hospital at Es Salt was now full of wounded from our two Divisions (Anzac and Australian Mounted), and the question was how to get them and our prisoners through the enemy's cordon down to the Jordan plain. The wounded men were tied on to horses and camels and sent down the only partially opened track under escort, before the main body moved. They were attacked, chiefly by irregulars, and had to fight their way through : it must have been an awful journey for the badly wounded, especially when their horses were

16

stampeded by some Bedouin, who suddenly opened fire on them. At 7 p.m. we called our mounted patrols down from the opposite hills, and an hour later, after making up large camp fires, we left our bivouac and proceeded along the highroad on the right of the Wadi Shaib. It was our regiment's duty to do rear-guard, and when the usual halts, owing to the blocking of the road by someone in front, took place one felt very uncomfortable, as it was expected that the enemy, as soon as they found our camp empty, would charge down the road. Before reaching the barricade across the road, near the Howeij bridge, our column turned right-handed and struck a track across very broken country, which was particularly difficult to negotiate in the pitch dark.

May 4th.

By 2 a.m. our Brigade had assembled in a cup-shaped depression on the top of the mountain, where commenced the Arsenyat track towards the Jordan. At 5 a.m. we were aware of other Australian Brigades on neighbouring hills, and the descent commenced. Each Brigade and regiment fought a rear-guard in turns, as the Turks were now pursuing us, at the same time picketing the hills on either side in order to protect the unit whose turn it was to go first ; the latter then picketed the next hills and allowed the regiments which were following to pass through. The Turks, who had got wind of our intention, and were out in considerable numbers and with machine guns and mountain guns on the various peaks, tried to hinder our retreat. Most of the way it was a gallop across very rocky ground and down descents where in quieter moments one would probably have led one's horse. Every now and then, as one came round a corner, one would find oneself under fire from some little mountain gun, the explosions of whose shells had a very small range and did not do much harm. Our outposts on the heights kept off the enemy infantry to the last moment, and then came scuttling down to join our main body. Our wounded we had to tie on to horses and get them along as best we could. As the sun rose Fritz came over and added to our discomfiture by bombing us as we descended the narrow ravines. Much equipment was lost, and the tracks in our wake were strewn with tin hats, sun-helmets, ammunition, dead horses, etc., but on the whole it was said the retirement was carried out according to plan. As we descended one felt the awful Dead Sea atmosphere again—a great contrast from the clear mountain air which we had been living in for the last few days. My last casualty we picked up just before debouching into the plain, and it was an uncomfortable sensation remaining behind while attending to him and tying him on to a horse, as Fritz was still overhead and the enemy, who were following our retreat, were still busy. However, our Brigade Commander was the last to leave the hills, and would not gallop into the plain until he had seen his three regiments clear. As our small party eventually made its appearance in the open, we were met by a salvo from the Turkish guns, but by galloping in extended order we managed to put about 4 miles between us and the hills in a very short time. Our escape from the hills to the plain was facilitated by the Sixtieth Division, who diverted the enemy's attention to a large extent by attacking Shunet Nimrim and the hills on the right of the Arsenyat track. After watering in the Nimrim brook, close to the spot where it flows into the Jordan, we crossed the latter river by the pontoon bridge, and after a long ride over the dusty plain eventually arrived at our old bivouac below Tel El Sultan, behind the Wadi Auja outpost line. With the exception of the prisoners captured by our force, some of whom had been killed by the fire from their own guns as they were driven before us into the plain, the whole thing had been a costly failure. It had been a gamble on the fall of Nimrim and on the assistance of the Arabs which did not mature, consequently a quick retirement had to be undertaken in order to prevent further disaster. We now heard of the experiences which our Third and Fourth Brigades had had when they were pushed up east of Jordan towards the north. When they had passed the line held by the Imperial Camel Corps west of Jordan, on the opposite bank, and were engaged with the enemy, the latter, crossing the river from the western side by a pontoon bridge, had attacked them in the rear. Two batteries which accompanied these Brigades had suffered heavily while in the foothills, and had to abandon seven of their guns. Some of our dismounted men whom we had left in camp a week ago had been called out with various oddments in order to strengthen these Brigades, and they told us how the enemy cavalry had pursued them during the retreat. It now appeared that the whole of our sudden move had a political meaning. On April 23rd a Meccan force of 7,000 rifles were said to have captured Madeba (18 miles south-west of Ammam), and it was reported that the Arabs east of Jordan, including the Beni Sakhr tribe, were ready to side with us. Hence the hurry and rush from Jaffa to Jericho in order to clear up the Es Salt–Madeba–Ammam triangle, as it was said that it only needed a spark from the British mounted troops to set the whole country ablaze and finally destroy the Hedjaz Railway. But the result had been a fiasco ; one wondered whether the whole thing had not been a German or Turkish ruse. Had the Meccans ever taken Madeba ? Was the message sent through native sources merely in order to lure our troops on while large reinforcements were coming down the railway line to Ammam ? A few days later we read the following " official " in the *Egyptian News :*

Between April 30th and May 4th a mixed force of cavalry and infantry carried out a successful operation east of Jordan. The enemy, who were holding a strong position defending the Ghoraniye–Es Salt road, about Shunet Nimrim, were contained by our infantry, whilst the cavalry, moving rapidly northwards up the east bank of the Jordan, entered Es Salt from the north and west. Three hundred and thirty prisoners, including 33 Germans, were taken, and much valuable war material, including six motor-lorries and a motor-car, was destroyed. During the night of the 3rd–4th May we withdrew to the plain on the east bank of Jordan, and on the night of the 4th–5th May our troops returned to their positions on the original bridge-head. During the operation our total captures amounted to 46 officers and 885 O.R.'s and 29 machine guns.

This somewhat bald narrative did not quite coincide with our experiences, and few of us would have described the operation, at any rate the part we saw, as " successful." It was said that most of the machine guns captured had been found packed in cases at Es Salt, where they had been left. We wondered what the native population of Es Salt would think when the next raid took place and we occupied the town again. We were afraid that the chits on which we had requisitioned for goats and sheep would not be honoured by the Turkish commander !

For the next week we remained in the same position, our Division suffering considerably from Fritz's visits, one Brigade sustaining as many as eighty casualties in four days. An attack was daily expected on the Auja outpost line, west of Jordan, at that time held by the Imperial Camel Corps, and our regiments took it in turn to provide working parties and reinforcements. Several Indian Cavalry Brigades arrived in the valley, and were amalgamated with the yeomanry regiments in a proportion of two to one. We were taken out of the Fifth Mounted Brigade, which had been temporarily re-formed, and the latter now became a composite brigade, consisting of the Gloucesters and two native cavalry regiments. Every day the heat seemed to increase, and yet we were not really into the summer yet. Scorpions, tarantulas, mosquitoes, flies, dust and thorns, and the oppressive heat will ever remain in one's memory when one thinks of the old Jordan Valley. In the evening we used to climb the hills on our left and get a view over the Wadi Auja towards Redhill, held by the Turks. On these walks one saw a certain amount of animal life, including vultures, who nested amongst the rocks, rock-pigeons and hares. On May 10th we received orders to rejoin the Twentieth Corps, with Headquarters at Jerusalem.

Needless to say, everyone was delighted at the prospect of getting into the mountains again, although we had had such a comparatively short time in the valley. At five o'clock we left our camp, riding for the first 3 miles through such thick white dust that one had difficulty in keeping one's direction, inhaling the sickening sulphurous stench which one generally notices in the Dead Sea Valley at sunset. Following the ancient Roman road through modern Jericho, we rode along the shore of the Dead Sea for a while, and then, ascending by the new Turkish road from − 12,000 to + 14,000 feet, reached Talaat El Dumm, below the inn of the Good Samaritan, just before midnight. On the way up many Indian cavalry regiments were passed, who were on their way down to the Jordan. Latron was eventually reached in the early morning of May 13th, after traversing the now well-known road from Dumm through Jerusalem and Enab, marching by night and sleeping by day. The Sherwood Rangers now left us and marched to Jaffa, while for the next month we remained in camp at Latron, where grazing was good, the unit undertaking the various duties which devolved on it as a Corps cavalry regiment. We were kept down here and not at Jerusalem on account of water difficulties at the latter place and the absence of level ground suitable for horse lines. Bilharzia having been discovered in the Latron brook, from which we took our drinking water, the usual precautions had to be taken in order to avoid infection. The Imperial Camel Corps bivouacked in our vicinity for the night, being on their way to rest after a very strenuous two months in the Jordan Valley. About 2 miles west of our camp the tracks forked to Jaffa and Junction Station, and at this point a considerable hill was situated, on the summit of which were the remains of what looked like an ancient temple. On several occasions two of us climbed this hill and found an old vulture perched on the ruins ; from this point he had a splendid view, and evidently kept a look out for any camels who might collapse on either of the roads. He was a wary old bird, and we were never able to get near enough in order to shoot him with our revolvers. We had often noted previously how, if a camel or horse died overnight and was left cut open, the vultures and jackals would only leave the bones on the following day. Sometimes one would see a crowd of jackals satiated with food lying around the carcass, but yet growling and trying to prevent the vultures from partaking in the feast.

At this time we did not suffer much from Fritz, but our own anti-aircraft guns were somewhat troublesome; several of the latter's shells fell in our camp without exploding, but on one occasion a shell exploded in the horse lines on striking the ground, and wounded the horses and also one man very seriously. We were used to small fragments and shell-cases from our " Archies " falling on us, but complete shells were too much of a good thing. One afternoon, when most of us were having a siesta, we watched a very exciting air fight overhead. Eventually our own aeroplane drove the German down, and the latter landed about a mile away. Everyone who was awake seized a horse off the line and galloped towards the scene. However, we were too late, as, just before arriving, the two Germans had set fire to their aeroplane. A few minutes later a car arrived from our Ramleh aerodrome, which took them away.

Our Second-in-Command, having ridden over the hill known as Abu Shushar (Biblical Gezer) during the advance last autumn, had noted the large number of tombs and excavations on it. Now that we were encamped in the vicinity we decided to investigate these tombs in our spare time and carry out some excavations. After interviewing the Omdah of the village, we engaged two natives, known as Ibrahim and Hassan, to assist us. The latter was able to explain, in Arabic, that he had assisted a certain " Macleest " in his excavations some years ago, and it eventually turned out that he referred to that eminent archæologist, Professor Macalister. In order to obtain all the local information we could with regard to these excavations, we called on the abbot of the monastery at Latron, who, with a few monks, had recently returned after their exile during the Turkish occupation. The conversation was carried on in French, and our host told us that he formerly possessed a very fine collection of coins which had been found in the neighbourhood. He told us that Abu Shushar (Gezer) extended over five stages in the world's history, and that the remains of four towns had been found one on the top of the other : (1) The Stone Age, as shown by the caves cut into the rock, with very small openings in order to prevent the larger wild animals from entering, and containing stone implements, etc. ; (2) a Canaanite town ; (3) the Egyptian period, during the captivity of the Jews ; (4) the Jewish period, when the Maccabeans made the town a very strong fortress and, during a siege, drove an enormous shaft down into the bowels of the earth in order to obtain water. It was during this period that some king gave his daughter to Solomon, and added Abu Shushar as a dowry. Most of the stone vaults were cut out at that time. (5) The Greco-Roman period. For several days we rode over every afternoon in order to carry on our excavations, but unfortunately we were very ignorant as to the type of tomb we happened to be opening. In almost every case the entrance to the tomb was entirely obliterated, and it was only after digging away a certain amount of earth that we were able to discover the large rock which usually blocked the entrance. It appeared that many of them had been previously opened and then carefully closed again, and one could not help wondering whether this had not taken place thousands of years ago. We found a number of skeletons, which I was able to reconstruct, and a small number of late Roman coins, lamps, broken pottery, pieces of old glass, and occasion- ally very thin gold sequins, probably part of a dress. In every case the vaults were full of very fine mould, and we came to the conclusion that this had silted in during the last few thousand years on account of the cracks in the walls of the tombs, caused probably by seismic disturbances. One noticed that underground the limestone rock was comparatively soft and could have been cut out with flint instruments; where, however, it had been exposed to the air it was as hard as granite. While exploring underground we always had our orderlies, who were looking after our horses, watching the hole by which we had descended, as we did not quite trust some of our local assistants. On arriving one afternoon, when our Second-in-Command was away on a reconnaissance, I found that Ibrahim and Hassan had brought their wives and children with them; the latter worked well and passed up the baskets of earth from one to another, while our Sudanese syce, who was interpreting for me, assisted in the sifting of the soil for antiquities. A little French Jew made his appearance during the afternoon, and asked if he also had permission to excavate. Naturally this was refused, and he appeared the next day with a long rigmarole about his being the agent for some colonization society to whom the land belonged. Eventually he became so troublesome that he had to be thrown down the hill; but this had an unfortunate sequel. A few days later our C.O. received an order from H.Q. L. of C. to stop any of his officers who might be carrying on excavations at Abu Shushar; however, we were able to find another locality and continued our work for some weeks.

At this time there were a considerable number of oases of snake-bite occurring in the Twentieth Corps, and it was said that recently three out of four men who had been bitten died at a neighbouring Casualty Clearing Station. A few days after this an order was received from the D.D.M.S. of the Corps to the following effect: "Medical officers are requested to collect any snakes they may see and forward them to Headquarters in order that an anti-venene may be produced; it is particularly requested that these snakes may be killed without destroying the brain or spinal cord." At the time one did not consider these instructions anything out of the ordinary, but when one put them into practice one discovered later how difficult it was to comply with them. We had seen a fair number of snakes during the last month or so, and I now instructed my orderly to inform me when the next snake was seen in our camp. A few days later, while at breakfast, I was called down to the horse lines, where I found a large black snake, some ten feet long, pinned down with two swords. One of our officers who had served in the Sudan and South Africa identified the snake as a very poisonous one known as the Black Mamba ; the natives also agreed that it was a dangerous snake, and could not be persuaded to approach it. As the head and some two feet of the snake were free of the first sword, we managed to catch the former with some wire-nippers and transfix it also with another sword. Eventually the whole snake was pinned out on the grass with some six swords piercing its body, but not interfering with the spinal cord. I now remembered my instructions, namely, that the snake must be killed without injuring brain or cord. Sending for a bottle of chloroform, we solemnly anæsthetized our patient, eventually giving it a considerable overdose and pouring an ounce into its mouth, which was held open by means of wire-nippers. The snake was now inert, and was rolled up in a large native fig-basket ready for removal by D.R.L.S.[1] to Headquarters at Jerusalem. An hour later a horrified orderly met me, saying that the snake had come to life again ! On going down to the medical tent we found that this was true, and that the snake was slowly emerging from the basket, apparently none the worse for its experience. One felt inclined not to obey the instructions this time, but to cut off its head with a convenient spade. However, in this fourth year of war one had learnt to obey, so we determined to take other measures. Again we went through the same performance, but after the snake had been pinned down I determined to take no chances, and with a couple of farriers holding the snake's head with their pincers, I emptied one pound of Burgoyne's best army chloroform into the reptile's mouth ; he didn't seem to like the drink, but was compelled to swallow it, and appeared to be

[1] Dispatch rider.

stone dead when the bottle was empty. However, this time we were not going to give him time to come to life ; he was packed into his fig-basket, which was securely tied up with ropes and was placed on the back of a dispatch rider's motor-cycle, which dashed off up the Latron road to Jerusalem. Half an hour later another D.R.L.S., who must have passed ours on the road, brought me an urgent note from Corps Headquarters : " *Re* my ——. Sufficient snakes have been received for this purpose, and no more are required, please." We often wondered what happened to our snake, and whether he ever came to life again, but thought it wiser not to investigate the matter any further. One evening, while opening an old tomb near our camp, we came across a still larger Black Mamba, which moved with lightning speed. Somehow our interest in the antiquities which might be discovered in that particular area seemed to fade away after that incident.

During these days frequent parties were made up to view the holy sites in Jerusalem and Bethlehem. The Fast Hotel near the Jaffa Gate had been taken over by the Army and Navy Canteen Board, and seemed quite a luxurious place to stay the night at. The guides, many of whom spoke English, did quite a good trade after their enforced idleness for the last four years. The Church of the Nativity at Bethlehem seemed to interest us most, as this appeared to be by far the most authentic of all the holy places. It seems unnecessary here to record one's impressions of the Holy City, as so much has been written on this subject, and this diary is written merely in order to narrate the experiences of the author and the regiment with which he was. While on one of these visits to Jerusalem, two of us suddenly received news that we had been granted leave to the U.K., as home leave is called in the Army. Many of us had had no home leave since we had left England in April 1915, and were naturally very excited at the prospect. The question was how to get down to Alexandria in order to catch the boat to which we had been detailed. The following morning, early, a passing Ford car, which was travelling from the Dead Sea to Jaffa, was stopped and commandeered, as it only contained the driver. The latter apparently was in a hurry to complete his journey, and we experienced a most thrilling descent as we zigzagged down the pass, whirling round the hairpin corners, often with a drop of hundreds of feet to the right or left. Our driver cheered us up by telling us how a few weeks ago the steering gear of a Ford car had refused to act on a similar road, with disastrous results to the occupants of the car. However, Latron was eventually reached, and we started on our journey from railhead at Ludd on the evening of June 21st. Three days later we embarked on the transport *Rose*, in Alexandria harbour, one of a convoy of three small boats which were taking an infantry battalion *en route* for France, and a few officers on leave, to Taranto. The three boats left the harbour at dusk, accompanied by five destroyers. There had been a considerable number of transports sunk outside the harbour, and consequently we had to stand to our stations for some two hours lest a similar fate should befall us ; at the same time the destroyers emitted an enormous amount of smoke, which we imagined was to act as a screen. On account of this submarine menace we were compelled to wear our life-belts all day. After passing through the Corinth Ship Canal, about four days later, we emerged into the Straits, and were met by some French destroyers, which escorted us to Taranto, the latter place being reached after an uneventful journey. Taranto had at this time become an enormous rest camp, as it was the port of embarkation for all troops proceeding to Salonika, Palestine, Mesopotamia and India. After a few days' delay a leave train was made up, and we travelled by the usual route, along the east coast of Italy, and thence through Bologna to Genoa, Havre being reached after about ten days' railway travelling, the latter being broken by a couple of days' rest at the Mediterranean L. of C. Rest Camps at Faenza and St. Germain au Mont d'Or, near Lyons.

CHAPTER V

ITALY

ON August 3rd, in company with two other Medical Officers who had also received orders to join the British armies in Italy, I crossed to Havre from Southampton on an American transport, which was crowded with United States troops. On arrival we were ordered to report at Padua, in spite of our protests, as we knew that that town had been evacuated by the Headquarters of the Italian Expeditionary Force. Three days later Turin was reached and we again received orders to proceed to Padua; on arrival at the latter town on the following night we found, as we expected, no orders and no signs of any British troops. However, as we had not been in this mediæval town before, a couple of interesting days were spent visiting the old place, which had suffered to a slight extent from recent bombing. As the result of our telephoning up and down the line we received orders to proceed to Vicenza, and accordingly set out for that town. However, on reporting, we were told that nothing was known about us, and it was suggested that we should try Cremona on the following day. Vicenza appeared to be full of French and British troops, but we were amused to find that the medical authorities did not apparently take any interest in our movements. On the following day, August 9th, we arrived at Brescia, and as usual did the town thoroughly, with the aid of a Baedeker. There were no British troops at Brescia, and it seemed that, if we had cared to, we might have stayed there for the rest of the war. On the following day, remembering that something had been said about Cremona, we took train to that city. After installing ourselves in a comfortable hotel, where the food was excellent, we reported at the British Headquarters on the following morning. It was a surprise when we discovered that something was known about us. Finally it was suggested that we should travel to Milan and then try the British Base at Aquarta Scrivia. This was rather a blow to one of us, who had hoped that he might spend the rest of the war travelling round the mediæval cities of Italy without being worried by anyone; indeed, we had been talking of visiting Florence and Naples, but I thought that the latter might be considered a little too far out of the way. Milan was reached on the following day ; here no one seemed to take any interest in us, and we spent quite a pleasant twenty-four hours. The following morning we entrained again, almost forgetting that we had anything to do with the war in Italy, and travelling through Pavia, eventually reached Aquarta in the afternoon. On reporting as usual, we were not received with much encouragement, and we hoped that we might be allowed to drift off at a tangent again. However, we eventually received instructions to report to two hospitals in Genoa ; unfortunately, the names of the hospitals were given, so we were compelled to report there on the following day. We had left England on August 3rd and were actually at our destination ten days later. The interesting part about this little Cook's tour in the north of Italy was that, owing to our having followed instructions implicitly, our hotel bills, or rather the allowances in lieu of them, were paid forthwith by the Field Cashier. After two weeks in a Base Hospital at Genoa, the author of this diary was transferred as Acting S.M.O. of Faenza and district ; this was one of the large rest camps on the Mediterranean lines of communication, situate between Bologna and Rimini. We had two hospitals, British and Indian, and a considerable district to be responsible for. Our patients for the hospital were chiefly taken off the leave and reinforcement trains which were passing through daily. The influenza epidemic was commencing, and the

Salonika leave train always supplied a large number of malaria cases which were unfit to travel any further. The rest camp was situated in a shady park just outside the old walls of the mediæval city, and was about as perfect as any rest camp could be ; every detail was attended to in order to make officers and other ranks comfortable. The trains which supplied our hospitals with patients carried all sorts of nationalities, from British troops and Serbian refugees to Labour Corps units from Malta, Fiji and South Africa. Sometimes these trains contained units suffering from infectious disease, about which we were generally warned from Taranto beforehand, and a certain amount of difficulty was naturally experienced with the Italian authorities. On one occasion a train containing Indians suffering with mumps was held up for half a day near the station, being shunted on to a siding ; when it had continued its journey the local sanitary authorities disinfected the permanent way, but later it transpired that the engine which had drawn the train had been waiting on another siding, and accordingly the rails on which it had stood were also solemnly disinfected ! While at Faenza one's duties took one to various places, up to 40 miles away, where there were small detachments of British troops, and while on these motor excursions one noticed how very thoroughly American propaganda was being carried out, even in the smaller villages. On one occasion an official cinematograph performance was given in the market square of the town, showing the work of the British Army in France. The Italians, however, who were so used to the American propaganda, thought that the pictures represented American troops, and cheered for the Americans accordingly.

.   .   .   .   .

Early in October I received orders to report to the Seventh Division, and accordingly joined a Field Ambulance which was in billets near Vicenza. On the following day we commenced a march up to the front, and after a busy time with the influenza epidemic, which was then raging, reached Vascon, a village between Treviso and the Piave, on October 20th. At this time the Seventh and Twenty-third Divisions had concentrated near Treviso, and were about to take over a portion of the Piave line from the Italians before commencing the offensive which culminated in the defeat of Austria. Our main dressing station was established in a building vacated by an Italian Sezzione Sanita (a Divisional Medical Field Unit), our advanced dressing stations being amongst the ruins of the church at Maserada, about 2 miles from the front line, and at Lovadina, a little higher up the river. At dusk the roads were full of the Italian troops who were being relieved by the British. There was very little shelling going on at night, but we were told by the Italians that we should be heavily shelled during the day. On the following day we found that the cross-roads at Maserada were very unhealthy, and looked about for a more suitable advanced dressing station. The C.O., however, was unable to find anything better than the ruined church, as most of the houses were merely piles of bricks and all the Italian dugouts were full of water. At this time we were ordered to wear Italian tin helmets and Italian great-coats when near the line, in order that the Austrian aeroplanes might not realize that British troops had taken over this sector from the Italians. This precaution seemed rather a farce, as a few miles back whole battalions of infantry were to be seen marching along the road in ordinary British uniforms. On October 22nd I joined another M.O. in an advanced dressing station at Casa Forte, some 200 yards behind the Piave bank, in some excellent dugouts which were partially occupied by the R.W.F.[1] We had a very quiet time, and one realized that it was a gentlemanly war on this front ; occasionally the Austrian guns would throw a shell over the Piave, and now and then the Italian guns in our rear would retaliate.

[1] 1st Royal Welsh Fusiliers.

THE RIVER PIAVE.

(By permission of the Imperial War Museum.)

October 23rd.

Our C.O. came over at midday and told us that our Brigade would cross to the Papadopoli Island that night, and that I was to accompany them with the bearer party. This island was some 3½ miles long and varied in breadth from a half to 2 miles. It was separated from the Italian bank of the Piave by a very swiftly flowing stream, dotted here and there with shoals whose position differed from day to day, according to the depth of the water ; the island was occupied by the enemy's infantry, and was connected with the " Austrian " mainland by means of wooden bridges, which connected some smaller islands with Papadopoli ; it was therefore a sort of outpost in front of the Austrian line, which extended along the left bank of the river. It was estimated that it would take us two days to capture and clear the island, and that then a pontoon bridge could be built which would enable two Divisions to join us and eventually cross and attack the Austrian main position. Our Brigade, therefore, was to have the post of honour, and, by establishing a bridge-head, was to open up a road for the offensive. The whole undertaking was to be as secret as possible, in order that the enemy might not know that a big offensive was maturing (but rather that he should think it was a large raid), and above all that he should not know that British troops were present until the last moment ; for this reason we had for the last few days been wearing Italian helmets and coats in the trenches on account of aeroplane observation. At 9 p.m. three of us M.O.'s, together with the bearers (all lightly equipped, as we had been warned that we might have to swim) marched down through Lovadina to Zeoti ; here we left one officer with a detachment, and then made our way down to the front-line trenches at Palazzina. Leaving the N.C.O.'s and men, we crept down to the river and crossed a plank bridge to a small islet ; here embarkation was proceeding, and our orders were to embark in the following order : 2nd H.A.C., 1st R.W.F., 8th Yorks

17

(one company), M.G.C., T.M.B., and lastly the bearer party of our Field Ambulance ; troops were being embarked in gondolas, each of which contained seven men and two Italian Pioneers ; the latter had been specially selected for these duties, as they were largely local men who understood all about the currents and shoals met with in the Piave. Two platoons of the leading regiment had just got over, when the enemy, by means of star-shells and searchlights, discovered what was going on. He immediately began to shell the embarkation point, the boats in mid-stream, and the place where the landing was being effected. Boats no longer returned empty, but contained wounded ; the latter reported that they had been met with rifle fire on landing. Meanwhile, casualties from H.E. and shrapnel were taking place amongst the troops who were waiting to embark. We read some weeks later in the newspapers that the landing was a complete surprise, and the two regiments were dug in before the enemy discovered them. If the correspondent who wrote this had taken part in the crossing on that night, his account would probably have been a different one. Whenever the shelling was bad, embarkation was postponed for a few minutes while we lay in some old trenches on the beach. The Italian Piave boatmen (Pioneers) were simply splendid, making repeated journeys under heavy fire.

October 24th.

At 1 a.m. our turn came to embark. It was not a pleasant prospect ; the shelling continued heavily, and our guns were not allowed to reply, as our presence was not supposed to be known. We went back to the Zeoti trenches to fetch our men, and found that our senior sergeant had been mortally wounded ; we now returned to the islet beach and commenced to embark. I went in our second boat, which contained also six men, a few stretchers and our two " gondoliers." As our boat pushed off into the swiftly running Piave, much swollen by recent rain, the scene resembled a pyrotechnic display,

with the flashes of the explosions and the white and green
lights which lit up the water. It seemed that our boat
could never get over whole, as great fountains of water
seemed to burst up all around us ; but most of the boats
crossed safely, including our own, which was eventually
floated and steered down to a shoal of shingle. Here
we got out and re-embarked into a second boat on the other
side. We were now ferried over another branch of the
river into the shallows, through which we had to wade
ashore in icy water, nearly up to our waists, for about
100 yards. We had come very lightly equipped,
carrying stretchers and surgical haversacks only, packs,
overcoats, etc., having been left behind, as we had been
warned that our boat would very likely be sunk or upset.
In this way the whole Brigade crossed to the island of
Papadopoli (northern portion), with luckily not many
casualties in transit. The crossing reminded one of the
upper reaches of the Danube. On emerging in the pitch
dark on to a sandy beach, we were met by rifle fire. We
could find no one. After proceeding cautiously in a north-
easterly direction, we got into touch with the regiment
(2nd H.A.C.) in front, which was engaged with four
companies of the enemy in a belt of scrub, and a little
later got into communication with the 1st R.W.F. on
our left. Whenever a star-shell went up, we all fell prone
on the sand, as there was absolutely no cover. As some
snipers, about 200 yards away, seemed interested in our
movements, we dug in in a sandy bank (each man a hole
for himself) and dropped the stretchers under the lee of
it. Eight men were then dispatched to collect wounded
from the regimental aid posts. By dawn we had got most
of the wounded, both British and Austrian, into our
dressing station, but as soon as it was light, shelling,
whizz-bang, rifle-grenade and machine-gun fire became
very severe. The plaintive cries of the Austrian wounded,
" Italiener, Italiener ! " showed that anyhow the rank
and file of the enemy did not realize that they were fighting
against British troops. At 7 a.m. some enemy aeroplanes
began to fly over the island, but none of ours were allowed

to appear, as those in authority did not wish this to be thought an important movement, and for the same reason our guns from the mainland were still dumb. To us it seemed a very one-sided show. At 7.15 a Fritz hovered over our dressing station and began to fly in circles, evidently signalling to his guns on the Austrian mainland. We knew that the worst had happened. He thought that we were a trench mortar battery or machine-gun emplacement, as our little rows of dugouts and parallel rows of stretchers under the bank might resemble something of this sort when seen from a certain altitude. The result was, we were subjected to an incessant bombardment by a great variety of " missiles " until 11 a.m. Luckily, we never got a direct hit by H.E., or not one of us would have escaped. Some of our wounded were killed and some died of wounds during the morning. There was no question of evacuation, as the boats had ceased to run before dawn. We deepened our holes and those containing the stretchers, without exposing ourselves, by digging with our hands in the shingle until the water level was reached. There we cowered for some hours, watching the rank grass being mown down a few inches above our heads. It was one of those uncomfortable occasions when tobacco was the greatest solace. Towards midday the shelling got less and we were able to collect some more wounded ; then it recommenced again, and the other M.O. and I debated about making a run for it. At 2 p.m. the two of us seized a stretcher with a man on it, and ran out towards the guns, in order to show their observation officer what we really were. However, he must have misinterpreted our action, as we were driven back again, my walking-stick being cut in two by a bullet. In the afternoon things quietened down a little, and we were able to move our dressing station forward, conforming with the movements of the Brigade, under a scrub-top bank. The supply of stretchers gave out, and we were reduced to using Austrian blankets. At night we were able to evacuate some of our wounded by boat, but unfortunately under fire, as the enemy turned a searchlight on the beach, as they feared

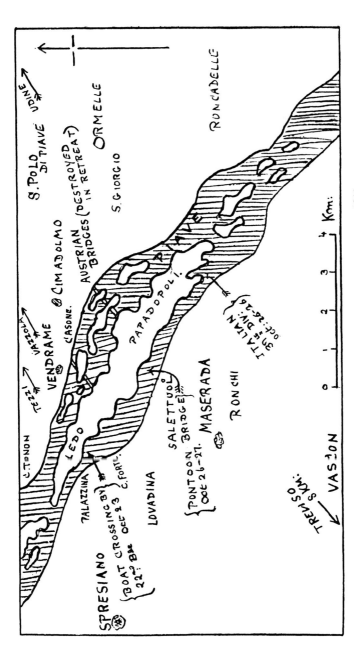

ROUGH SKETCH MAP OF PAPADOPOLI ISLAND, OCTOBER 1918.

that we were receiving reinforcements. The transference of the stretcher cases across the middle shoal, from one boat to another, was very difficult. It was said that one boat had been hit by a shell, and that, the boatmen being killed, the wreck was washed down the river ; we heard the cries of the wounded far below us later on, but were unable to locate them in the dark, and we never heard whether they were saved ; possibly they drifted on to a sandbank on the Italian side and were rescued, as we could see no sign of them at dawn. After dispatching some wounded, two of us were standing about 200 yards from the shore, while 100 prisoners were standing in the water waiting for the boats which would fetch them ; suddenly the enemy's searchlight showed up the Austrians, and they were mown down pitilessly by their own machine guns, under the impression that they were more British reinforcements. We lay flat on our faces while the bullets whistled a few feet above us. After this episode no rations could be got over, and, as ammunition was running low and the Piave was rising, our connection with the shore seemed somewhat precarious. The island had now been cleared to a depth of 2 kilometres.

October 25th.

Just before dawn our dressing station was moved forward, still on the beach, under cover of a friendly bank, in order to conform with our Brigade, which was advancing. The second regiment (1st R.W.F.) now took the lead. Shelling continued all day, and we were very short of stretchers, as none could be returned from the mainland. At 10 a.m. we saw an Italian observation balloon (the observer escaping in a parachute) shot down across the Piave on the Italian side, also an Austrian aeroplane in the same place. The British guns from the mainland opened at about midday for the first time. We heard that our big attack had been postponed, owing to the state of the river, and that we were to remain on the island and be shelled for the present. During the afternoon the enemy shelled and sank some of our boats which had been anchored as a decoy a little lower down the river. It was very pretty shooting, which we enjoyed watching, as the targets were some 300 yards away from us, and we knew that the Austrian artillery were known to be very accurate. Many prisoners came in, mostly Magyars and Czechs. By midday most of the island was in our hands, both the northern or Ledo portion and also Papadopoli proper. A little later strong reinforcements were brought up by the enemy, and a sharp counter-attack by troops from the Austrian mainland took place, the latter getting in some places within 10 yards of our line and being eventually driven back with the bayonet. The evacuation of the wounded was again a difficult problem at night, as our beach was still overlooked, on account of the flatness of the island, by the enemy on the Austrian mainland. After dusk we were joined by the Royal Warwickshire Regiment, the rest of the 8th Yorks, and some bearer reinforcements.

October 26th.

We were dressing wounded from 6 a.m. till 11 a.m., mostly the result of the enemy's counter-attack on the previous night and at dawn. A blessed white river fog, which lasted almost till midday, undoubtedly saved many lives, as the boats were able to take off wounded without being seen. One hundred and sixty prisoners were dumped on us, and as there appeared to be no one else to take charge of them, I made them make a cage out of their own barbed-wire entanglements, into which they put themselves. Their officers told me that they had no idea that there were British troops on the Piave sector until they made their acquaintance somewhat forcibly on the island. During the morning I found a very unkempt little Italian officer near our advanced dressing station, who seemed very perturbed. He said that he had important news, and that no one could understand him or would take any notice of him. We conversed in French ; he had just arrived from the mainland, and said he was liaison officer of the Italian Thirty-seventh Division, which

had just effected a landing on the island some 3 kilometres lower down, and that this Division wished to join
hands with our Brigade. He said that he had come at
great personal risk, and must see our Brigadier at once.
Accordingly, I sent him up to the leading regiment at once,
and only just in time, as half an hour later I had a wounded
man through from the 2nd H.A.C., who said that they
had suddenly run into a regiment, which they were just
about to fire on, when they received a message that
part of the Thirty-seventh Italian Division had joined
them ! We discovered that a large supply of emergency
rations had been dumped indiscriminately on the beach
on the previous night, but, owing to their being inadequately
guarded, they were quickly looted by those nearest, consequently many never got their fair share. At midday we
had to organize several relief bearer posts, as our Brigade
was advancing again, and the " carries " to our dressing
station were getting longer. Shelling and rifle-grenade
fire continued incessantly, and one was continually under
observation, except when in the hastily made Austrian
trenches. Just before sunset three Austrian aeroplanes
flew down the Piave, only about thirty feet above the
water, looking to see if we had built a bridge; they found
none, but it (the pontoon bridge) was built during the
night. At 11 p.m. our intense artillery preparation
(preliminary to the advance) commenced, and continued
for six hours. Every British and Italian gun on the mainland took part, and bombarded the enemy's position on
the Austrian bank of the Piave; as these shells passed
directly over our heads and exploded only a short distance
beyond us, the din was terrific.

October 27th.

Our bombardment ceased abruptly at 6 a.m., and then
recommenced at 7 a.m. as a creeping barrage, advancing
over the Austrian side. Meanwhile, during the previous
night and early morning the whole of our Seventh (less
the Twenty-second Brigade, which had been on the island
since October 23rd) and Twenty-third Divisions crossed

by the pontoon bridge, which had been made in the night from the Italian mainland at Salettuol to the island, followed by the Italians ; thence our Divisions, fording an arm of the river, stormed the enemy's position on the Austrian mainland. The enemy shelled the whole island vigorously in order to prevent more reinforcements from collecting, especially our side of it, and the bridge, which was washed away more than once. Enormous craters suddenly appeared in our vicinity—trees, rocks and balks of timber were hurled into the air, and the latter seemed to be full of small stones which had been thrown up from the shingly beach. The Austrians were using 30 and 40 centimetre guns, which were bigger than anything I personally had experienced before. We were bruised by the showers of stones which were thrown up from the shingly beach, one of our bearers was blown to bits, and an officer standing by the dressing station was killed. We were now joined by other Field Ambulances which had arrived on the island. An Alpine battery established itself just in front of our position, and consequently made things so uncomfortable for us that we had to move again. Soon after midday the gun fire slackened, the gap (entirely dependent on our Twenty-second Brigade bridge-head) had been made, and the Tenth Italian Army streamed through. Many of our regiments were now across, heavily engaged on the mainland, after sustaining considerable losses by drowning before reaching the latter ; accordingly, we established alternative lines of evacuation from the mainland across the island to the bridge (when it was not broken), and to our boats at the northern end of Papadopoli. We heard afterwards, from some Hungarian prisoners captured on the Austrian side of the river, that they had suffered heavily from our barrage, and that they had held out until they saw the British troops emerging from the river without any trousers on (the 2nd Gordon High-landers), when they thought that, being confronted by such mad troops, it was time to give in. The fighting now gradually moved northwards, and we were left in comparative quiet, looking after the wounded on the island.

TYPE OF BOAT USED IN CROSSING THE PIAVE.

(By permission of the Imperial War Museum.)

Our Brigade also was given a short respite before being thrown into the line again with the rest of the Seventh Division. A bright moonlight night followed, and five Austrian aeroplanes flew over and bombed our Brigade slightly, and also an Italian Division very severely, who were waiting at Salettuol for the pontoon bridge, which had been broken that evening, to be mended. About a hundred were killed and as many wounded were treated by sections of our Field Ambulance on the Italian side.

October 28th.

During the morning a few occasional shells continued to fall on the island and then gradually ceased. For the next six days we remained on Papadopoli, evacuating the wounded from the Austrian mainland at Vendrame and Casa Nuova, where they were collected by the other two Field Ambulances, who had advanced with the rest of the Division, across the island to the Italian side, utilizing a large number of bearers, some of whom were lent by other Brigades. It was heavy work, especially as the Austrian bridges on the farther side were not rebuilt for some days by our R.E., and consequently the bearers had to wade through a swiftly running arm of the Piave, in some places almost four feet deep. Several Brigades of Italian cavalry passed through, looking very resplendent, the officers particularly being wonderfully turned out. I was living in an old Austrian battery position, in a sunken road, and one morning my groom announced that my horse had been joined by two others. I discovered that they were two very fine black Italian chargers, and, remembering the axiom well known to us in Palestine that " Finding is keeping," appropriated them forthwith ; however, to my grief, they were later on claimed by an Italian squadron-sergeant-major, and as they were so obviously Italian horses, they had to be handed over. Owing to the large number of wounded which were coming down from the front, which was now several miles in advance of us, all of which seemed to come via the island, I managed to borrow some fifty Austrian prisoners from one of our cages ; the former always had to be returned at night, but sometimes we were unable to return the correct number, as they drifted away, owing to the scarcity of guards ; when this happened, however, it was always possible to make up the deficiency by catching a few more, as our island seemed to be swarming with them. On one occasion, late at night, I suddenly received some fifty British and Austrian wounded from the mainland, and found it almost impossible to have them carried the 3 miles across the island, as my bearers, who had themselves been hard at work all day, were almost collapsed. At that moment two or three Carabinieri sergeants appeared in charge of about a hundred prisoners. I informed them that I required the prisoners to act as bearers, and added that amongst my wounded were several Italians. The Carabinieri refused, and said that, as these prisoners had been captured by the Italians, they must be handed over to an Italian cage, and that if they were loaned to me they would probably eventually find their way into a British cage, and could not be then included in the total number captured by the Italians. This seemed rather an absurd excuse, as at that time whole regiments of Austrians were beginning to come over to us, and one could not see that it made very much difference whether the prisoners were accredited to England or Italy, as they had been captured by an Anglo-Italian army. However, my knowledge of German stood me in good stead ; and telling the senior N.C.O.'s to fall out, I told them to give orders that the fifty stretchers should be picked up, and that the whole crowd should follow me across the island in the dark and over the bridge to Salettuol. The Carabinieri did not understand what was happening until we had started, and eventually, much to their chagrin, after seeing my wounded dumped at our Field Ambulance, I handed the prisoners over for further fatigues, which led to their being taken for the night to a British cage.

It was interesting at this time, after crossing to Vendrame on to what had been the Austrian mainland, to stand on the river embankment and see how the Austrians observed almost all our movements during those first three somewhat lurid days on the island. On October 31st we received the following official résumé of G.H.Q. Intelligence :

On the night of October 23rd–24th the Tenth Italian Army (including the Fourteenth British Corps, Seventh Division, and Twenty-third Division), commanded by General Lord Cavan, undertook operations against the island of Grave di Papadopoli on the Piave. The Seventh British Division, crossing the river in small boats under circumstances of considerable difficulty, surprised the garrison, which consisted of troops of the Seventh Austrian Division, and occupied the northern half of the island. In this operation some 360 prisoners were captured. The remainder of the island was cleared of the enemy on the night of October 25th–26th by a combined movement of British troops in the north and troops of the Thirty-seventh Italian Division, who crossed the Piave and attacked the southern portion of the island. Two hundred and fifty more prisoners were taken. At 8 a.m. on the 26th the Austrians made a violent counter-attack on the British troops holding the northern portion of the island. The enemy advanced with determination, and reached within 10 yards of our foremost line— everywhere they were repulsed with heavy losses and more prisoners were taken. On the 27th, at 6.45 a.m., an attack of the Tenth Army across the Piave, in the area of the island of Grave di Papadopoli, commenced. The Italian troops on the right met with strong resistance, which was overcome. The British reached their first objective, Tezzi, after midday, the Italians reaching Cimadolmo. On the 28th the British Corps had reached the line C. Bonotto– C. Damian. On the 29th, at 11.15 a.m., the British infantry and cavalry forced a passage of the River Monticano north-east of Vazzola. On the 30th the British had reached the River Livenza at Lancenigo. His Excellency General Diaz telegraphs : " I beg to convey to the Fourteenth British Army Corps the expression of my high satisfaction with the valour and dash shown in the great battle, which unites in brotherhood in the decisive triumph the fighting units of England and Italy."

During this time American troops crossed the island, marching as fast as possible in order to reach the front line before the Armistice, of which there were already vague rumours, should mature. It seemed very hard luck on these troops that they would probably see no fighting, after having come all the way from America. We heard afterwards, however, that they had arrived on the Tagliamento just before the Armistice was concluded.

During the Austrian retreat, piles of bombs and hand grenades had been left behind, and many had been partly trodden into the ground ; some Italian horses were destroyed in this way, and in order to prevent further accidents we put our Austrian prisoners, who were acting as stretcher-bearers, on to collect all bombs, ammunition and weapons which were lying on the tracks used by the troops. Eventually I had quite a stock of assorted souvenirs in the sunken road behind our dugouts, and was able to supply almost any want expressed by officer souvenir-hunters, from an Austrian automatic pistol or trench dagger to a small trench mortar, one of the latter being actually taken away by an officer of high rank. On November 1st, while we were still busy man-handling the wounded which were coming down from the front across the island, we received a secret order that Phase I was over, this meaning, in conjunction with the previous order, that the line Cornari–Jajarine had been reached, and that our Division, which was now many miles ahead of us, would have a temporary halt. In the evening some Italian troops on the other side of the river became very excited and kept up an incessant shower of star-shells and Verey lights, having, as usual, received another premature peace rumour. Just before midnight our C.O. dropped in on his way down from Vazzola to Masarada ; he brought with him a young R.A.F. officer who had been shot down that morning over the Austrian lines, escaping to a house where friendly Italians dressed him as a civilian ; the Austrian troops did not recognize him, and in the afternoon, when the Italians entered the village, he was liberated.

November 4th.

Soon after dawn the church bells on the right side of the Piave, which had not rung for a year, were pealing joyfully. The churches on the left bank of the river, however, were silent, as the Austrians during their occupation had removed all the church bells in order to make use of the metal. After breakfast a captain of Arditi

AUSTRIAN PRISONERS CARRYING WOUNDED TO MAINLAND.

(By permission of the Imperial War Museum.)

and an Italian gunner officer rushed into our little camp
in a great state of excitement—they told us that Trieste,
Pola and the Trentino had fallen, and that an Armistice
between Italy and Austria would be signed at 3 p.m.
They consumed a complete bottle of whisky between
them, which they drank neat, and toasted the Italian and
British armies, saying that we should advance " Per
Austria a Berlino," eventually departing with many
expressions of perpetual friendship.

On November 5th our unit assembled at Casa Nuova,
where we handed over our accumulated stores to a
Casualty Clearing Station, and then marched through
the ruins of Cimodolma and Tezzi to the little town of
Vazzola, which we reached in the afternoon.   This place,
which had been out of reach of the Italian guns during
the Austrian occupation, had only suffered from aerial
attacks.   We were billeted in a comfortable house owned
by an Italian married to a Frenchwoman, the latter making
conversation easier.   We ascertained that a Hungarian
cavalry regiment had recently been quartered locally,
and that the house in which we were living had been
the headquarters of an Artillery Brigade.   Our host told
us that the Austrians were not aware that the British
were on the Piave sector until an artillery officer discovered
an English nose-cap which had been blown off a shell
just outside Vazzola.   Our good hostess was quite overcome with joy at the retreat of the Austrians, and supplied
us with champagne and red wine, which had been buried
in the garden during the enemy occupation.   All the
people in the town looked very starved, especially the
children, whom we were able to supply with Bovril and
biscuits which we had brought up specially for this purpose.
In my bedroom I discovered some interesting Austrian
Army Orders, including a congratulatory letter from the
Emperor Karl of Austria addressed to his troops.   The
people in the village told us that they feared the Hungarian
soldiers much more than the Austrian, as the former had
shown themselves particularly cruel, especially where
women were concerned.   On the following day we marched

early to Codogne, crossing the river Monticano, the passage
of which our troops had forced a week previously. The
villages were now not so dilapidated, but showed occasional
traces of bombing. Here and there the road was cut up
by shell-holes, where the Austrians had made a stand during
their retreat—dead horses and mules were lying about the
roads, and the ditches were littered with rifles, helmets
and ammunition which had been thrown away in the
general rout. The populace again looked very pinched
with famine, and some of the women were almost too
weak to walk, and assailed us with pitiful cries, " Pane,
pane ! " ; although this territory had now been reoccupied
for almost a week, it appeared that very little had been
done on a large scale to relieve the distress. Everywhere
we came across enormous numbers of guns of varying
calibre which had been abandoned on the roads. After
marching through Rovero Basso and Jajarine, we crossed
the River Livenza at Francenigo ; at this point we began
to meet parties of starved-looking Italian soldiers in rags,
liberated prisoners dating from the Caporetto disaster,
who were returning homewards ; many of these were too
weak to walk and were lying in the doorways of ruined
houses, hoping to get a lift out of that famine-stricken
country and over the Piave. One could not help feeling
for these poor ex-prisoners, about whom no one seemed to
worry, and they appeared to be looked upon with some
contempt by the advancing troops ; their appearance
showed a marked contrast to the car-loads of distinguished
Italian civilians who were rushing up to the front bedecked
with Italian flags and flowers, who had already heard that
the Armistice had been signed. Sachile was reached at
dusk, with the snow-capped mountains in the background.
A large railway bridge had been blown up and was lying
like a broken child's toy in the beautiful Livenza. There
had been some street-fighting in this town, which had done
a certain amount of damage to its buildings. Owing to
the rapid departure of the enemy subsequently, they had
been unable to destroy many houses ; but that this had
been their intention was shown by the fact that the ground

floor of the house in which I was billeted had been filled
with inflammable material, such as shavings, hay, etc.,
laid ready to be lit at a moment's notice. At first we
had to be rather careful about our immediate surroundings,
on account of traps, one man having been killed in this
way. The market-place of Sachile contained the finest
collection of abandoned (one could hardly say captured)
Austrian guns that we had seen up till now. In the evening
we heard that the Armistice with Austria was really
authentic, and the town was bedecked with Italian flags.
A few days later, on November 12th, we heard that an
Armistice had been signed between the Allies and Germany
on the previous day, and we realized that the Great War,
which had caused many of us to leave our homes on
August 4, 1914, was over at last.

INDEX

18

UNITS, FORMATIONS AND SHIPS

BRIGADES (MOUNTED).

1st Australian Light Horse . .	65, 66, 70, 74, 90, 95, 98, 100, 101, 113, 176, 177
2nd Australian Light Horse .	53, 65, 74, 100, 176, 177
3rd Australian Light Horse . .	67, 95, 98, 101, 113, 117, 118, 124, 126, 134, 135, 149, 150, 167, 182, 183, 184, 187, 189, 191, 194, 204, 224, 243
4th Australian Light Horse . .	134, 146, 149, 150, 151, 167, 174, 175, 187, 189, 191, 194, 224, 226, 243
1st Mounted (M.E.F.) . . .	15, 26, 27, 45, 226
1st South Midland, Mounted .	13, 225
2nd Mounted (M.E.F.) . . .	27, 32, 45
3rd Mounted (M.E.F.) . . .	22, 26, 27, 45
4th Mounted (M.E.F.) . . .	27, 32, 45
5th Mounted (M.E.F.) . . .	26, 27
5th Mounted (E.E.F.) . . .	56, 63, 73, 97, 98, 99, 100, 106, 110, 113, 116, 117, 128, 129, 134, 135, 148, 149, 164, 170, 174, 175, 194, 213, 219, 222, 224, 226, 228, 245
6th Mounted (E.E.F.) . . .	110, 115, 116, 117, 119, 120, 122, 124, 126, 129, 133, 134, 138, 139, 149, 150, 152, 153, 159, 163, 164, 166, 201, 207, 226, 227
7th Mounted (E.E.F.) . . .	166, 167, 173, 175, 192, 201, 219
22nd Mounted (E.E.F.) . .	114, 164, 219
New Zealand Mounted . .	57, 58, 63, 66, 76, 79, 98, 100, 101, 103, 113, 173, 179, 181
Scottish Horse	49, 56, 64, 66

BRIGADES (INFANTRY).

22nd	263, 264
156th	92, 125
166th	86

CORPS.

Desert Column	96, 97, 98, 99, 112, 226
Desert, Mounted	171, 175, 204, 206, 226

CORPS (continued).

IXth	43
XIVth	267
XXth	173, 174, 175, 180, 200, 223, 226, 227, 228, 245
XXIst	193, 195, 197, 222, 223

DIVISIONS.

Australian Mounted	160, 161, 164, 170, 172, 173, 186, 192, 226, 241
Imperial Mounted	110, 114, 115, 116, 119, 120, 134, 141, 149, 150, 159, 226
Anzac Mounted	92, 93, 114, 115, 116, 119, 120, 131, 132, 140, 145, 149, 150, 163, 170, 171, 172, 173, 175, 188, 215, 221, 234, 241
2nd Mounted	13, 14, 43, 45, 226
7th (British)	256, 263, 267
7th (Meerut)	218, 222, 226
10th	25, 26, 200, 213
11th	22, 23, 27, 47
23rd	256, 263, 267
29th	26
42nd	57, 64, 66, 72, 77, 85, 90
52nd	49, 56, 66, 71, 90, 91, 92, 106, 111, 115, 125, 126, 131, 132, 186, 193, 199, 218, 222, 226
53rd	27, 57, 66, 111, 115, 116, 119, 121, 126, 131, 132, 154, 155, 168, 170, 174, 213, 217
54th	27, 115, 116, 119, 121, 128, 131, 132, 133, 204, 217, 222
60th	154, 171, 181, 182, 183, 184, 185, 198, 199, 221, 233, 243
74th	127, 128, 131, 132, 146, 181, 199, 200
75th	142, 165, 195, 196, 198, 222, 224, 227
Yeomanry, Mounted	159, 170, 188, 192, 199

East Force	153, 163
Egyptian Labour Corps	93, 94, 96, 152, 208, 217
Imperial Camel Corps	53, 81, 84, 86, 98, 100, 101, 120, 123, 129, 131, 149, 164, 173, 174, 175, 181, 202, 244, 245, 246
Bikanir Camel Corps	47, 53
Camel Transport Corps	111

FIELD AMBULANCES AND CASUALTY CLEARING STATIONS.

1st Australian Light Horse F.A.	67, 74, 77
2nd Australian Light Horse F.A.	67
3rd Australian Light Horse F.A.	103, 106
East Lancs F.A.	67

SHIPS.

GLOSSARY

Abu	.	.	.	. Father of
Ain .	.	.	.	. Spring
Bahr	.	.	.	. Sea
Beit .	.	.	.	. House
Bir .	.	.	.	. Well
Biyuk	.	.	.	. Large
Burnu	.	.	.	. Cape
Dagh	.	.	.	. Mountain
Darb	.	.	.	. Road
Dere.	.	.	.	. Valley
Deir	.	.	.	. House
El .	.	.	.	. The
Gebel	.	.	.	. Hill
Goz .	.	.	.	. Sand Hill
Hod	.	.	.	. Depression in Sand with Palms
Ibn .	.	.	.	. Son of
Karakol	.	.	.	. Fort or Guard House
Katib	.	.	.	. Sand Hill
Kebir	.	.	.	. Great
Khirbit	.	.	.	. Ruin
Kuchuk	.	.	.	. Small
Maghara	.	.	.	. Cave
Nag .	.	.	.	. Mountain Pass
Ras	.	.	.	. Summit
Rijm	.	.	.	. Stone Heap
Sabkhet	.	.	.	. Salt Lake
Sana	.	.	.	. Rain-water Pit
Tell .	.	.	.	. Mound
Um .	.	.	.	. Mother of
Wadi	.	.	.	. Water-course (often dry)

Lightning Source UK Ltd.
Milton Keynes UK
UKOW04f2314180315

248111UK00001B/24/P